T0332837

More and More and More

More and More and More

An All-Consuming History of Energy

JEAN-BAPTISTE FRESSOZ

Translated by the author

ALLEN LANE
an imprint of
PENGUIN BOOKS

ALLEN LANE

UK | USA | Canada | Ireland | Australia
India | New Zealand | South Africa

Allen Lane is part of the Penguin Random House group of companies
whose addresses can be found at global.penguinrandomhouse.com

First published in French under the title *Sans transition: Une nouvelle histoire de l'énergie*
by Éditions du Seuil 2024
This translation first published 2024

003

Set in 12/14.75pt Dante MT Std
Typeset by Jouve (UK), Milton Keynes
Printed and bound in Great Britain by Clays Ltd, Elcograf S.p.A.

The authorized representative in the EEA is Penguin Random House Ireland,
Morrison Chambers, 32 Nassau Street, Dublin D02 YH68

A CIP catalogue record for this book is available from the British Library

ISBN: 978-0-241-71889-6

To Michel and Josette, Cecilia, Leonor and Esteban

Contents

Preface   ix

Introduction: A Symbiotic History of Energy   1

1. A History of Energy by Candlelight   15
2. 'The Age of . . .': Material Stagism and Its Problems   29
3. Coal and Wood: A Tangled History   43
4. The Timber Palace   56
5. *Liaisons carbone*   67
6. The Carbon Fallacy   86
7. The Roots of Growth   96
8. The *Pétrolization* of Wood   117
9. Technocracy Inc.   128
10. Atomic Malthusians   142
11. The Invention of the Energy Crisis   160
12. 'Play the technology card'   180
Conclusion: The Weight of History   212

Notes   221

Preface

This book was born out of an unease felt when reading general histories of energy. At a time when coal consumption has just experienced major growth on most continents, academic works, representing the state of the art on the subject, are *still* telling stories of transitions between energy systems. The main arguments in this book matured in the intellectual atmosphere created by David Edgerton at the Centre for the History of Science, Technology and Medicine at Imperial College London, where I began my career in 2011. His *The Shock of the Old* is a major book that redefines the field of the history of technology, broadening its scope and interest; a book whose lessons for the climate issue had yet to be learned. Finally, the writing of this book was made possible by the time and intellectual freedom offered by the Centre National de la Recherche Scientifique and the École des Hautes Études en Sciences Sociales in Paris, and I would like to thank all their staff.

Thanks also to the many colleagues who, in one way or another, encouraged me to pursue the argument of energy symbioses: David Edgerton, Christophe Bonneuil and Charles-François Mathis who discussed, commented on and enriched previous version of this text, and also Dominique Pestre, Sabine Barles, Simon Schaffer, Soraya Boudia, Romain Huret, Franck Aggeri, Stefan Aykut, Harry Bernas and Béatrice Cointe, together with Christophe Cassen, Amy Dahan, Michel Damian, Jawad Daheur, Giuliano Garavini, Frédéric Graber, Sebastian Grevesmühl, Elie Haddad, Ciaran Healy, François Jarrige, Jean Jouzel, Michel Lepetit, Thomas Le Roux, Fabien Locher, Sophie Lhuillier, Valérie Masson-Delmotte, Antoine Misse-mer, Raphaël Morera, William Oman, Thomas Piketty, Antonin Pottier, Daniela Russ, Vincent Spenlehauer, Alessandro Stanziani, Thomas Turnbull, Adam Tooze and Paul Warde. Many thanks to the editorial teams and anonymous reviewers of *Annales des Mines, Revue d'histoire moderne et contemporaine, Revue d'histoire du XIXe siècle, Histoire et mesure* and *Terrestres*: their feedback helped me to clarify the argument of this book. Thanks also to the team at Penguin, particularly Simon Winder, and to my copy editor Charlotte Ridings.

In recent years, I had the pleasure to teach energy history to students in Paris at the École des Ponts et Chaussées and the École des Hautes Études en Sciences Sociales. Special thanks to those who worked under my supervision on related subjects: Nelo Magalhães, Gaëtan Levillain, Sam Allier and Jules Calage.

Finally, I had a lot of interesting discussions with some of the people involved in the story I'm telling. In particular, I would like to thank Nebojsa Nakicenovic, Cesare Marchetti's assistant in the 1970s, who played an important role at the International Institute for Applied Systems Analysis (IIASA) and within Group III of the Intergovernmental Panel on Climate Change (IPCC), Jean-Charles Hourcade, with whom I had many discussions on the last chapter of this book, and Youba Sokona, the current vice-president of the IPCC, who encouraged me to explore the disturbing history of its third group.

I have presented the arguments of this book on numerous occasions and in a variety of settings, not only academic and scientific, but also associative, governmental and international. Each time I have been struck by the interest aroused by a discussion based on figures, without taboos or positions of principle. On all these occasions, I have never received any serious objection to the thesis of energy symbioses, which seems original only in the light of a very strange standard historiography. The point of this book is not to say that the transition between energy systems is impossible because it did not happen in the past. The point is rather to take a fresh look at history in order to identify the factors that lead to energy accumulation – symbiotic processes that are still with us and that are not about to disappear.

Introduction:
A Symbiotic History of Energy

It is possible that effects [of global warming] become significant before the middle of the next century. This time scale is similar to that required to redirect, if necessary, the operation of the world economy, including agriculture and the production of energy.

(World Meteorological Organization, Declaration of the First World Climate Conference, Geneva, 1979, p. 2.)

This book tells a new story of energy, one that makes it possible to understand the radical oddity of the notion of *energy transition*. Instead of presenting the succession of energy systems over time, it explains why all primary energies have grown together and why they have accumulated *without* replacing each other. Instead of considering energies as separate entities in competition with each other, it reveals the history of their entanglement and interdependence. The stakes could not be higher, as these symbiotic relationships explain the permanence of primary energies right up to the present day and constitute major obstacles on the road to decarbonization.

This book also offers the first history of the 'energy transition', not as a historical and material phenomenon but as a futurology, a technological project and a way of understanding the dynamics of change. It explains why stage-theory reasoning has been applied to a field – energy and the material world – that did not lend itself to it at all. It recounts the strange trajectory of the energy transition, a heterodox and mercantile futurology – a mere industrial slogan – which, from the 1970s onwards, became the future of experts, governments and companies, including those that had no interest whatsoever in seeing it happen.

This book is certainly not a critique of renewable energies. It does, however, explain why the concept of energy transition is preventing us from thinking properly about climate change. For half a century now, this notion has produced more scientific confusion and political procrastination than anything else. Transition projects a past that does not exist onto an elusive future. To have any chance of forging a climate policy that is even remotely rigorous, it is essential to have a completely new understanding of the dynamics of energy and materials. That is the aim of this book.

In search of transitions

The notion of energy transition makes a radically strange future seem natural. Yet it is from history, a false history, that it draws its persuasive force and its appearance of plausibility. As if echoing the transitions of the past – from wood to coal, then from coal to oil – we should now, in the face of global warming, be making a third transition to nuclear power and / or renewable energies. The climate crisis demands that we continue the history of capitalism and innovation, even accelerate it, to hasten the advent of a carbon-free economy. Thanks to the transition theory, climate change calls for a change of technology, not a change of civilization. The history of energy, its chronological routines, its stagist narratives of the past – the age of wood, the age of coal, the age of oil, the organic economy and the mineral economy, the first and second industrial revolutions – has played a discreet but central ideological role in the creation of this comforting future.[1]

Let us start by stating the obvious. After two centuries of 'energy transitions', humanity has never burned so much oil and gas, so much coal and so much wood. Today, around 2 billion cubic metres of wood are felled each year to be burned, three times more than a century ago.[2] Wood currently provides twice as much energy as nuclear fission, twice as much as hydroelectricity, and twice as much as solar and wind power combined (2019 figures).[3] Wood remains an essential source of heat for the poorest third of the world's population – 2.3 billion people – who are also the first victims of pollution. But rich countries have also seen their consumption of wood energy increase: the United States burns twice as much as it did in 1960, and Europe three times as much as it did at the beginning of the twentieth century.[4] However, historians have been most interested in wood when it seems to disappear: its alleged ousting from the English energy mix in the nineteenth century has been the cause of more spilled ink than its rise throughout the world since 1950.

The same bias applies to coal: historians have mainly written about the situation in Europe in the nineteenth century, even though this is neither the main place nor moment in coal's history. The overwhelming majority (95 per cent) of coal was mined after 1900, and most of it was mined outside Europe (86 per cent).[5] Medium-sized Asian powers such as Australia and Indonesia currently extract twice as much coal as the giants of the 1900s such as Britain and the United States. In many ways, coal is a new energy. The strongest growth in its history occurred between 1980 and 2010 (+300 per cent), leading to an increase in its share of the global energy mix, to the detriment of oil. It was also in the 2010s that the number of miners reached its peak.[6] Lastly, coal-fired power stations are on average younger (around fifteen years old) than atomic power stations (thirty-two years), and are often much more efficient.[7] Coal was the great energy of the 2000s: it fuelled the internet revolution, which is basically just another electron network, just as much as the industrial revolution.

While China plays a central role – each year it burns fifteen times more coal than England at its peak and more than France throughout its history – this country is exceptional only in terms of its size. Since 1980, coal consumption has increased tenfold in China, but it has multiplied by 12 in Taiwan, by 11 in Vietnam, by 10 in the Philippines, by 8 in India, by 7 in Turkey, by 6 in South Korea and by 50 in

Indonesia. India, South Africa and Poland all have electricity mixes that are more coal-intensive than China's. And coal is not just the energy of development. Between 1980 and 2010, coal consumption doubled in the United States, Japan and the Gulf States, before falling back, mainly because of the rise of natural gas. Bush's America consumed four times as much coal as Roosevelt's.

That leaves us with Europe. The first to enter the 'coal age', Europe is also, we are told, the first to escape from it. This European exception, like so many others, needs to be put into perspective. The decline in coal use that began in the 1960s looks like a long, slow and cautious retreat. In 2020, Europe still consumes 400 million tonnes of coal a year, and the continent's major industrial power, Germany, remains one of the world's leading producers of lignite, the most polluting of fuels. Angela Merkel's Germany consumed three times as much coal per year as Bismarck's Germany. What is less well known is that Europe is also a world leader in manufacturing mining equipment, and it is partly thanks to European machines that world coal production soared in the twenty-first century.[8] Last but not least, the European Union, like all rich countries, engages in large amounts of foreign trade, and more than a quarter of the manufactured goods it imports are based on coal energy. However 'green' their energy systems may be or become, the rich countries, for the simple reason that they are rich, are resolutely on the side of the big coal consumers.

If we take into account the coal incorporated into imports, the UK would consume around 50 million tonnes – instead of the 9 million officially burned.[9] One study even puts that figure at 90 million tonnes – almost as much as on the eve of Margaret Thatcher's assault on the country's mines. Similarly, France consumes not 6 million tonnes of coal a year but rather 70 million, a quantity close to its peak extraction in the 1960s.[10] Whatever the accuracy of these figures, the important point is that in a globalized world, the decarbonization of a national economy is a difficult phenomenon to measure and that the 'transition' of the rich countries of Western Europe away from coal is, in part, a statistical artefact linked to a convenient convention: the attribution of CO_2 emissions to the countries producing the goods and not to the consumers.

Other imputation criteria would produce different results.[11] Let's take the case of Switzerland. This prosperous country has never been a major coal consumer, and its last mines closed in 1945. But it should be noted that its prosperity is partly due to the fact that Switzerland is part of a global economy that still consumes a lot of coal. For too-well-known reasons, international mining companies such as Glencore have their headquarters in Switzerland. They control the extraction of at least half a billion tonnes of coal per year. What's more, 40 per cent of the international coal trade is conducted in Switzerland, with Trafigura being a key player in this field. In total, at least a billion tonnes of coal contribute directly to the prosperity of the Swiss Confederation, which is quite a lot for a country of 8 million inhabitants.[12] Other similar examples include Luxembourg, home to ArcelorMittal, the world's leading steel company, or Norway, with its luxury electric cars bought with oil revenues.

The epic of energy transitions

Despite its fundamental dynamic of accumulation, the history of energy is generally told as a series of transitions or shifts in energy systems, on the scale of nations, continents or even the world as a whole. In what has become a genre in itself – the epic of energy transitions – we generally find the same chronological structure: initial chapters deal with muscle power, wood and water power in the pre-industrial era; central chapters deal with coal and steam in the nineteenth century; this is followed by chapters on oil, electricity and nuclear power (gas is often less studied); and finally, concluding remarks on the transition to 'green' energy in progress or to come. As each era is defined by the new – a bias common to the history of technology, rightly highlighted by the historian David Edgerton – massive phenomena are erased, such as the rise of renewables in the

nineteenth century, biomass and muscle power in the twentieth century, and the recent rise of coal.[13] 'King coal reigned for about
seventy-five years, before ceding the throne to oil in about 1965'
wrote a leading figure in American environmental history recently.[14]
The transitionist model is so deeply rooted that even a book of reference such as *Power to the People* contains some questionable assertions.
For example, oil and electricity are presented as two 'energy transitions', whereas electricity increases coal consumption and oil does
not necessarily reduce it.[15] The case of Vaclav Smil is also revealing.
A leading expert on energy issues, he is currently one of the most
influential voices warning of the enormity of the challenge represented by a global transition away from fossil fuels in thirty years'
time. But his scepticism about the current transition does not prevent him from reiterating in his historical epics on energy the classic
narrative of a modernity made up of transitions.[16]

Of course, there are other ways of telling the story of energy.
Professional historians generally prefer to focus on a particular
energy source. There is a wealth of literature on coal and oil, and
other works on wood, hydroelectricity and, more recently, wind
and solar power. The problem with these approaches is that they
are 'mono-energetic'. They study one form of energy separately
from others and from materials in general. However, we cannot
understand much about the history of coal without studying the
history of the wood used to extract it. Similarly, the rise of oil in the
twentieth century is inexplicable without concrete, steel and, by
extension, coal. This book aims to show the importance of a host of
objects and techniques – mine props, railway sleepers, oil pipes,
creosote, plywood panels, concrete mixers, dump trucks, cardboard
boxes, wooden pallets, etc. – that are absent from standard accounts
and yet are key to understanding the material history of energy.[17]

Since the 2010s, a number of historians have sought to renew the
genre by challenging the primacy of economics, relative costs and
resource availability in favour of the political determinants of
'energy transitions'. In *Fossil Capital*, for example, Andreas Malm
explains the spread of the steam engine in England in the 1830s as a

result of capitalists' desire to escape the locational constraints imposed by water power. Steam enabled them to move production to the cities to better exploit the abundant labour force that resided there.[18] In his famous book *Carbon Democracy* – to which we will return in Chapter 6 – Timothy Mitchell also offers a political account of the switch from coal to oil: the fluidity of oil is said to have enabled capitalists to circumvent the power and demands of European miners at the end of the nineteenth century.[19]

While the desire to inject politics into the somewhat smooth narratives of the economic history of energy is laudable, it should be stressed that these authors are repeating the standard transitionist story, and even exacerbating it by applying chronological periodization derived from the history of politics to the history of energy. As far as Malm's thesis is concerned, historians have shown that the steam engine of the 1830s was more a symbol than a trigger for 'fossil capital'. In nineteenth-century Britain, coal was burned primarily to produce domestic and industrial heat, and secondarily for steam and mechanical power. From the seventeenth century onwards, the demand for heating had led to a gradual increase in the price of firewood and a corresponding increase in coal mining. It should be added that steam did not replace hydraulic power. In fact, the use of water power in the British textile industry remained stable during the nineteenth century. Steam engines were used especially where rivers were overcrowded with watermills, like in Manchester.[20] Industrialists who were able to do so used both a water turbine *and* a steam engine. In France, for which precise administrative statistics are available, in 1860 half the companies using steam had another engine too, usually hydraulic, and steam engines were often used to pump water into the reservoirs when rivers were running low.[21] As for the hypothesis that capitalists had a particular appetite for urban crowds, it seems contradictory to the many projects to relocate industry to the countryside, synonymous with relative social calm. In the United States, in Massachusetts, textile capitalists had no difficulty in prospering thanks to hydraulic power, by completely transforming the River Merrimack.[22]

Timothy Mitchell's book comes up against the same stumbling block: oil does not bypass miners because, simply, it does not replace coal. Oil is used primarily to power cars, which in turn require a lot of coal to manufacture. Moreover, in the twentieth century, electricity gave coal a new economic centrality; the number of miners declined not because of oil but because of productivity gains in the mines. The attraction of the 'political' history of energy, which is also its flaw, is that it tends to present climate change as a capitalist conspiracy. This apparently radical but ultimately reassuring story underestimates the immensity of the climate challenge. Getting out of carbon will be far more difficult than getting out of capitalism, a condition that is probably necessary but certainly not sufficient.

A major criticism of transition epics has come from historians with a thorough knowledge of nineteenth-century modes of production, and consequently less impressed by coal and steam than their energy-specialist colleagues. They showed the importance for industrialization of energies that are wrongly regarded as traditional: whether human muscle, water power in factories, wood in the iron and steel industry, animals in transport, agricultural work or as industrial mechanical power.[23] But as a critique of transition, this history of technological persistence remains middle of the road.[24] The idea that traditional energies would 'resist' in the face of fossil fuels still takes the transitionist narrative too seriously. To understand the history of energy, we need to get rid of both Schumpeterian Darwinism – the too-simple idea of 'creative destruction' – and the dialectic of winners and losers. In the nineteenth and twentieth centuries, renewable energies did not put up barriers to fossil fuels, but progressed and developed thanks to them. As we shall see, coal and oil greatly increased the production of wood and its availability for energy purposes. Renewables improved thanks to steel and cement, two materials that are closely dependent on coal, enabling them to capture diffuse energies much more efficiently. In France, the steel turbines of the 1900s produced three times as much energy as the wooden mills of the 1800s, at a much lower cost, even before the rise of the large hydroelectric dams that were obviously dependent on oil

Wind turbines at the Chicago World's Fair in 1893. By the end of the nineteenth
century, at least a million windmills were pumping water in the Great Plains of
the Midwest. The development of wind turbines is inextricably linked to that of
fossil fuels. Wind turbines have benefited from advances in metallurgy, sheet
metal stamping, ball bearings, steel tube production and cement. Their
lubrication system was inspired by that of car casings, and, between the wars,
the blades took on their modern shape thanks to advances in aviation.
Conversely, in the arid regions of Texas, wind turbines were used to supply
water to locomotives burning coal.[25]

and coal for their construction.[26] Similarly, oil and gas have made it
possible to increase agricultural production and hence the availability
of human energy. For these and many other reasons, the story we tell
in this book is not one of resistance, or even of additions, but of the
entanglement and symbiotic expansion of all energies.[27]

When every tonne counts

There is no reason why historians should choose transition as the
main motif of their accounts. Energy sources are as much symbiotic
as they are in competition, and their symbiotic relationships explain

9

why, over the course of the nineteenth and twentieth centuries, primary energy sources tended to add up rather than substitute each other. This observation leads to an obvious question: how is it that the idea of transition has become so widely accepted? Why did this future without a past became the future of governments and experts from the 1970s onwards? And how has it rubbed off on historians' accounts of the past? The last four chapters of this book will provide detailed answers to these questions. Let us simply mention for the moment that if the concept of transition poorly describes past transformations, it is because that was not its purpose: the idea comes not from an empirical observation of the past, but from anticipation of the future; it comes not from historians, but from futurologists. The history of energy was born out of futurology: it was to estimate future consumption that the first works on the quantitative history of energy were carried out. It is also in order to anticipate changes in the energy mix that certain experts, proponents of the atom, have considered energy dynamics not in absolute but in relative terms. From this matrix, historians have inherited certain ways of thinking about and representing energy. They have chosen to focus their analyses not on absolute values but on changes in relative shares, and they have adopted, without too much reflection, the lexicon of certain futurologists of the 1970s: expressions such as 'energy system' and 'energy transition'.

More often than not, historians have been content to characterize the transition in qualitative terms, as the shift from one 'technical system', to another, with all the economic, social, political and cultural consequences that this would entail. When we see the flagrant errors in the history of energy made by the French historian Bertrand Gille, who introduced the notion of *système technique*, we understand that this latter notion must be handled with care.[28] Its main problem is that by focusing on the 'coherences' linking techniques, materials and energies in each period, 'technical systems' have fostered a discontinuous vision of the history of energy, based on the dynamics of technological substitution.

The divergence between history in relative terms and history in

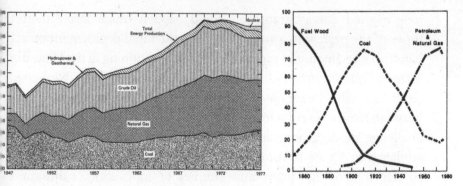

Two ways of representing the US energy mix: in absolute terms on the left, and in relative terms on the right. This second method appeared in the mid-1970s, first in the energy forecasting field and then in the US administration after the 1973 oil crisis. It was also at this time that a new body of expertise focused on transition was born. (Energy Information Administration, 'Annual Report to Congress', 1978, p. 2 and Executive Office of the President, *National Energy Plan*, 1977 (Cambridge, MA, 1978).)

absolute terms is not just a matter of academic debate on the interpretation of modernity. It is also about the politics of history in the face of climate change. Since the 2000s, some experts have been searching for clues and fragments of answers in the history of energy to address the most pressing contemporary questions: how long could the transition take? How can we speed up the process? What is the role of the market? of the state? of innovation? Historians have willingly lent themselves to this game, and we have seen colleagues who specialize in the Industrial Revolution offering advice on transition, even though they have only ever studied energy additions.[29]

History – although not historians – also occupies a prominent place in an academic field that emerged in the 2000s: *transition studies*. The founding article, written by the sociologist Frank Geels, studied the spread of steam navigation in the nineteenth century in order to infer a theory of transition supposedly useful for decision-makers.[30] This article, which recycled Schumpeterian studies of innovation, was surprisingly successful. Currently, another author, Benjamin Sovacool, is working to spread a reassuring discourse: the long-awaited energy transition could happen much faster than those of the past, with 'evidence' such as the rapid deployment of a handful of technologies ranging from air conditioning in the United States to butane stoves in Indonesia, to natural gas in the Netherlands.[31] As with steam navigation, it is difficult to discern the link between the success of a few polluting technologies and the current challenge of decarbonization. The sleight of hand of transition studies is to equate transition with the diffusion of innovation and to reformulate the quantitative studies of innovation, common since the 1970s, in the lexicon of sociological theories. This prolific literature is fuelled by the ambiguity of the word 'transition' (technological? energetic? relative? absolute? deep? shallow?) and by endless discussions between approaches ('multi-level perspective', 'socio-technical transitions', 'large technical systems', 'social construction of technology', 'actor-network theory') that are theoretically different but really very close.[32] But this doesn't matter; because of their optimistic and constructive tone, well-funded by the European authorities and in vogue in business schools, transition studies have acquired a scientific weight out of all proportion to their empirical contribution. In its March 2022 report, Group III of the IPCC drew on this literature to make the strange assertion that 'energy transitions can occur faster than in the past', and that 'a low-carbon energy transition needs to occur faster than previous transitions'.[33] What is most worrying here is not so much the extent of the influence of transition studies as the fact that a stagist and false history of energy can thus pass all the validation procedures put in place by the IPCC.[34]

Faced with the climate crisis, we can no longer be satisfied with a history written in relative terms. A 'transition' towards renewables that would see fossil fuels diminish in relative terms but stagnate in terms of tonnes would solve nothing. We can no longer be satisfied with the vagueness of transition and its innumerable epithets, nor with the misleading analogies between the pseudo-transitions of the past and the one we need to make today. The climate imperative does not call for a new energy transition, but it does require us to voluntarily carry out an enormous energy amputation: to get rid, in four decades, of the proportion of the world's energy – more than three-quarters – derived from fossil fuels. To think that we can draw some useful analogies from history dramatically underestimates the novelty and scale of the climate challenge.

The history of energy recounted in this book is different from accounts that have gone before, in that it is concerned with absolute values rather than relative dynamics; it deals less with the replacement of engines and more with the persistence of materials; it does not separate the production of energy from that of materials; it does not recount the epic struggles between energy systems but rather the alliances and mutually supportive relationships that exist between them. We will see how energy sources are in a symbiotic relationship as much as a competitive one, and how these symbiotic relationships explain why, over the course of the nineteenth and twentieth centuries, primary energies have tended to add to rather than substitute each other. The 'transitionless' history that this book proposes does not mean that nothing changes – quite the contrary – but that change is better understood when we leave behind the stagist narratives of the material world.

As we have said, the history of energy is often called upon to 'illuminate' the present. The approach of this book is exactly the opposite: it is the contemporary challenges of transition that throw a harsh light on the gaping holes in our historical understanding of energy. The slowness, even the stagnation, of the much-desired transition necessarily renders the 'great transitions' of the past suspect. The material and energy imbroglios revealed by industrial ecology and life-cycle analyses point to fundamental entanglements that historians, overly concerned with periodization, systems, dynamics and modernity, have left in deep obscurity.

I.

A History of Energy by Candlelight

In 2018, the Nobel Prize in Economics was awarded to two Americans, William Nordhaus and Paul Romer, for their work on climate and innovation respectively. The message of economics to the rest of the world was unambiguous: it is through innovation, through the 'creative destruction' so dear to Joseph Schumpeter, that we can effectively combat global warming. At the awards ceremony, Paul Romer chose to illustrate this thesis with an edifying story about light. He referred to an article written twenty years earlier by 'his friend Bill' (Nordhaus), notable for measuring the collapse in the price of light from Roman oil lamps to contemporary light bulbs.[1] The fight against global warming, Romer explained, had to be part of this story of innovation, growing efficiency and increased well-being. From this vision of technological progress, economists drew an almost unique recommendation: the carbon tax, designed to put companies on the right track of 'green innovation'.[2] In addition to the tax stick, there is the carrot of subsidies to help companies break free from their 'path dependency', a path that would lead them down the fossil fuel-dead end. Instead of moping around, Romer concluded, all we need to do is point 'our innovative efforts in a slightly different direction'. And that '[decarbonizing the economy] will be so easy that looking back it will seem painless'.[3]

This rather surprising understatement is based on a widespread error that tends to confuse technology with innovation.[4] Since climate change is caused by second nature as a whole, by all the techniques and infrastructures accumulated in the world over the last two centuries, acting on the technological frontier, 'slightly modifying' the direction of corporate R&D as Romer suggests, will obviously change the quantity of CO_2 emissions only marginally and in the distant future. Innovation is preventing us from having an adult conversation about climate change. Even though it is constantly invoked in relation to climate, innovation is, in reality, simply a way out, a procrastination tactic. Instead of wandering around dreaming about hydrogen-powered aircraft, nuclear fusion or the third industrial revolution, we should be basing climate policy on existing, available and cheap technologies, on the relevance of their use and on the fair and efficient distribution of CO_2 emissions.

Romer's understatement reflects a strange intellectual phenomenon: the extraordinary success of the simplistic idea of 'creative destruction'. It is striking to see the extent to which this shortcut has been taken seriously by countless experts and economists, including experts on 'energy transition'. Not only is this idea generally false from the point of view of the history of technology – the new does not make the old disappear – but as far as climate change and the environment are concerned, it is entirely and totally refuted by the history of materials. In fact, it was refuted even before Schumpeter formulated it.

As an American forester remarked in 1928, whatever the technological innovations – and he was thinking of cement-and-steel skyscrapers – 'raw materials are never obsolete'.[5] Work in ecological economics has confirmed this remarkable conjecture.[6] Any serious discussion of climate change should start from the somewhat worrying observation that technological innovations have never, right up to the present day, caused any flow of material consumption to disappear. Over the course of the twentieth century, the world's range of raw materials expanded, and each was consumed in increasing quantities.[7] Of the major raw materials, only the use of sheep's wool has fallen, because of the diffusion of synthetic fibres, which is not good news for the environment. The total weight of materials used by the economy has increased twelvefold, and after the year 2000 there was a further acceleration, far greater than the famous 'great acceleration' of the 1950s.[8] For the time being, therefore, substitution processes have always been trumped by the expansion of markets, by rebound effects and by the reorientation of raw materials to other uses.

This chapter takes the supposedly illuminating example chosen by Romer to understand the climatic failure of technological futurism. Even in a field – artificial light – where progress and efficiency gains have been spectacular, in a field that has been turned upside down by a real technological revolution – namely electricity – 'creative destruction' has ultimately destroyed nothing in terms of material consumption. Quite the contrary.

Modern candles

The material history of light is different from the history of lighting technologies and has nothing to do with the edifying history proposed by the new Schumpeters of the climate. In the picture painted by Nordhaus of the benefits of economic freedom guiding inventors, it is gas that is bizarrely presented as the essential breakthrough between 1820 and 1850, even though very few people were using it at the time.[9] 'There were virtually no new devices and scant improvements', writes Nordhaus, 'from the Babylonian age until the development of town gas in the late eighteenth century.'[10] Presenting gas as progress poses another problem. The process consisted of distilling coal in cast-iron vessels heated with coal. The gas obtained was stored in a gasometer before being distributed through a network of lead pipes. At the outlet of the gas burner, a mixture escaped that was mainly composed of hydrogen, which had little lighting power. Between the losses in heating the retorts and the leaks in the network, the efficiency of the process was disastrous.

In 1819, a chemist wisely pointed out that if the oil lamp had been invented after gas, everyone would have admired this simpler, less capital-intensive, less dangerous and more efficient innovation, which also used a renewable resource – seed oils. Until the end of the nineteenth century, history did not prove him wrong: the real advances in lighting in the 1800s were not in gas, but in lamps and candles. These techniques were just as 'modern' as gas and, in many respects, superior to it – their efficiency, as we shall see, was much higher. The stearic candle, which was invented *after* gas, is the result of advances in organic chemistry and the extraction of stearin, a fatty acid that remains solid at 60°C. Stearic candles are nothing like the tallow candles of the eighteenth century: they don't drip, smoke or smell.[11] From the 1830s onwards, candle factories sprang up all over the world, first in the major cities of Europe, then worldwide by the end of the nineteenth century.[12] From fuel to wick, the candle was a veritable cornucopia of innovations. Candle production, taking place both in small workshops and in gigantic factories, was mechanized with machines using compressed air to remove candles from their moulds.[13] The main economic interest of the candle industry is that it converted just about any organic fat – slaughterhouse waste, cooking residues, etc. – into a product with high added value.

Much more than gas, the candle was a global technology. Palm oil from West Africa was particularly sought after by candle manufacturers for its richness in stearin. Both French and British imports quadrupled between 1850 and 1900, with around half going to candle factories.[14] Great Britain, world leader in coal-gas consumption, also consumed a lot of palm oil – four times as much as France: gas and candles were clearly not mutually exclusive. To capture the greasy windfall from Africa, candle factories moved to the ports: the two leading candle companies of the nineteenth century – Price's Patent Candle Company in Liverpool and Fournier in Marseilles – exported candles to the four corners of the world. Great innovations were born from the candle: it was in a chemical laboratory working for the pioneering Parisian company L'Étoile that the Italian chemist Ascanio Sobrero synthesized nitroglycerine for the first time – he was looking for a use for glycerine, a residue from the extraction of stearin. Alfred Nobel, who was apprenticed to Sobrero at the time, benefited immensely from his colleague's discovery.[15]

Without going into too much detail, the oil lamp was also completely reinvented from the end of the eighteenth century onwards. Hollow cylindrical wicks and glass tubes increased the flow of oxygen

Candles are just as 'industrial' as gas and because they were much easier to transport than gas their production was far more concentrated. In France in the 1870s, there were around a hundred candle factories, including three very large ones, and almost five hundred gas factories. In England, Price's Patent Candle Company, based in London and Liverpool, dominated the market. It reached its peak at the beginning of the twentieth century: its Battersea site in London covered 5 hectares, employed 2,300 workers and produced 160,000 tonnes of candles a year using palm oil and petroleum wax.

and made the flame much brighter. The first people to see these new lamps were amazed.[16] The fuel – mainly rapeseed oil, with petroleum making its appearance in the 1860s – was purified more effectively using powerful acids. The regular feeding of the wick was improved by numerous inventions in the field of mechanics and sealing. A visitor to the 1834 Paris Industrial Exhibition noted that 'lamp-making has now become as difficult a science as algebra'.[17]

The materials behind the techniques

It's easy to see why gas didn't replace lamps or candles in the nineteenth century, but rather supplemented them in a modest way, its use concentrated in cities, and by the bourgeoisie, factories, theatres and shops. The transition from organic to mineral sources of lighting did not really start until the very end of the 1800s, with kerosene lamps and candles made from petroleum paraffin. But the important point is that this 'transition' in no way prevented increased consumption of the original materials concerned. After petroleum replaced organic oils, consumption of palm oil, rapeseed oil and even whale oil continued to rise. Between the two world wars, global palm-oil exports increased fivefold (from 100,000 to 500,000 tonnes) for lubricants, soaps, food and pharmaceuticals. At the end of the twentieth century, with the rise of 'biofuels', the energy use of vegetable fats increased tremendously. Nowadays, French cars alone burn between 300,000 and 500,000 tonnes of palm oil a year, about as much as the world consumed in the 1930s. French motorists also burn between 2 and 2.5 million tonnes of rapeseed oil, at least ten times more than all French candles and lamps in the mid-nineteenth century.[18] Similarly, once electricity had blown out the flame of gas burners, coal

Grand ball given by the whales in honour of the discovery of oil in Pennsylvania. (*Vanity Fair*, 20 April 1861.)

gas found many other uses for domestic heating and cooking, and coal has never been distilled as much as it is today, to produce coke for the steel industry, methanol and many other chemical products.

Then there is the case of whale oil, rightly famous as one of the rare historical examples of the disappearance of an energy source. But it is important to understand the significance of this exception. In his article, William Nordhaus does not hesitate to repeat an old cliché, dear to the hearts of American oilmen: oil saved the whales. Nordhaus even adds that the good fortune of these cetaceans was that, in the days of Edwin Drake and John D. Rockefeller, there were no environmentalists or impact studies to prevent the rise of the oil industry. There's no point in dwelling on this absurd argument, which has long since been refuted.[19] Let's just note that even before petroleum wax was introduced, there were several less expensive and far more abundant light fuels available than whale oil. Oil did not save the whales because innovations such as the stearic candle had already made spermaceti obsolete for lighting.[20] In England, according to the work of Roger Fouquet and Peter Pearson, at the beginning of the nineteenth century whale oil represented only 5 to 10 per cent of the light produced by candles.[21] In France, it was even less. At its peak, in the mid-1800s, six to eight ships brought back less than 2,000 tonnes of oil a year. Imports from the United States peaked in the 1840s at 5,000 tonnes, and then fell back below 1,000 tonnes for the rest of the century.[22] If whaling had been prohibited in 1850, an alternative would have been to increase rapeseed production by a few per cent, or to import slightly more palm oil.

In addition, the peak of the whaling industry was reached in 1960, a century after the advent of oil. In the twentieth century, during the so-called 'age of oil', three times as many sperm whales were killed (760,000) as in the nineteenth century (around 250,000).[23] Oil played a key role in this carnage: more powerful and more reliable boats powered with diesel engines chased whales to the furthest reaches of the southern hemisphere. Whale oil was no longer used as a source of light, but for many other purposes: margarine, pharmaceuticals, paint and explosives. Actually, petroleum *increased* the demand for whale oil: top-of-the-range lubricants for gearboxes and machine tools used to contain between 5 and 20 per cent whale oil. Until the mid-1970s, aircraft turbojet engines were lubricated at least in part with whale oil. In 1970, with the prospect of the end of whaling, companies began to stock up, and it was then that sperma-ceti oil reached the highest price in its history. If anyone wants to credit a substance with 'saving the whales', it is the jojoba, a tree native to Mexico whose fruit produces an oil very similar to sperma-ceti.[24] And this transition took place only because it was imposed on the industry by the ban on whaling that non-governmental organizations fought so hard to obtain. Contrary to what Nordhaus writes, it was environmentalists who saved the whales, at least those few that had survived the carnage of the twentieth century.

The labour behind the materials

The history of light illuminates a second important point for this book: the blurred nature of energies. The names we give them – 'oil', 'petroleum', 'gas' – are linguistic conveniences that obscure material processes that are much broader, more intertwined and more composite than we think. Stearic candle production, for example, involved an enormous amount of human labour, mainly due to the extraction of palm oil. Depending on its quality, it took between 130 and 630 working days to produce one tonne of oil. With all the limitations inherent in this kind of calculation, it can be assumed that 1 calorie of human energy produced just 3 calories of palm oil.[25] The candle economy was based on very low labour costs and often on slave labour. It is no coincidence that African palm-oil exports began to rise after the abolition of the slave trade: European merchants, deprived of the triangular trade, saw in this commodity a new way of making the most of the labour force available in West Africa. The abolition of the slave trade did not mean the end of slavery, but rather its expansion in Africa itself. In the middle of the nineteenth century, a palm-oil merchant from Marseilles admitted that the stearic

PRICE'S DISTILLED PALM CANDLES

Advertisement for Price's Patent Candle Company. The candle burns the rope of servitude. By offering a legal trade to African sovereigns, the stearic candle may have helped to dry up the sources of the slave trade, but palm oil was largely produced by slave labour. Price's Patent Candle Company directly employed 2,300 workers in Britain but the palm oil it used required tens of thousands of men and women in West Africa.

candle had certainly helped to dry up the slave trade, but only because the West African kings had an interest in keeping slaves on site to harvest and extract the oil.[26]

The European lights of the nineteenth century were therefore based partly on slavery in Africa, but also on many other workers, other materials and other sources of energy: on the toil of the peasants who grew rapeseed and poppy, on the mills that crushed oilseeds, on the millions of hectares of grassland in Europe and America used to fatten cattle.[27]

The emergence of fossil fuels adds a new level of complexity but does nothing to change the interweaving of materials and energies that lights up the world. Indeed, gas lighting was produced from coal extracted from mines, which in turn were significant consumers of lighting oil. In the 1860s, a miner extracted an average of 200 tonnes of coal a year with the help of 60 kilos of oil or candles. The gas itself therefore depended on a large quantity of organic light. The cost of lighting was considerable: less than the cost of labour and pit-props but more than capital remuneration.[28] Similarly, the petroleum that made European lamps shine at the end of the nineteenth century had a much broader material and energy base than the chemical energy it contained. Its extraction required wooden derricks, it was pumped by steam engines, it crossed the Atlantic in sailing ships, it was stored in wooden barrels that required coal and muscle power to make, and so on.[29] When we consider the materiality of their production, the words 'oil' or 'coal' become problematic. The candle sheds light on a point that is both trivial and rarely taken into account in thinking about energy and writing its history: energies are symbiotic entities that depend on complex webs of materials from which this book draws some threads.

The mismeasure of energy

The material history of illumination sheds light on a final, more historiographical point. In books on the history of energy, in particular Kander, Malamina and Warde's *Power to the People*, we can admire spectacular curves showing the early triumph of coal in industrial countries: by 1800, 80 per cent of British energy was derived from coal. In France and Germany, by the middle of the nineteenth century, more than half of all energy depended on coal. These curves have rehabilitated a coal-centric history of industrialization, a vision that a generation of economic historians had criticized.[30] Undoubtedly, coal had a major economic impact on industrial countries by the close of the nineteenth century. The problem is that the methods used to measure this impact have the effect of anticipating and exaggerating its consequences.

Let's take the case of lighting in France in 1872, an example which has the merit of providing all the necessary statistical information. With only 470 gasworks, gas lighting was unknown in the countryside. The Seine department, and Paris in particular, consumed half of the gas produced nationwide. However, there were only 92,000 subscribers in the capital out of a total population of 2 million.[31] Gas was therefore used mainly to light the streets and homes of the bourgeoisie. Even in Great Britain, where gas was cheaper, only a quarter of the population had domestic access to gas lighting by 1885.[32] In Europe, and even more on other continents, rural and poorer people used lamps and candles for lighting. Not much, admittedly: in 1872, every French person had on average an hour and a half of candlelight a day. Although gas provided little light, it did consume a lot of coal: around 1 million tonnes in France in 1872, i.e. four times the mass of fat consumed by oil lamps and candles. Given the disastrous inefficiency of gas, this million tonnes of coal produced as much light as 120,000 tonnes of oil and candles. In short, gas consumed twice as much energy as candles and oil lamps to produce half as much light.[33]

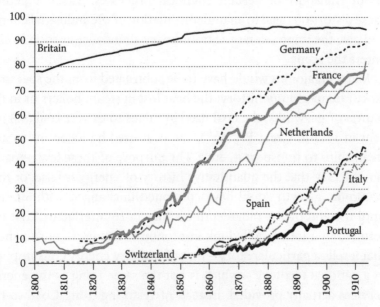

Share of coal in total energy consumption. In Astrid Kander, Paolo Malamina and Paul Warde, *Power to the People. Energy in Europe Over the Last Five Centuries* (Princeton, NJ, 2013), p. 137. This graph represents primary energy (the amount of energy contained in a tonne of coal, for example) and not the energy actually used by final consumers (the work produced by a steam engine burning a tonne of coal, for example). In doing so, it exaggerates the importance of coal in 19th-century economies.

As gas lighting vigorously stimulates coal consumption, the latter is duly measured by energy historians who, on the other hand, do not bother with vegetable oils and animal fats, arguing that they contribute very little in comparison with coal.[34] This is entirely true from the point of view of primary energy consumption, but completely false when we look at the energy services provided. This distortion is general: it is due to the difficulty of accounting for so-called traditional energies and the low efficiency of machines using coal. The case of the steam engine is similar to that of gas lighting. According to the efficiency parameters used by energy historians in their calculations, an industrialist who replaces his water mill with a steam engine of *equivalent power* multiplies his energy consumption by a factor of between 5 and 10.[35] Similar remarks could be made about transport or certain chemical processes. Taken together, these distortions lead to an underestimation of pre-industrial energy and give the impression of extraordinary abundance as soon as coal enters the scene.

Many gigajoules would have to be subtracted from the spectacular curves of energy history: the heat lost in steam boilers or in the retorts of gasworks, the coal used in mines to extract coal (8.8 per cent in 1922 in Great Britain[36]), the coal used by locomotives and steamships to transport it, etc.[37] The purpose of these few remarks is not to say that the quantitative history of energy is false, or that economic growth could have continued unchanged without coal until the end of the nineteenth century (a counterfactual that has resulted in a lot of spilled ink in economic history[38]), but to show that it tells a particular story – that of primary energy consumption in a national territory – which is not the same thing as the energy services actually provided. Instead of restoring 'King Coal' to the throne of the industrial revolution, such a story would probably echo the findings of the cliometricians of the 1970s and 1980s on the progressive nature of economic growth. It would also show, along-side steam engines and gasworks, the role of candles, wheelbarrows, ball bearings, cranks, winches, lubricants, barrels, dollies, trolleys, bicycles, pedals, sewing machines, etc. – machines that consumed little energy but played a fundamental role in the economic growth of the nineteenth and twentieth centuries.

To conclude, let's turn to the amphitheatre of the Royal Swedish Academy on 8 December 2018. In his speech there, Paul Romer highlighted a little-known but important innovation, the Welsbach mantle, which at the end of the 1800s had increased the luminous power of gas tenfold. Welsbach, the inventor of the mantle, had made the lights of the industrial world shine brighter by covering the gas nozzles with a mesh of metal oxides.[39] The next slide of Romer's presentation illustrated the progress of lighting. Instead of the usual evocations of Times Square or Shibuya at night, it showed an anonymous street, probably that of a town in Africa: under the pale light of the street lamps, teenagers were revising with their textbooks. From light would come other lights, Romer explained, and, who knows, maybe one of these students, embarking on a scientific career, would discover the incandescent gas mantle of the twenty-first century, thus helping to solve the climate crisis.

Once again, the example was poorly chosen. The gas mantle, with its classic rebound effect, had considerably *increased* gas consumption and therefore CO_2 emissions. In 1900, Paris consumed more gas than the whole of France twenty-five years earlier. If we continue the story, it's true that electricity blows the wick out of kerosene lamps in rich countries, but it also leads to a huge increase in petroleum consumption for lighting. In 1973, a quarter of the world's electricity was produced from oil, and around a fifth of this electricity was used for lighting. Subsequently, oil's share in electricity production declined. But in the 2000s, the electricity used by car headlights alone consumed more than a million barrels of oil a day, twice the world production in 1900, to which must be added the 1.3 million barrels (in 2005) used to fuel lamps in poor countries.[40] Since 2000, on a global scale, despite the rapid spread of LEDs (which accounted for half of all lighting in 2020), electricity consumption for illumination has remained stable. Our light bulbs, however efficient, send almost a billion tonnes of CO_2 per year into the atmosphere, thousands of times more than in the days of gas lighting and kerosene lamps.[41] Finally, it is unlikely that some student in Africa or elsewhere will invent the equivalent of the gas mantle: LED lamps are already so efficient that progress in this domain is largely behind us.

The 2018 Nobel Prize award illustrates the obsolescence of Schumpeterian economists' modernist ideology: their answers no longer correspond to the question being asked. The two laureates learned their academic trade in the debates on growth initiated by the Club of Rome report and the energy crises of the 1970s.[42] In response to the warnings about the depletion of resources, they argued, partly correctly, that higher prices would encourage substitution between raw materials and innovation. According to the cake metaphor that economists relish, growth could continue endlessly thanks to new recipes (innovations) while consuming fewer and fewer ingredients (natural resources). Almost forty years later, our two climate Schumpeterians were rehashing the conventional refutation of Malthusian thinking about resources. The problem is that the climate crisis has nothing to do with this easy target. It is not a problem of gradual scarcity to which price rises, substitution and innovation could provide a response. It is not a question of whether there will be enough cake, but rather of what happens to the cake, however big and delicious it may be, after it has been eaten. Global warming is a tragedy of abundance rather than scarcity, a tragedy made all the more intractable and unjust by the fact that its victims are generally not responsible for it. Combating global warming means achieving an unprecedented transformation of the material world by sheer force of will, and in an extraordinarily short space of time. To claim that 'innovation' – be it incremental, granular, green, frugal or disruptive – is up to this unprecedented challenge is just smoke and mirrors.

2.

'The Age of . . .': Material Stagism and Its Problems

In the second half of the nineteenth century, an expression flourished in Anglo-American literature: *the age of*. In particular, it took over the titles of the technical journals founded at the time: *The Railway Age* (1856), *The Age of Steel* (1857), *The Iron Age* (1867), *The Gas Age* (1884), *The Petroleum Age* (1887), *The Electrical Age* (1897), *The Motor Age* (1898), *The Cement Age* (1904) and *The Coal Age* (1911). By vying with each other for the name of their era, these magazines testify, in spite of themselves, that industrialization was the sum and symbiosis of all these techniques and all these materials – and a thousand more besides. But taken one by one, they claimed to distinguish their era by a particular technique or material.

These titles reflect the rise of a new kind of stage theory: reading history as a succession of distinct material epochs.[1] This was a novel historical sentiment. In the previous century, the idea of living in the 'age of wood' or the 'age of the horse' or any other material would hardly have made sense. At the beginning of the nineteenth century, new ages did begin to appear, inspired by the 'golden', 'silver' and 'iron' ages of Hesiod and Ovid, but in a Romantic vein to deplore the triumph of materialism.[2] The difference, in the second half of the nineteenth century, is that these tropes were increasingly being taken seriously. But why? Who disseminates material stagism? What accounts for the success of the 'ages of'? And what are the historiographical consequences?

The seductions of material stagism

The problem is not periodizations in general, some of which are perfectly legitimate, but this empirically unfounded way of singling out certain materials, energies or innovations (and always the same ones) as defining their era. Take, for example, the idea of an 'age of coal' that is often used to characterize the nineteenth century.

In Britain, it is true that this material became a ubiquitous part of daily life. Between 1830 and 1900 its consumption increased tenfold.[3] The problem is that the use of many other materials also grew during the same decades: wood consumption increased by a factor of 6 and bricks by a factor of 5 – two materials which, as much as coal, marked the English landscape in the nineteenth century.[4] What's more, while in Britain the real progress of coal preceded talk of its age, in all other countries the opposite was true. In the mid-1800s, French mining engineers claimed that coal had become 'the backbone of the modern world',[5] 'the food' of the nation and even that 'industry lives only by it'.[6] According to the coal-mine owners, without them 'there would be no more industry, no more trade, no more power' as coal was 'force, movement and light',[7] even though its role in mechanical power and for lighting was still modest at the time. In any case, a 'realistic' interpretation of the *ages of* would not work for other materials. Oil never acquired the importance that coal had. Between the wars, when the 'motor age' was in full swing – in the press more than on the roads – the mass of oil consumed weighed less globally than milk or potatoes, and four times less than wood or coal.[8] In the 1920s, economists calculated that the value of world oil production was equivalent to that of horses and mules, and barely a quarter of that of rice or a third of that of wheat.[9] Finally, the 'atomic age' enjoyed extraordinary lexical success and marginal economic importance. One of the reasons why the history of energy has been so badly told is that it has tended to take this kind of trope seriously, to focus on a limited number of

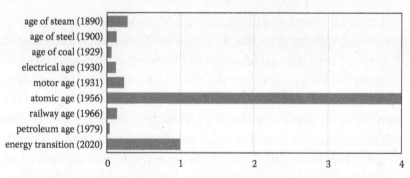

Material ages endure, in fact and in the language. These expressions tend to reinforce themselves over time because they function by opposition. Never were so many people talking about the steam age as in the early days of electricity and oil: it was a way for new entrants to mark a break with the past while at the same time inscribing themselves in an august lineage. Similarly, the 'railway age' flourished in the 1960s, at precisely the time when train lines were being sacrificed to the car. The graph shows the frequency of 'age of X' at the time of its peak use (date in brackets) compared with the frequency of the expression 'energy transition' in 2020. For example, 'atomic age' was four times more common in 1956 than 'energy transition' in 2020. (Google Ngram English-language corpus between 1800 and 2020.)

techniques considered to be absolutely fundamental and to confuse the beginning of their use with their mass take-up.[10]

As the titles of the magazines mentioned above remind us, these formulas are nothing more than commercial slogans. It is hardly surprising, in itself, that oil companies should extol the age of oil, or gas sellers the age of gas. What is more surprising, and needs to be explained, is the infatuation of intellectuals with these promotional tropes.[11]

This way of thinking about matter and time was first given a certain prestige by two disciplines that revolutionized our understanding of the distant past through the use of material markers: geology and prehistory. The expression 'Coal Age' first referred to a geological period – the Carboniferous – before being applied to the nineteenth century. In England, an intense ideological relationship was established between these two periods: it was not historical contingency but Providence that, by stockpiling thick layers of coal in the ground, had ensured power and empire for the Victorians. By the 1830s, pre-historians, following in the footsteps of Christian Thomsen (the director of the National Museum of Denmark in Copenhagen), had constructed a stage theory of the distant past based on three materials: stone, bronze and iron – the Stone Age, the Bronze Age and the Iron Age.[12] In popular technology literature, the three-age system was sometimes presented as an introduction for the arrival of coal.[13] Krupps, Bessemer and Carnegie became the heroes of 'an age of steel' following the mythical ages of bronze and iron.[14] The three-age system made it possible to associate this or that innovation with the majestic course of human history, and this was precisely the effect sought by the high-sounding titles of the magazines mentioned above.

Secondly, the 'age of' notion corresponded well to a bourgeois interpretation of history. Marx, in his time, had already highlighted the fascination of economists with steam. He insisted on the primordial role of *machines*, which in textile factories had preceded the introduction of steam by several decades. The energy that powered them could vary: water, animals (including humans), or steam, and the three were not mutually exclusive.[15] In contrast, the technological literature of the 1860s depicted the steam engine as the essential breakthrough, connecting matter with genius. It is no coincidence that the 'age of coal' was also the age of the glorification of inventors, with James Watt dominating their pantheon. Louis Figuier, the famous French science popularizer, presented modernity as the result of human ingenuity. In his encyclopaedic history of technology, it is the scientists who unleash the forces of nature, almost in spite of the workers. The latter are strangely relegated to the side of inertia and resistance, even though they were clearly the most essential contributors to progress: no steam without miners, no railways without navvies.[16]

In the 1920s, the energy statistics that were beginning to appear were even more oblivious to human muscle. With the rise of oil and then hydroelectricity, statisticians were no longer content to count tonnes of coal and barrels of oil separately, but opted for energy units that aggregated all sources of heat, electricity and power.[17] Thanks to the ambiguity of the word 'work' the statistics justify some quite extraordinary assertions, such as one engineer explaining that 'in the United States two-thirds of the work is done by coal and most of the last third by gas and oil'.[18] On the basis of available power per capita statistics, the Americans, farmers and workers included, were depicted as oriental princes: 'each American is endowed with 40 invisible and obedient genies', and each worker was even said to have '3,000 energy slaves' at his disposal, according to Bassett Jones, the great elevator specialist of Manhattan in the 1930s, who was also one of the first to use this term which promised such a brilliant future.[19]

Thirdly, material stagism also corresponded to a certain futurology, that of the dread of running out of resources. Materials are seen as ages when considered from the future as closed episodes. Stanley Jevons played a fundamental role here. His book *The Coal Question* (1867) launched a genre in its own right, that of energy forecasting.[20] But it is also a perfect example of material stage theory and mono-materialism. Coal, he writes, is the 'alpha and omega' of industrialization, trade and power.[21] Other materials receive only cursory treatment; the few passages devoted to wood deal with its scarcity in seventeenth- and eighteenth-century England. The general pattern is one of substitution: wood by coal, then coal by . . . nothing at all.[22] And this, despite the fact that Jevons could have extended his theory of the rebound effect to the English consumption of many other materials. Written in just three months and based on the strange hypothesis of a continuous exponential growth, *The Coal Question* launched a fifty-year debate on the exhaustion of coal and a wave of speculation on the material age that might follow. In French, one of the first occurrences of the expression *âge du charbon* is found in a review of Jevons's work: '*à l'âge du bois a succédé l'âge du charbon, à l'âge du charbon succédera l'âge d'une autre puissance*'.[23]

Who will the electric age belong to?

Around 1900, the identity of this mysterious *autre puissance* fascinated the public, in part because it seemed to be intertwined with the political fate of industrialized countries. What would be the consequences of electricity in the struggle between capitalism and socialism? In numerous futuristic texts from that era, coal, viewed as both environmentally harmful and socially problematic, was predicted to become obsolete. Electricity would reign supreme – even if it was not clear how it would be produced.[24] The social question underpinned these discussions: for capitalists, the end of coal could also mean the end of the challenges posed by the labour movement. The French chemist and minister Marcelin Berthelot predicted that by the year 2000, renewable energies would have rid the world of 'coal mines and consequently miners' strikes'.[25] With the development of hydroelectricity, some entrepreneurs hoped that a new wave of industrialization in rural areas would enable them to escape the cities contaminated by socialist ideas. This was one reason why in the 1920s Henry Ford decided to relocate part of his business from Detroit to some twenty villages in Michigan powered by hydroelectric dams.[26]

But socialists, too – and Engels was one of the first – were convinced that electricity would work to their advantage.[27] In a remarkable book published in 1910, *Fields, Factories, and Workshops*, Peter Kropotkin showed that small-scale manufacturing was still dominant in most industrial countries: electric motors, simpler and more affordable than steam engines, would modernize these countless workshops, making mass production and large factories obsolete. Thanks to electrification, production could continue in the countryside, reconciling agricultural and industrial work and thus strengthening workers' autonomy.[28] The German socialist August Bebel, returning from the 1900 Paris Exposition, was convinced that electricity held the promise of liberating women from domestic chores.[29] Innovation, however tenuous or, frankly, speculative ('vegetable electricity', to which

Bebel and Kropotkin devoted long pages), became emblematic of a world on the cusp of a profound transformation. Other socialists, like the English Fabians of the 1900s, insisted on the centralizing effect of the electricity network, which would make competition obsolete and impose economic co-operation. The monopolistic tendencies at work, 'gas-and-water-socialism', the placing of gas, electric and water companies under municipal control, seemed to indicate that capitalism had reached its limits in the face of techno-logical development. Socialism became the condition for the electric age to fully blossom. For the Fabians, the key word for this transform-ation was 'transition', which they contrasted with the 'revolution' that had already taken place in the world of production.[30] The transi-tion to socialism was an adaptation to the revolutionary changes in technology. In *Transition: A Novel* (1895), the novelist Emma Brooke portrays her heroine's choice between two lovers: an attractive for-eign anarchist and a dull but solid English socialist reformer modelled on Sidney Webb, the figurehead of the Fabian movement.[31]

In 1925, the sociologist Patrick Geddes also used the word 'trans-ition' in a lecture he gave to the Royal Society. England was going through a 'coal crisis'. The coal industry, penalized by the country's return to the gold standard and faced with competition from the mines on the Ruhr, was deprived of export markets. With miners refusing wage cuts, the mining companies decided to stop operations. A general solidarity strike was organized in May 1926. According to Geddes, this crisis was not the consequence of an inept monetary policy, but the sign of a Britain stuck in the 'coal age' (characterized, with irony, as a form of Stone Age), while the continent, 'from Fin-land to Palestine', was in the process of switching to hydroelectricity. Clean and inexhaustible, this energy promised to revolutionize Europe, beginning with its peripheries – the Alps, the Pyrenees and Scandinavia. There, along the rivers, in the countryside, virtu-ous people would cultivate 'the highest technologies'. According to Geddes, hydroelectricity would become the great redeemer of modernity: it would reconcile industrialization, the environment and eugenics, and would help to regenerate the soil and nature through the production of nitrogen fertilizers.[32] The transition was a matter of racial survival, and the English risked suffering the same fate they had inflicted on primitive peoples if they missed the 'neotechnical' transformation.

A 'common bugaboo'

By the time Geddes announced an imminent 'neotechnical' transition away from coal, economists, oilmen, geologists, foresters and even anyone consulting statistics knew that this hope was illusory. They knew that the nineteenth century had been the age of wood as much as the age of coal, and they predicted that the twentieth century, heralded as the age of oil and electricity, would burn ever more coal and use ever more wood.[33] They considered the idea of substitution to be simplistic and insisted, quite rightly, that the consumption of most raw materials was almost always increasing. The specialists made no secret of their annoyance at the propaganda of industrialists – and the intellectuals who followed them – about the 'age of oil' or the 'age of electricity', abrogating the deleterious reign of coal. One of them described the idea of substitution as 'common bugaboo'[34]: when a material is no longer used in a sector, its producers find other uses for it. Wood provided the most striking example of this maxim. Instead of its use being eliminated by coal and industrialization, wood was consumed more and more for construction, railways, mine timbering, crates, barrels, cardboard, paper, newspapers, hygiene products and so on. Egon Glesinger, the great specialist in forestry statistics between the wars, emphasized the enormous weight of wood used in the world economy (1.2 gigatonnes) compared with oil (0.27 Gt). Only coal was consumed in greater quantities (1.3 Gt).[35] Conservationists were far more concerned about the depletion of forests than about the depletion of coal, whose global reserves had been evaluated by geologists at 6,000 years of consumption at the 1913 rate.[36]

The same applies to the substitution of oil for coal. Oil, whose limited reserves are always stressed, is described by the experts as simply 'accelerating the progress' of an industrial world still based on coal.[37] Robert Brunschwig, a mining engineer at the French Office Nationale des Combustibles Liquides, described the 'end of coal' or the 'age of oil' as 'a brilliant and misleading oversimplification'. Although coal's relative share in the world's energy mix was declining because of the rise of oil, it remained by far the dominant energy source. Even though oil was overtaking coal in navigation and heating, experts believed that for a long time to come coal would remain 'the chief energizer of modern industry',[38] or 'the basis of the world of machines'.[39] The hope of a transition to

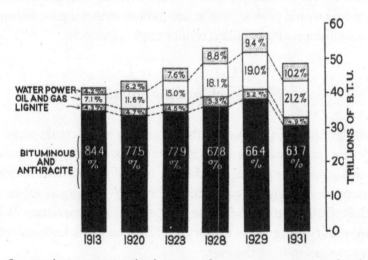

The first graphs representing the dynamics of energy systems appeared at the end of the 1920s in the United States, when economists began to represent coal, oil and hydroelectricity in a single curve, relating them to energy units. For the experts, the fall in world coal consumption between the wars was in no way a sign of a transition from coal to oil or hydroelectricity. It was a temporary phenomenon linked to the high price of coal during the First World War and was mainly due to improvements in efficiency. By replacing steam engines with steam turbines, the efficiency of American thermal power stations doubled between 1917 and 1930. Electrification, by scrapping inefficient steam engines, made it possible to save coal, while paradoxically reinforcing its economic importance. (Scott Turner, 'The Mineral Industry', Department of Commerce, US Bureau of Mines, 1932, p. 12.)

hydroelectricity was also quickly refuted. Long before Geddes' flights of fancy, calculations had already shown that flat England would save just over a million tonnes of coal thanks to its rivers: a ridiculous amount compared with the 200 million tonnes burned at the time.[40] In the United States, where the potential for water power was much larger, hope lasted a little longer, but experts generally regarded hydropower as a means of conserving coal, certainly not as a replacement for it.[41] It is also striking to see the extent to which conservationists were concerned with the very long term, with the availability of coal in three or four centuries' time: proof if it were needed that the idea of transition was alien to them.[42] In 1915, Herbert Jevons, Stanley Jevons's son, stated that British coal consumption would peak in 2100 at 400 million tonnes a year, followed by stabilization at 300 million tonnes until . . . 2200.[43]

'The age of' and the historians

In the last third of the nineteenth century, the intellectual routine of indexing epochs with materials appeared in an ideological potpourri of industrial promotion, Malthusian fear of exhaustion, national anxiety, electric utopia and social reformism – all expressed in the prehistoric lexicon that befits the great evolutionist narratives. What is most surprising is the extent to which historians have accepted this strange vision of the past.

In early works on the 'Industrial Revolution' – by Arnold Toynbee, for example – coal was not central. The heart of the action was at the end of the eighteenth century, with the mechanization of the textile industry. Historians were more interested in the deleterious social effects of mechanization than in the replacement of muscle by steam. The inspiration came from Adam Smith and Marx rather than Jevons.[44] But at the beginning of the twentieth century, various concepts – organic economy, the first and second industrial revolutions – acclimatized 'the age of' narratives in history. For historians with philosophical pretensions – or philosophers with historical pretensions – erecting matter as a temporal marker provided ready-made explanations and gave an appearance of materialism to narratives which, ironically, were rather inspired by idealist philosophies of history. Material-stage history provided a convenient alibi for intellectuals who claimed that they had to rethink social, economic, historical and other issues from top to bottom because the material foundations of the world had suddenly changed. These *tabula rasa* intellectual tactics are ancient, commonplace and constantly renewed.

As early as 1903, the German historian Werner Sombart interpreted industrialization as a departure from the 'organic economy' and even proposed calculations of 'ghost acres' to illustrate its impact; for example, steam locomotives generated such an amount of energy that a quarter of Germany's surface area would have had to be dedicated to feeding the horses required to provide an equivalent amount of power.[45] While contemporary historians of the Industrial Revolution such as Rolf Peter Sieferle, E. Anthony Wrigley and Kenneth Pomeranz have adopted the term and the method, for the very conservative Sombart, the 'organic economy' served above all to characterize German identity. 'What differentiates the Germans from other nations,' he wrote, 'is the forest. The material culture of the northern countries was rooted in the forest before iron and other inorganic materials created a new one.'[46] Sombart contrasted this *Gemeinschaft* of forest, wood and use-value with the mineral economy of English capitalism based on machines, coal and iron. The Anglo-Saxon capitalist in his city of steel and concrete is like the wandering Jew in the desert: both 'are deprived of their relationship with mother earth. The sense of communion with all living things is destroyed, as is any true understanding of organic nature.'[47] The nineteenth century, he laments, saw the destruction of the organic economy through quantification, science and mechanization, and the substitution of mineral matter for living matter: coal for wood, steam for horses, phosphates for manure, chemical dyes for natural dyes.[48]

In the 1930s, the idea that the English industrial revolution was fundamentally an energy phenomenon became commonplace in the writings of public intellectuals trying to make sense of the economic crisis and 'technological unemployment'. They explained that the early 1900s saw the advent of a 'second industrial revolution' – American and electrical – a 'power revolution' that should be analysed in the light of the first: that of England and coal.[49] Machines receded into the background: 'the new thing, the really fundamental thing, the profoundly important thing that defines the Industrial Revolution is the substitution of other powers for human physical effort as the working energy of the world's production,'[50] wrote the London socialist Fred Henderson. The *Chicago Tribune* journalist Harper Leech made the same observation: intellectuals idolized or blamed machines without understanding that they were merely an emanation of coal: 'Modern mankind has been the passive beneficiary of the great Palaeozoic accident.' The first industrial revolution took place when 'the steam engine shifted the economic basis of Britain from her soil to the coal seams underneath',[51] and the second when energy became ubiquitous thanks to electricity. Here, energy thinking served a conservative ideology: just as Malthus and Ricardo were already obsolete in their time – because they had not grasped the upheaval introduced by James Watt – so, in the USA, Marxism and the class struggle no longer made any sense 'when labor, the muscular work of man is responsible for only a trifling fraction of all actual work performed . . . when 94% is done by coal, oil, natural gas, and waterpower'.[52]

Technics and Civilization is undoubtedly the masterpiece of the stagist literature of the 1930s. Its author, Lewis Mumford, takes elements from Geddes, Sombart and Oswald Spengler and claims to provide a history of 'the material foundations of Western civilization'.[53] In his book he identifies three successive phases – eotechnic, palaeotechnic and neotechnic – a more distinguished way of speaking of the ages of wood, coal and electricity that goes back to the prehistoric origin of all these tropes. The history of materials is conflated with the history of technology, which leads Mumford to certain aberrations. Iron is described as the 'universal material' of the nineteenth century, and Mumford is even astonished to see the techniques of wood surviving the age of metal.[54] Like Geddes, but later than him, Mumford was still convinced that 'neotechnics' would abrogate the reign of coal, that they would save industrialization from the original sin of coal. Thanks to hydroelectricity, 'blue skies and clear waters will return'.[55] Better still, it would give birth to a planetary conscience, to 'geotechnics' concerned with forests and the climate, because humanity would henceforth have to take care of nature – or at least of watercourses – to produce its energy.[56] It should be noted that in 1938, Mumford was recruited by the Pacific Northwest Regional Planning Commission (PNWRPC), an institution similar to the better-known Tennessee Valley Authority, which poured an enormous amount of concrete to develop the Columbia river with hydroelectric dams and other infrastructure.[57]

Hiroshima and Nagasaki caused an outburst of stagism. 'We enter a New Era: the Atomic Age' was the headline in the *New York Times*.[58] In France, *Le Monde* and *L'Aurore* announced 'a scientific revolution'[59] at the time of the destruction of the two Japanese cities. On 18 August, well before Gunther Anders, an American journalist announced 'the obsolescence of man'. In the 1950s, the 'atomic age' was everywhere. Everything had to be reread in its light: physics, war, peace, law and ethics, of course, but also *Le savoir vivre à l'âge atomique* and *L'éducation catholique de nos filles à l'âge atomique*. A French doctor even dared this title: *Comment prévenir la cellulite, fléau de l'âge atomique* ('How to prevent cellulite, the scourge of the atomic age').[60] Virgil Jordan, the editor of *Business Week*, wrote without batting an eyelid in 1946: 'Thanks to atomic energy, anything can now be made from anything, or even from nothing, anywhere in the world, in any quantity and at no cost.'[61]

Despite the disappointments of the atomic age, stagism did not disappear. After the atom, it was the computer that designated the new era, and like many of the other 'ages of' that had preceded it, 'Information Age' appeared in the title of a computer magazine in 1978, before becoming the title of a famous sociological trilogy.[62] In the 1970s, there was a vogue, especially in the United States, for the 'solar age'. And today, in the face of global warming, a fantastical history of energy is fuelling the return of the crudest stagism, for example Jeremy Rifkin's books announcing a 'third industrial revolution' based on hydrogen, which would follow the first one based on coal and the second industrial revolution based on oil.[63]

More surprisingly, in the historical studies too, the 'ages of' endure. The British Library catalogue even shows a resurgence of publications with a material chrononym in their titles.[64] Recent historiography, rightly concerned with the environment and resources, has given a second life to the energy stagism of the last century: the 'industrial revolution', relativized by twenty years of economic history, has been rehabilitated as a 'transition' from wood to coal, as the passage from an 'organic economy' to a 'mineral economy'. However, since the beginning of the twentieth century, as stagism spread through popular culture and among intellectuals, experts had painted a very different picture of material history: a history not of phases and ages, but of stratification and symbiosis.

Whether for obscuring human muscular work, for advocating social reform or for claiming power for engineers, age-of-ism has always had political overtones. But with climate change, its persistence has become truly dangerous. For it is this ordinary historical culture that explains the ease with which, in the face of climate change, the notion of an 'energy transition' has become self-evident and could appear as a solid and reassuring notion, a notion anchored in history. Whereas in reality, this future had no past whatsoever.

3.

Coal and Wood: A Tangled History

Let us take it a step further. The aim of this book is not simply to show that energies and materials have piled up on top of each other over the nineteenth and twentieth centuries – a statistically trivial observation – but to show that they are in symbiosis and that we understand nothing of their history if we do not take into account their relationships of mutual dependence. In this chapter and the next, we will show that, far from replacing wood, coal has driven the consumption of wood, including for energy purposes.

Energy historians describe industrialization in the 1800s as an energy transition, with wood losing out to coal, which took over from the eighteenth century in England and from the mid-nineteenth century in other industrial countries. This way of presenting things is based on a prior quantification exercise that consists of converting tonnes of wood and coal into energy and then considering the evolution of these quantities in relative terms. Indeed, once these two steps have been completed, it seems clear that in most industrial countries the energy contribution of wood in 1900 was low or even negligible compared with that of coal. There are two objections to this interpretation. The first is that it is based on a particular viewpoint, that of economic historians studying the 'industrial revolution'. From the point of view of trees and the ecosystems they support, and also from the point of view of the climate, it is of course the *absolute* values that matter, the number of trees felled and reduced to ashes: a number that is only increasing. The second problem is that, even from the point of view of economic history, presenting wood as 'secondary' in the energy production of industrial countries is a serious and widespread error.

The real subterranean forests

The idea of a transition from wood to coal is all the more wide-spread for its antiquity. It was born of a promise made by entrepreneurs at the end of the seventeenth century: in exchange for mining concessions, they promised their sovereigns 'subterranean forests' capable of preserving the real ones. Coal was said to be a gift from Providence, placed there by God to replace wood when it ran out.[1] Even leaving God out of the equation, this vision of the future seems to have been fairly commonplace. For example, the French naturalist Buffon, who also owned a forge in Burgundy, explained that the voracity of blast furnaces and chimneys would sooner or later exhaust the forests. Coal would therefore have to be used in the coming centuries, especially as, according to his planetary theory, the Earth would cool down inexorably. Condorcet conceived of another scenario close to the English experience: population increase would lead to the expansion of fields to the detriment of the forests. The point of coal was not to preserve the forests but, on the contrary, to be able to get rid of them and devote the area thus freed to cereals.[2] Whether it was the saviour (Buffon) or the gravedigger (Condorcet) of the forests, coal was conceived in opposition to wood, as a substitute, as its successor.[3] In reality, the image of the *Sylva Subterranea* must be taken literally: extracting coal was effectively tantamount to burying entire forests.

The bourgeoisie who ventured into the mines often insisted on the surprising smell that reigned there: a smell of softwood and sawn timber, the smell of the millions of pit props that supported the galleries. In the open air, before the slag heaps marked the landscape in the twentieth century, it was the enormous reserves of timber that signalled the presence of the mines.[4] In a remarkable book entitled *La vie souterraine*, the French mining engineer Louis Simonin described the fauna and flora of the galleries, such as the strange luminescent mushrooms that thrived in their moist heat.[5] Lewis Mumford described coal mines as 'the first completely inorganic environment created by man'.[6] Most likely, he never set foot in one. At the same time, George Orwell, who visited the mines of Wigan in the north of England, reported how exhausting his excursion had been, more than a kilometre underground before reaching the coal face: he had to bend at every step to avoid hitting a wooden beam.[7] And yet historians have preferred to follow Mumford rather than Orwell. The shortcut of coal as 'mineral energy', the cliché of coal as a way out of an 'organic economy', has prevailed.

Let's take the case of Britain, the leading country of the so-called first energy transition. According to data provided by the historian Paul Warde, and used by Anthony Wrigley in a graph that has become famous,[8] wood no longer played any role in the English energy mix from the middle of the nineteenth century onwards. And indeed, blast furnaces burned coal and very few English people heated their homes with wood.

In fact, wood played a fundamental role in energy production: without timber to prop up the mines, England would have had very little coal, and therefore very little steel and very little steam. Although

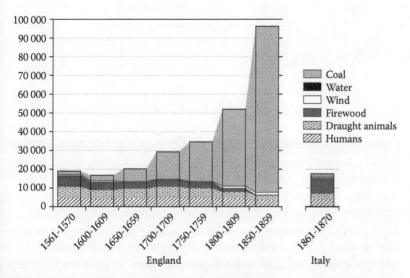

Annual per capita energy consumption in megajoules. (E. A. Wrigley, *Energy and the English Industrial Revolution* (Cambridge, 2010), p. 95.)

pit props are classed as construction timber, this is a misleading convention: their function was indeed to produce energy. At the beginning of the twentieth century, British mines consumed between 3 and 4.5 million cu. m of props every year. By way of comparison, a century and a half earlier, the British burned just 3.6 million cu. m of firewood.[9] In terms of volume, Great Britain consumed more wood for energy in 1900 than in pre-industrial times. What's more, with timber production requiring around four times as much land as firewood, Britain was actually using six to seven times as much woodland to produce energy in 1900 as it had a century and a half earlier.[10] That such a process can be described as an 'energy transition' or an escape from the 'organic economy' is somewhat disconcerting.

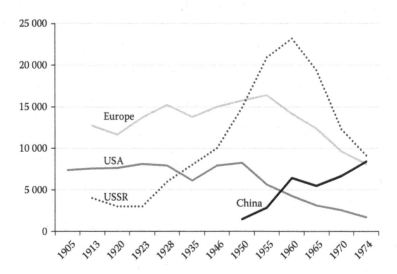

Consumption of timber in mines in thousands of cu m. (FAO, *European Timber Statistics, 1913–1950* (Geneva, 1953); FAO, *Forest Products Statistics, Part II, Apparent Consumption, 1950–1975* (Rome, 1975); J. J. MacGregor, 'Timber statistics', *Journal of the Royal Statistical Society*, 116, 3, 1953, pp. 298–322; US Department of Agriculture, Forest Service, 'Timber Resources for America's Future' (1958); Robert Stone, 'Wood products used by coal mines', *Forest Products Journal*, 35, 6, 1985, pp. 45–52; S. D. Richardson, *Forestry in Communist China* (Baltimore, MD, 1966) p. 164.) Statistical sources do not distinguish between props for coal mines and other types of mines. However, in most countries, coal mines are the main consumers of props.

The British case is exceptional only in the disproportion between the mining industry and forest resources: in the nineteenth century and well into the twentieth, all coal-producing countries depended on forests for their energy. Over the course of the 1800s, France's consumption of pit props increased fiftyfold.[11] Not only did the coal face have to be wooded, but so did the main galleries, which were left open for the circulation of air, people and equipment. Under the pressure of the surrounding rock, the props tended to bend and fracture and had to be replaced regularly. After labour, timber was the second-biggest expense for mining companies. Even if they tried to economize on timber, doing without seemed impossible. 'Mines and forests', noted an engineer at the end of the nineteenth century, 'maintain numerous, continuous and necessary relations . . . which highlight all the resources that wood offers to the mineral industry and that *only* wood can offer.'[12]

Wood was vital for industrial economies, but even more so for miners. At the end of the nineteenth century in Europe, between one in a thousand and one in two thousand miners died every year under collapsing roofs, and three times as many were seriously injured. Far more than firedamp explosion, the breaking of a beam was a common, almost daily, danger. That is why these accidents hardly caused a stir, or were viewed with fatalism: they killed, injured and mutilated, in small numbers but regularly, and as the miner was held responsible for timbering work, the collapse of a roof was considered to be the consequence of his negligence.[13] As payment was by the tonne of coal produced, timbering was unremunerative and miners were constantly forced to arbitrate between their wages and their safety. 'The worker is the best judge', the companies explained, to absolve themselves of responsibility. At the end of the nineteenth century, mining mortality rates varied greatly from one country to another – by as much as double between France and England on the one hand and Germany and the United States on the other, where mines were more dangerous. One of the reasons for these differences was the youth of the Ruhr and Pennsylvania coalfields: according to the experts, the miners had not yet acquired the skills needed to timber the galleries. In the 1920s, Jules Mousseron, a Picard-speaking French poet and underground miner at Anzin, explained, *bon mineur sait carpinter*. Who should bear the cost of safety? Should the payment per tonne of coal be supplemented by a payment for timbering? This question was a recurring battleground. Zola made no mistake when he used it as the starting point for the strike in *Germinal*. In 1913, in Colorado, pay for 'dead work' – vital, in reality, since it mainly included the timbering of galleries – was one of the demands of the strike that ended with the Ludlow Massacre, perpetrated by Rockefeller's henchmen. Rockefeller, oil magnate that he was, also owned coal mines, coal being essential – as we will see later – for extracting and transporting oil.[14]

Cross-trade in timber and coal

In contrast to global oil, coal is sometimes described as a 'national' resource: in reality, it was entirely dependent on the international timber trade. This is particularly true of the major European coal-producing countries. In the 1930s, Belgium used half of its annual timber production to support its mines, and still had to import 800,000 cu. m from abroad. Belgian coal mines consumed more wood than the country's forests produced.[15] At the same time, Great Britain was importing almost all (96 per cent) of its timber from abroad. In terms of volume, it was the country's biggest import. In terms of value, timber exceeded oil imports and, in some years, even coal exports.[16] Pit props accounted for between 20 and 30 per cent of this timber. They came from regions stretching from the Baltic to Portugal, half of them from the Landes 'forest' in south-western France. Created under Napoléon III, this was probably the largest plantation in the world at the time. By way of comparison, in the 1920s, Firestone's rubber plantation in Liberia was half its size. By the end of the nineteenth century, 800,000 hectares of pine trees had reached maturity and were exploited for their resin. After twenty years, they were cut down and sent to British mines. Ships unloaded coal in Bordeaux and left Bayonne with their holds full of props. This trade was so strategic that England sought to secure it by signing a 'props for coal' barter agreement with France in 1934.[17]

At the end of the Second World War, European mines were still totally dependent on timber. In 1945, coal production was two-thirds of pre-war levels. The cause: damaged mines, malnourished miners and a shortage of timber.[18] Lumberjacks were short of horses and lorries. The Ruhr mines lacked the timber from the forests of East Germany and Poland. And last but not least, European trade was at a standstill: starved of German and British coal for five years, Sweden began to burn more wood, depriving the mines of the Ruhr and Britain.[19] The first European economic organizations – the Solid Fuel Section of the American army and then, from May 1945, the European Coal Organization based in London – gave priority to allocating American coal and oil to the Scandinavian countries, as this was the *sine qua non* for relaunching the European trade in wood and coal.[20]

The situation was obviously different in the United States, which was self-sufficient in timber. In the 1900s, pit props accounted for just 3 per cent of the country's wood consumption, compared with 30 per cent in Great Britain.[21] Nevertheless, in America too, coal depended on a wood trade of continental dimension. The mines in Pennsylvania, despite their immense forest properties, brought in props from North Carolina and Virginia. Some even fetched their props from as far away as Oregon, which they transported via the Panama Canal.[22] Similarly, in the USSR, the huge Donbass coalfield was supplied by the remote forests of central Russia. In the 1950s, this material synergy between Ukraine and Russia was a major theme of Soviet propaganda.[23] The Lenin Canal, inaugurated in 1952, connecting the Volga to the Don, was presented as the vital artery linking Ukrainian coal to the forests of central Russia.[24]

The case of the Chinese mines further illustrates the importance of timber for coal extraction. In the 1900s, American and European engineers established in China insisted that the country was poor in coal because it was poor in wood.[25] This was Herbert Hoover's opinion, for instance. Before becoming President of the United States,

Unloading pit props for the Welsh coal mines, port of Cardiff, 1936. (Getty Images/Fox Photos.)

Hoover had made his fortune from Chinese coal. In 1901, thanks to the Boxer War, and with the assistance of Belgian and British capital, he managed to take control of the Kaiping mine, the country's largest.[26] In his view, Chinese mines consumed little wood but a lot of men: their production costs were low thanks to rudimentary timbering and, ultimately, thanks to their contempt for human life. One of Hoover's initiatives was to finance tree plantations around Kaiping.[27] In the Fushun mine, Manchuria, the Japanese owners were also faced with a shortage of wood, which they had to import from Korea. After a decade of unfruitful efforts, they resigned themselves to opencast mining, buying expensive German and American excavating machines.[28]

While Western engineers generally regarded Chinese mines with condescension, the American engineer William Shockley (the father of the inventor of the transistor), who spent time in China, believed that they were simply adapted to their environment. For example, in Shanxi, where coal is extremely abundant and wood scarce, miners had developed original working methods that were very economical with wood. They exploited veins located under resistant rock layers. Or, when the deposit was close to the surface, they mined it using countless vertical shafts, extended by short horizontal tunnels that were not timbered. The miners even kept pet rats, trained to warn them of an imminent landslide. With no capital and almost no timber, these miners managed to supply the local population with several million tonnes of coal a year at unbeatable prices.[29]

A slow separation

The difficulty of extricating coal from its dependence on wood is clearly seen in the case of England. In 1915, with the outbreak of the submarine war, this country, which had almost no forestry industry, found itself dangerously dependent on foreign countries for its energy supplies. The price of wood tripled, and consumption of props was halved.[30] At the end of the war, the government launched a reforestation programme in order to meet its needs, at least temporarily, in the event of another conflict. It bought and reforested half a million hectares between 1919 and 1934. Paradoxically, it was coal that forced England to look after its forests and plant new ones.

The English mines also tried to use steel supports at least for the main galleries. In 1930, they buried 600,000 tonnes of steel, mainly in the form of arches.[31] But wooden props have undeniable advantages at the coal face or in temporary galleries: they could easily be shortened with a hatchet; their creaking sound warned miners of danger; and, above all, as they were cheap, they did not need to be recovered.[32] On the other hand, adjustable steel props had to be removed before blasting the galleries and miners complained about

Belgium	4
Czechoslovakia	2
France	4.2
Saarland	2.5
Federal Republic of Germany	2.5
Netherlands	2
Poland	2
United Kingdom	1.34
Europe	2.2

Mine wood consumption in cu. m per hundred tonnes of coal in 1950. Variations are largely explained by the greater extent of opencast lignite mining in Central Europe. (FAO, *European Timber Trends and Prospects* (Geneva, 1953).)

this dangerous operation. This was the subject of a strike in the mines of Northumberland in 1929.[33]

In the 1920s, the fall in the cost of maritime transport, the return of Soviet timber exports and then the Great Depression led to a fall in the price of pit props. For all these reasons, British consumption of mining timber remained stable at a level roughly proportional to the coal extracted until the end of the 1940s. Depending on the year (mines stocked up timber when prices were low) 1–2 cu. m of timber were needed to extract 100 tonnes of coal. In February 1938, a convoy of wood was transported from Siberia to Scotland by a fleet of three Russian icebreakers, built in England and powered by oil.[34] In 1958, the first nuclear-powered icebreaker was used to facilitate trade from the Siberian ports, which were then exporting a lot of timber. Oil certainly, and probably nuclear power thus helped to transport the timber used to extract coal.

In other European countries, mines consumed more wood than in Great Britain: between 2 and 4 cu. m per 100 tonnes of coal extracted. During the major strikes in 1948 in the collieries of northern France, miners used props to erect their barricades. At the start of the 1950s,

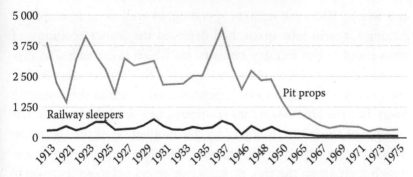

English timber consumption in thousands of cu. m for sleepers and props.
(FAO, *European Timber Statistics, 1913–1950* (Geneva, 1953) and FAO, *Forest Products Statistics, 1950–1975, Part II, Apparent Consumption* (Rome, 1975).)

mines still accounted for 10 per cent of European timber consumption. From the mid-1950s onwards, however, there is a notable decline. This was due to the use of metal props and rock bolting, followed, in the mid-1960s, by the introduction of powered roof supports, impressive hydraulic machines which protect the coal face as it advances. The coal is evacuated laterally, and the void is filled with sterile earth.

In Soviet mines, the use of wood was both greater and later than in other countries. In the 1960s, wood consumption reached a record level of 24 million cu. m per year, representing around 8 per cent of the country's total forest production. At the time, the United States produced as much coal as the USSR using five times less wood. This difference can be explained by a technological lag, but also by specific geological characteristics. In the country's main mining basin, the Donbass in Ukraine, the coal seams were narrow, making it difficult to install powered supports. As a result, miners worked with jackhammers in wooded galleries only 60 to 90 centimetres high.[35] Between 1950 and 1970, coal production in the Donbass coalfield increased dramatically, from 70 million to over 220 million tonnes. Demand for timber soared so that the Soviet Union struggled to supply Ukraine with wood, despite the presence of vast forests and a huge forestry workforce of 800,000 loggers, some of whom were forced labourers.[36] According to a CIA report, the props remained a bottleneck for the mining industry and hence for Soviet industry as a whole. Excessive military spending, as well as on Sputnik and putting Gagarin into space, had deprived the Soviet economy of investment in the forestry industry on which it depended to produce its energy.[37] From the 1970s onwards, the 'timber intensity' of Soviet coal fell, thanks to the opencast coal mines in the Kuznetsk basin. But the Donbass mines continued to use a lot of wood. The collapse of the USSR, followed by the devaluation of the Ukrainian hryvnia against the rouble, plunged Ukrainian miners into a catastrophic situation: the lack of sufficient wood led to an increase in accidents, and coal production collapsed.[38]

In China, the lack of wood has long been an obstacle to coal extraction. In the 1950s, Chinese mines represented 18 per cent of the country's wood consumption.[39] Amazingly, pit props were the largest expense for the state-owned mines, ahead even of labour.[40] The high price of wood may partly explain the remarkable competitiveness of Shanxi's small-scale artisanal mines. After Deng Xiaoping's reforms, these began to multiply and by the end of the 1990s, 60,000 'village mines' were extracting more than 600 million tonnes of coal a year, around 40 per cent of China's total production. The mining conditions were similar to those described by Western engineers in the 1900s. According to one specialist:

> It is hard to imagine the working conditions of most village mines. The most typical in north-east and north-west China are small well-style mines, whose major vertical shaft is about one metre square . . . Once the main shaft is established, the workers dig as many horizontal sub-shafts as possible radiating from the main vertical shaft to extract more coal. While state-run mines use pit props to prevent shaft collapse, village mines, in order to save costs, usually do not.[41]

Wood consumption in Shanxi mines was minimal, but mortality rates were also two to four times higher than in European mines a century earlier.[42]

★

Without abundant wood, Europe would simply have had no coal, and hence little or no steam, little or no steel, and few or no railways. The curves showing the extraordinary dominance of coal in the energy systems of industrial countries mask an equally extraordinary dependence on wood. To say that there has been no transition does not mean that nothing has changed, but rather that the change is not the one described in the standard historiography of the industrial revolution. The dynamic that governs the relationship between coal and wood is not that of a transition. Rather, we should be talking about a symbiotic relationship that intensified during the nineteenth century, followed by a gradual disengagement that really began in the second half of the twentieth century. In today's opencast mines, coal is extracted by shovels and lorries, which consume a huge amount of diesel: coal has effectively broken free from wood but has entered a new and even more solid dependence on oil.

4.

The Timber Palace

Let's consider the famous 'Crystal Palace' of the 1851 Great Exhibition in London. Its contemporaries, and intellectuals ever since, have constantly praised its material modernity, a modernity of iron and glass.[1] However, according to documents relating to its construction, the building contained at least three times more wood than iron and glass.[2] Although it illustrates the 'industrial revolution' in most textbooks, the Crystal Palace was a monument to an agricultural and aristocratic society: it was designed on the model of a greenhouse and its architect, Joseph Paxton, worked in the service of a duke who made his fortune from an estate of 80,000 hectares.[3] This is not to say that the building was not 'modern', but rather that its modernity is not the usual cliché about the industrial revolution. For example, one of the innovations employed in its construction was the use of wood lathes powered by steam engines.

The gap between the cultural interpretation of the Crystal Palace and its material reality bears witness to a general distortion: the historical processes commonly associated with industrialization depended as much on materials and energies wrongly relegated to the side of tradition as on modernity's steel and coal. It's not enough to say that wood is 'resisting' the advance of coal, or that coal energy is simply adding to that of wood – evidence that is well documented by the FAO's statistics. No: wood consumption is soaring, not in spite of coal but because of it. This is an important point because it affects the interpretation of the material dynamics of industrialization. Usually approached from the angle of transition, they must be understood as a process of amplification, of the symbiotic expansion of all materials.

The iron horse made of wood

While coal should be associated with wood (see Chapter 3), steam should not be equated with coal. In many countries, the engines and techniques invented in England to run on coal led to a surge in wood consumption, as industrialists adapted to the price of local resources.[4] Take the emblematic case of the railways. Until the end of the nineteenth century, the world's largest rail networks, in the United States, India and Russia, burned more wood than coal.[5] In Brazil in the early 1950s, the railways burned 12 million cu. m of wood a year, ten times the volume of coal and twenty times the volume of oil.[6] The first eucalyptus plantations in Brazil were financed by the railway companies.[7] It is likely that wood also fuelled stationary boilers in the large and forested countries. In the United States, until 1914, the sector that used the most steam power after the railways was the timber industry: the thousands of sawmills, some of them gigantic, most of them small and itinerant, scattered throughout the forests, consumed more horsepower than the iron and steel industry and three times as much as the textile industry. And most of them used wood residues as a source of energy.[8] This means that, in American industry, not only did hydraulic power take precedence over steam engines until the late 1860s, but the latter were also largely powered by wood.

Even when the locomotives ran on coal, the railways used huge quantities of wood. Railway sleepers, which had to be replaced on average every five years, represented a major consumption item. At the end of the nineteenth century, for example, the French railways consumed 2.5 million sleepers a year.[9] At the same time, American railways required 120 million sleepers a year, the equivalent of 20 million cu. m of wood, or around 10 per cent of American timber consumption.[10] By way of comparison, iron consumption for rails was only 2.3 million tonnes. In terms of mass, the railways consumed six times more wood than iron.[11] The case of sleepers also illustrates the porosity between timber and firewood: all over the

United States, along the tracks, you could see piles of old sleepers destined to be burned in the locomotives.[12] For railways, replacing the sleepers was a considerable expense: the third largest item after wages and coal. At the beginning of the twentieth century, American companies spent more on wood than on locomotives or wagons.[13] In addition to sleepers, timber was also used for stations, platforms and bridges. Outside the East Coast, American bridges were almost all made of wood.[14] Companies built at low cost, betting on a future return to rebuild later in bricks and iron. They drew inspiration from the methods used to build makeshift bridges during the American Civil War: bridge piers were sometimes built from logs that were simply stacked on top of each other. On forest railways, even the rails were made of wood.[15] In England, where iron was undoubtedly the most widely used, the majority of viaducts were made of wood until the 1870s.[16] In addition to railway infrastructure, wood was also used in wagons and coaches, which were far more numerous than locomotives. And even in the latter, parts subject to high stresses were often cast from charcoal steel, which was reputed to be less brittle than coke steel.

In forest-rich countries, the production of cast iron and steel from charcoal remained massive well into the twentieth century. In Sweden, charcoal dominated the steel industry until the 1930s.[17] By then, coke from coal took over, but this was mainly because wood found a more lucrative outlet in the paper industry.[18] In nineteenth-century Russia, the ironmasters of the Urals used charcoal and slave labour. Between 1800 and 1900, their production rose from 100,000 to 800,000 tonnes, reaching 1.5 million tonnes in 1913.[19] This growth, based on forests rather than mines, was made possible by the modernization of blast furnaces, whose yields increased considerably over the nineteenth century.[20] The chronology is similar in the United States and Canada, where charcoal steel began to decline only after the First World War.[21]

In the twentieth century, the carbonization of wood was perfected at the same time as that of coal. As Heinrich Caro, one of the founders of the BASF chemical company, wrote, the distillation of wood and coal 'are two sister industries'.[22] Thanks to the Lambiotte retort, wood can be carbonized in a much more efficient way to produce charcoal and many chemical products: methyl alcohol, acetic acid, as well as formaldehyde, a key component of plastics. Although this material is now derived from petroleum, until the 1930s, plastic was a wood-based product. Rayon, the first synthetic fibre in history, was produced from wood, as was cellophane, a transparent packaging material that predated petrochemical plastics by half a century. When the chemist Leo Baekeland began work on the phenol-formaldehyde resins that would become the famous 'Bakelite', it was with the aim of obtaining a product that would harden wood.[23] The radios, pens, telephones and car dashboards of the inter-war period, as seen in the films of Hollywood's golden age, were mainly made of wood, with manufacturers incorporating a significant amount of wood flour into their phenol-formaldehyde resins in order to cut manufacturing costs.[24]

In any case, the end of the use of charcoal in the steel industry in many countries should not obscure the fact that, on a global scale, metallurgy uses far more charcoal than it did a century ago. The Brazilian steel industry alone consumed 24 million cu. m per year in the 1990s, i.e. 25 times more than the American steel industry at its 'charcoal peak' a century earlier, and 80 times more than the French steel industry in 1860.[25] Other metallurgies are making increasing use of charcoal. To reduce emissions from the production of solar panels, and also because charcoal contains few impurities, some silicon refiners in Norway, Brazil and China are using it instead of, or in addition to, coke.[26] The 'solar age' and the 'silicon age' will continue to use coke and charcoal for a long time to come.

Bricks and wood

Although in some sectors fuelwood did lose to coal, this decline was offset by the increase in timber consumption, which was itself driven by coal. Between 1830 and 1930, England's wood consumption

	United States (1910)	Canada (1923)	Great Britain (1920)	France (1913)
Firewood	43	32		56
Construction	44	33	41	26
Railways	5	7	3	4
Pulpwood	3	21	30	9
Pit props	1.5	1	23	4
Cooperage	1.1		1.5	
Wagons and furniture	1			

Breakdown of wood consumption (in per cent). (International Institute of Agriculture, *Les Forêts* (1924); Egon Glesinger, *Le Bois en Europe. Origines et étude de la crise actuelle* (Paris, 1932).)

increased by a factor of 6, and by a factor of 3 in relation to the number of inhabitants.[27] A champion of coal, England was also the country that imported the most wood in the world: 12 million cu. m at the end of the nineteenth century, twice the production of timber by French forests. In the last third of that century, Great Britain increased its timber imports at prices that were falling thanks to the progress of a merchant navy that used coal. Other European countries followed similar paths: Belgium saw its wood imports multiply by 6 between 1860 and 1900 and Germany, despite its high-yield lowland softwood forests, doubled its imports in the last decade of the nineteenth century. France, which had mainly coppice forests for firewood, was forced to import 3 million cu. m of timber, i.e. half its national production.[28] Not to mention the United States, where timber consumption increased a hundredfold in the 1800s, if such a figure makes any sense.[29]

What was all this wood used for? In all countries, construction came first, followed by paper, railways, mining and packaging (barrels and crates). And all these uses of wood were growing in line with coal consumption.

Industrial cities, even built with stones or bricks, made increasing use of wood. At the beginning of the twentieth century, from Rivoli to Broadway, cities' main thoroughfares were paved with wood-blocks, much appreciated for their smoothness. In Paris in 1900, a fifth of the road surface was paved with wood.[30] In the United States, it was estimated that a brick house consumed in wood three-fifths of the amount used in a house made directly in this material – for the frame, floors, window frames and scaffolding.[31] As a result, wood consumption kept pace with brick consumption, which exploded during the nineteenth century. In England, annual brick production rose from 1 billion to 4.8 billion between 1830 and 1907.[32] American production rose from 6 billion to 12 billion bricks between 1900 and 1910. At that time, the construction of New York alone consumed a billion bricks a year, eating away the banks of the Hudson river over dozens of kilometres. Brickworks were extremely energy-intensive: in the United States, they were the third-largest consumers of coal, after the railways and the steel industry.[33] Finally, bricks often incorporated coal ashes from the cities they contributed to build. In material terms, industrial towns at the end of the nineteenth century were an alloy of clay, coal and wood – glass and iron weighed much less. If we bear in mind that 1 tonne of brick required between 200 and 500 kilos of coal, the weight of cities in CO_2 is equivalent to or even greater than their weight in bricks: they weigh as much in the atmosphere as they do on the ground.

Coal and forest conservation

It is not hard to understand why, around 1900, foresters sounded the alarm: they feared a shortage of wood in the near future. And then, without abundant wood, how to extract coal, run trains, build houses or print newspapers? Conservationists were far more concerned about the depletion of forests than about the depletion of coal mines predicted by Jevons. While the latter could happen in a few centuries' time, wood, which was just as essential to industrial countries, seemed likely to become scarce in a few decades.[34] Pennsylvania, for example, would only have enough wood in its vast forests for thirty-five years of its mines' consumption.[35] In 1905, US President Theodore Roosevelt took up this theme in a famous speech: a shortage of wood could bring American growth to a screeching halt.[36] If this wood crisis, predicted on both sides of the Atlantic, never happened, it was because the technologies that were responsible for it also provided the means to contain it.

First, the railways created both an enormous demand for wood and a powerful tool for satisfying it. They reduced the physical resource – especially in the United States – but increased the economic resource by facilitating transport and expanding supply.[37] The fall in freight costs compensated for the growing scarcity of the resource. The forest railroads, which were often temporary, have never been accurately counted, but by the end of the nineteenth century they were vast in extent, and in some regions even larger than the official network. The Landes region in France, for example, was criss-crossed by 500 kilometres of forest railways. In the United States, in the first half of the twentieth century, there were almost 50,000 kilometres of logging railroads, or a fifth of the American network, which was then at its peak.[38] In the centre and west of the United States, the railway concessions included immense forests, the exploitation of which helped to finance the construction of the lines. While historians of industrialization have focused on the virtuous circle between coal and rail, relations are just as lucrative between train and forest, railway magnates and timber barons. In 1900, for example, the railway entrepreneur James Hill sold 400,000 hectares of woodland in Washington State. The buyer, Frederick Weyerhaeuser, built on this estate the timber empire that still bears his name. At that time, his fortune rivalled that of John D. Rockefeller.[39] We could also mention the case of Ephraim Shay, an entrepreneur who started out in sawmills and went on to become the third-largest builder of locomotives in the United States at the beginning of the twentieth century.[40] In the 1900s, timber was the third-most-important rail freight in the United States, behind coal and all agricultural products.[41] In the USSR, wood remained the most important rail freight until the 1930s, when it was overtaken by coal.[42]

Advances in maritime transport had a similar effect on the price and therefore the use of wood. In the last third of the nineteenth century, ships made greater use of steam power, became larger, spent more time at sea, used less coal and employed fewer sailors per tonne transported. As a result, freight prices on English timber trade routes were halved. In 1880, half of the timber from the Baltic was transported to England by steamship, compared with 90 per cent ten years later.[43] In addition, the rise of coal in the iron and steel industry and in urban centres during this period led to a fall in the price of firewood, which encouraged its use to continue in rural areas. In wealthy countries, firewood consumption remained stable overall until the 1950s, while it rose sharply in the USSR – its transportation being facilitated by oil-powered trucks.[44]

Secondly, the paper industry also had the paradoxical effect of increasing both the demand for wood and its availability. Since the early nineteenth century, numerous attempts had been made to replace rag as the raw material for paper manufacture. Similarly, the mechanical foundations of continuous paper production had been

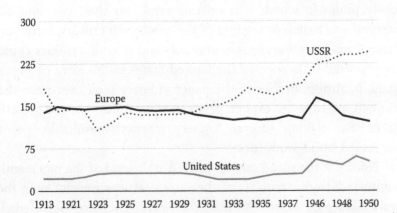

Firewood consumption in millions of cu. m. (FAO, *European Timber Statistics, 1913–1950* (Geneva, 1953).)

laid by the 1800s. If, in the last third of the nineteenth century, industrialists finally succeeded in freeing paper manufacture from
rag-pickers and were thus able to produce enormous quantities of
paper, it was thanks to the energy contained in coal. After a long
period of stagnation, paper production took off in the last third of
the nineteenth century. Between 1860 and 1910, British production
rose from 100,000 to 1 million tonnes, and that of the United States
from 100,000 to 4 million tonnes.[45] In 1920, world paper production
reached 15 million tonnes, half of which was in the United States.
To extract cellulose, wood was crushed and reduced to pulp by the
action of chemicals – soda, sulphate or sulphite – before being transformed into rolls by huge machines delivering up to 200 metres of
paper per minute.[46] Each stage of this process was extremely energy-
intensive, requiring coal to manufacture the chemicals, power the
shredders and digesters, feed the evaporators and dryers, etc. By the
end of the 1800s, the paper industry had become by far the world's
largest chemical industry. Paper became a hybrid product, a mixture
of wood and coal, with each kilo of paper requiring 1.5 kilos of coal
and around twice as much wood.[47] Between the wars, in wealthy
countries, paper was often the third-largest consumer of wood and
one of the top five consumers of coal.[48] But, thanks to the energy
provided by coal, the paper industry was able to make use of previously unusable wood. It is on this symbiosis that its economic
interest was based. At the end of the nineteenth century, softwood
from Canada or Scandinavia, branches and sawmill residues could
be exported to Europe or the United States in the form of paper
pulp. In American forests, the paper industry took over from the
timber industry to exploit previously worthless second-growth
trees. By making shorter forestry rotations profitable, paper
increased wood production.[49]

Thirdly, if the wood crisis predicted at the end of the nineteenth
century did not occur, it was because coal was transforming the
very nature of wood.[50] In 1838, the British engineer John Bethell
filed a patent for the preservation of wood using creosote, a substance derived from the distillation of coal. This product was far

superior to copper, zinc or arsenic salts, which were used for the same purpose: creosote does not dissolve in water, it makes wood impermeable, rot-proof and therefore much more durable. One engineer raved about this technique, which 'transformed timber into poison'.[51] The economic, ecological and historical importance of creosote cannot be overestimated: instead of lasting a few years, railway sleepers could now stay in place for several decades. Creosoting was carried out on an industrial scale: the wood, placed in an autoclave, was subjected to a vacuum before being immersed in a bath of creosote under pressure and at high temperature. At the Bethell factory near Greenwich, around 100 kilos of creosote were injected per tonne of timber, turning it into a composite material. From the 1850s, British and Indian railway sleepers were systematically creosoted. The process spread rapidly in Europe, and later in the United States, which helps explain the enormous quantities of sleepers used by American railways at the end of the century.[52] By making wood more durable, coal helped to satisfy the demand it had created. Creosote was undoubtedly one of the most important tools of forest conservation in the twentieth century. One journalist was enthusiastic: thanks to the creosoting of wood, forests would once again cover the planet.[53] More modestly, at the cost of a long-lasting pollution, creosote made it possible to contain the disaster that coal was causing in the forests.

That wood, like coal and iron, was an essential ingredient of industrialization was obvious to all the experts at the beginning of the twentieth century. 'Our consumption of wood', wrote a forester in the 1920s, 'is almost as universal and unconscious as the act of breathing. And it is about as essential to modern life.'[54] Another expert laughed at the 'superficial judgements' of those who 'imagine that thanks to the use of iron, steel and coal, wood is an increasingly neglected product'.[55] If historians had read these authors rather than Sombart and Mumford, the material understanding of industrialization would undoubtedly have been quite different. Finally, let's return to the Crystal Palace. In 1936, the wood of which it was made, which had been subjected for eighty-five years to the intense greenhouse effect produced by its glass roof, had become perfectly dry, and this is the reason why the monument burst into flames like a box of matches. In the end, the Crystal Palace is not such a bad metaphor for modern capitalism.

5.

Liaisons carbone

In *The Road to Wigan Pier*, George Orwell made this point a long time ago: 'You could quite easily drive a car right across the north of England and never once remember that hundreds of feet below the road you are on the miners are hacking at the coal.' Yet, he added, 'in a sense it is the miners who are driving your car forward'.[1] In their haste to recount the epic of oil and electricity, energy historians are also speeding towards the future: after the 1900s, coal fades into the background, presented as a simple 'persistence of the old'[2]; the action is elsewhere, even though in reality coal is modernizing at breakneck speed and playing a leading role in the history of electricity, steel, cement, the motor car and even oil. In recent works, written by the best specialists in environmental history or energy history, coal and oil are presented as two distinct 'energy regimes' or two 'development blocks'.[3]

On the contrary, the two great fossil fuels of the twentieth century should be seen as profoundly intertwined. The history of oil cannot be understood without the history of coal, and vice versa. This point is all the more important given that this symbiosis is the foundation of the entire material dynamic of the twentieth century: most materials – wood, agricultural products, metals – are produced, extracted and transported using steel machines, manufactured using coal and powered by oil. At the molecular level, carbon, by uniting with itself, acquires the ability to combine with many other atoms. Like the carbon–carbon bonds of organic chemistry, this essential symbiosis of oil and coal in the twentieth century enabled the growth of everything else.

Bonds strong as steel

In a remarkable book, the historian On Barak has recently shown that the rise of oil in the Middle East was prepared by the rise of coal. Oil, he writes, 'slipped comfortably into the boots of the British Empire', taking advantage of infrastructures and social relations created by and for coal. According to the book's subtitle, this Eastern encounter between coal and oil 'sparked global carbonization'.[4] In fact, well beyond the spark, and well beyond the Middle East, the enormous quantity of heat produced by coal has been, and remains, indispensable to oil. In the twentieth century, as today, oil is pumped by machines made of steel, transported by ships, railway tank wagons or pipelines made of steel, refined in plants made of steel and, finally, burned in engines made of steel. And most of this steel is produced using coal.

As Orwell rightly pointed out, oil was obviously no substitute for coal, as it served mainly to power cars, the manufacture of which consumed a large amount of coal, more by weight than the oil they would burn in their lifespan. From 1920 onwards, the American car industry published a remarkable brochure entitled *Automobile Facts and Figures*.[5] To demonstrate its role as a driving force for the entire American economy, the automobile lobby reported duly and proudly its material consumption year after year. Although coal is not mentioned, it is omnipresent in the form of steel, aluminium, copper, glass, nickel, tin, lead and electricity. The car industry was also closely dependent on steam locomotives to transport heavy goods: iron ore, steel, oil and coal. In the United States, between the two world wars, around one-sixth of rail traffic was used for this purpose, and the figure was even higher if we include the sand and cement needed to build the roads needed for cars. As a sign of this dependence, in 1922 strikes by miners and railway workers interrupted both car and road building; as blast furnaces shut down, cement works came to a standstill and building materials could no longer be transported.[6] Following the strike, Henry Ford decided

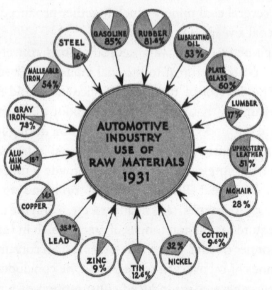

Additional Raw Materials Used in Motor Industry

No attempt has been made to estimate quantities used of each material

Sulphuric Acid	Soda ash	Platinum	Soap	Machine Tools	Asbestos
Hydrochloric	Caustic soda	Gold	Celluloid	Coal Coke	Carborundum
Alkali Acid	Turpentine	Silver	Chamois	Gas	Emery
Carbon Black	White lead	Mercury	Polish	Fuel oil	Garnet
Acetylene	Formaldehyde	Radium	Paper	Electricity	Silicon
Butanol	Phenol	Tungsten	Cork	Wool	Onyx
Cellulose Acetate	Arsenic	Phosphorus	Charcoal	Silk	Agate
Sulphur	Litharge	Molybdenum	Flaxseed	Hemp	Talc
Carbon	Cadmium	Magnesium	Linseed Oil	Jute	Silica sand
Nitro-cellulose	Alcohol	Vanadium	Animal Fat	Canvas	Limestone
Pyroxylin	Glycerine	Bismuth	Corn	Felt	Salt
Resin	Glue	Porcelain	Sugar cane	Moss	Tanning mat'ls
Shellac	Rope	Mica	Borax	Curled hair	Dyes

Automotive freight represented 1 out of every 8 carloads of traffic originated on railroads in 1931.

	Average 1921–1939
Steel	16%
Aluminium	22%
Copper	14%
Pewter	14.5%
Lead	25%
Rubber	81%
Freight wagons	14%
Petrol	90%

Share of the automotive industry in US resource consumption. (*Automobile Facts and Figures* (1920–1939).)

to acquire several coal mines, which together produced 3.5 million tonnes of coal a year.[7]

In Europe between the wars, several reports converged on the idea that oil posed no threat to the coal industry; indeed, quite the contrary. The director of the French Office for Liquid Fuels calculated, for example, that a car consumed about as much coal in its manufacture (around 7 tonnes) as it burned oil during its lifespan.[8] Oil, concluded another expert, 'shoulders coal'.[9] In 1934, the chief engineer of the Anglo-Iranian Company made a more complete calculation: in Great Britain between 1918 and 1934, the oil infrastructure – refineries, tanks, tankers, etc. – and the car fleet had together required 13 million tonnes of steel, which in turn required 53 million tonnes of coal. Given that Great Britain consumed only 21 million tonnes of oil over the same period, he concluded that each tonne of oil generated an induced consumption of 2.5 tonnes of coal.[10]

Where oil extraction took place, in the United States for example, the consumption of coal driven by oil was greater. Until the 1910s, oil was pumped using steam engines. Thereafter, companies sometimes used oil or gas engines, but most simply connected their oil pumpjacks to the electricity grid, which depended on coal.[11] In the 1930s, tanker wagons were pulled by steam locomotives, and oil refineries burned a million tonnes of coal a year.[12] Oil production also consumed a lot of coal because of its colossal demand for steel. At the beginning of the twentieth century, a new category appeared in trade statistics: 'Oil Country Tubular Goods'. By the end of the 1930s, the US oil industry was gobbling up more than 2 million tonnes of steel tubing a year[13]: by way of comparison, that is as much steel as the American railways used at their peak in 1890.[14] The much-vaunted fluidity of oil was in fact based on heaps of iron and coal.

Ford factory in Dearborn, Michigan, 1947. In the middle: reserves of coal, iron ore and chalk (capacity of the storage area: 2 million tonnes). Henry Ford owned blast furnaces, coal mines, iron mines and huge forestry operations. By weight, coal is the main ingredient in the manufacture of cars. (Getty Images/Underwood Archives.)

Under the road: the coal miners

In 1937, Orwell's carefree driver was speeding on a new kind of road that depended on coal. Over the course of the twentieth century, the road network in the rich countries increased, but not massively: in the United States, its length rose from 4 to 7 million kilometres, in France from 500,000 to 800,000 kilometres and in England from 283,000 to 350,000 kilometres.[15] On the other hand, the nature of those roads changed completely. In the United States, for example, their mass increased twentyfold.[16] The weight, number and speed of vehicles disintegrated road surfaces, reducing them to dust in summer and mud in winter. Until the 1960s, traffic in northern

France was partly seasonal: at the end of winter, the roads were too fragile to bear the weight of lorries and the police prohibited their circulation, rendering vast swathes of the country inaccessible to them. As Nelo Magalhães recently showed, in order to make possible the promise of speed offered by the internal combustion engine and the transport of goods by lorry, new kinds of road were needed. They became wider, straighter and their curves softer. Above all, the roads swelled, becoming heavier, covering themselves with a carapace made up of successive layers of aggregates, hydraulic binders, cement, concrete and tar – all sorts of materials dependent on coal.[17]

Tarmac's spread was synchronized with that of the motor car. In 1902, the British engineer Edgar Purnell Hooley patented a mixture of tar, steel slag and gravel – in short, a road surface that depended heavily on coal.[18] Initially, its role was limited to keeping dust off the road and so avoiding the clouds that bothered the motorized bourgeoisie. In France, it was a Swiss doctor based in Monaco, Ernest Guglielminetti, who promoted road macadamization.[19] In the first half of the twentieth century, millions of tonnes of coal tar, a carcinogenic substance, were poured onto the roads on the pretext of public health, until the arrival of natural gas in the 1960s reduced the tar supply. Tarmacadam was then replaced by a mixture of aggregates and bitumen derived from oil refining.

Instead of tarmac roads, American engineers from the Bureau of Public Roads preferred concrete roads, which were more expensive but also more resistant to wear. Concrete roads took off after the First World War. The trigger was not so much the motor car as the lorry. In 1914, lorries were still rare in America: there were only 80,000 of them, compared with 1.6 million cars. Their use was limited to short journeys to and from railway stations. That the truck could replace the horse was a given, but that it could compete with the train still seemed unlikely. However, during the winter of 1917 the railway companies struggled to get military equipment to East Coast ports on time. The Council of National Defense set up a special committee for highways transport headed by Roy Chapin, a car manufacturer who successfully organized the rotation of a fleet of 30,000 trucks between the Midwest and the Atlantic ports.[20] In France, the truck was also proving its worth as a means of long-distance transport.[21] While the efficiency of the truck had been demonstrated, its effect on the roads appeared catastrophic. 'Hundreds of miles of roads failed under the heavy motor truck traffic within a comparatively few weeks or months ... These failures were not only sudden but also complete, and almost overnight an excellent surface might become impassable.'[22] As would later be discovered, the damage caused by a vehicle on the road increased to the power of four of its weight. Yet, despite its destructive nature, road freight began its irresistible rise. In the United States, the number of trucks went from 80,000 in 1914 to 500,000 at the end of the war, then to 3 million in 1928.[23]

It was also at this time that the concreting of roads began in earnest. The American cement manufacturers orchestrated a powerful lobbying campaign with magazines, posters, press articles and a 'popular' movement of petitions in favour of 'good roads'. Chapin headed a 'Good Road Association', which worked hand in hand with the cement manufacturers and the Bureau of Public Roads. In 1921, the Federal Highway Act was passed, ensuring that dollars and cement rained down on American roads.[24] The modern cement industry is the offspring of this investment. Between the wars, roads consumed up to 60 per cent of American cement in some years, and their construction employed up to 4 million people.[25] The Panama Canal was only a small project in comparison.[26] The cement industry's trade association admitted that roads were the key sector: it is since America became the 'nation on wheels' that industry has changed scale.[27] Cement production tripled between 1919 and 1929. The average size of rotary kilns increased sharply during this period, and in the 1930s monsters over a hundred metres long appeared.[28] The law of increasing returns led to concentration in the cement industry. It was also in the mid-1920s, thanks to the boom in concrete roads, that an innovation closely linked to oil and coal appeared: the truck mixer. This concrete mixer on wheels enabled public works contractors to order ready-to-use, certified and standardized concrete.[29] The logistical mastery required to deliver ready-mixed concrete – it sets if delivery is delayed – drove further concentration in the sector.

At the end of the 1920s, the United States manufactured 84 per cent of the world's cars and owned 77 per cent of the world's vehicle fleet. Logically, it also produced more than half the world's cement, half of which was used in road construction.[30] Most of this cement was produced with coal. In total, it can be estimated that about half a tonne of coal was needed for every *metre* of concrete road.[31] This is how, in the United States of the 1920s, a fundamental alliance was forged between public funding of the road network and private means of transport, a symbiosis between coal, steel and oil that has only become stronger as dependence on the car has grown.[32]

Tanks filled with coal

Finally, Orwell's remark should be taken literally: in his day, coal did indeed power many cars. Between the wars, the German, French and British governments were concerned about their dependence on oil, and considerable efforts were made to develop and manufacture 'national fuels'. In England, low-temperature distillation of coal was promoted as a means of producing both a 'smokeless' combustible for domestic use and a fuel for cars.[33] In France, the government encouraged the use of a mixture of benzol, produced from coal, and ethyl alcohol, produced from wine – this was also a way of disposing of surplus wine. In Germany, motorists could fill their tanks with 'Monopolin', a mixture of benzol, petrol and wood alcohol.[34] In all these mixtures, benzol plays a little-known but important role. Not without exaggeration, a French journalist claimed that 'it is benzol that developed the automobile'.[35] During the First World War, European governments required gasworks and coking plants to recover benzol because it was used in explosives. Once peace returned, this substance was relatively abundant and

The dump truck is one of those neglected yet fundamental innovations of the 20th century. Its use spread in the United States during the First World War.[36] Coal-delivery companies were among the first to buy them. 'In no other sector', noted a specialist in 1918, 'has the truck replaced the horse so quickly.'[37] At the turn of the century, New York had some 300 coal-delivery companies employing thousands of horses. By the end of the First World War, there were just 25, equipped with around a hundred lift trucks.[38] In rural areas, dump trucks enabled coal sellers to extend their catchment area. The advantage of the dump truck was that it mechanized both transport and delivery. Compared with horse-drawn carriage, sacks, shovels and wheelbarrows, the time saved was considerable. Experts estimated that dump trucks increased labour productivity sixfold and cut the cost of coal delivery threefold.[39] Where the layout of the site was unsuitable, delivery drivers could also use conveyor belts powered by the truck's engine. While oil competed with coal, it also ensured the much more fluid and efficient distribution of coal beyond the rail and river networks. (US War Department technical manual, 'Coal Handling' (1947).)

Annales de l'office national des carburants liquides (1936).

cheap. In the 1930s, the quantities of benzol used as fuel for automobiles were not negligible: 150,000 tonnes a year in England, 300,000 in the USA and the same in Germany, where benzol accounted for a tenth of motor fuels.[40]

Coal – and this is much better known – has been used to power engines thanks to the hydrogenation industry. During the Second World War, most of Germany's aviation fuel was derived from coal. An autarkic technology par excellence, coal hydrogenation paradoxically had been an international project carried out by French, British, Russian, Dutch, German and American chemists.[41] The patents belonged to a consortium, founded in The Hague in 1931, comprising IG Farben, Imperial Chemical Industries (ICI), Standard Oil and Shell. This technology was disastrous in every respect: as the reaction took place at very high pressures and temperatures, at least 4 tonnes of coal were needed to produce 1 tonne of oil. In 1939, a barrel of German synthetic oil was 15 times more expensive than a barrel of American 'natural' oil.[42] Even from a military point of view coal hydrogenation was of dubious interest, as the size of the plants made them easy targets for bombing raids.[43] Despite all these shortcomings, England and France also threw themselves whole-heartedly into this industry, collaborating with German chemists right up to the eve of war. In 1935, ICI set up a large coal-liquefaction plant at Billingham with the help of IG Farben.[44] From 1934 onwards, the French government tried to catch up, and until 1938 mining engineers worked with their German counterparts.[45] Even the United States, which had plenty of oil, and Japan, Spain and Italy, which had little coal, were investing in synthetic fuels.[46]

For all its faults, coal liquefaction did not disappear with Nazism. In South Africa today, a single plant, SASOL (South Africa Synthetic Oil), produces 7.6 million tonnes of synthetic petrol a year, a third of South Africa's fuel and three times more than Nazi production at its peak.[47] The plant also emits more CO_2 than Portugal or Switzerland. SASOL's production has recently been eclipsed by Chinese mining companies operating in Shanxi and Inner Mongolia. Non-existent before 2008, Chinese production of synthetic fuels consumed 33 million tonnes of coal in 2019, to which can be added methanol, produced in China from coal, which is also used as a motor fuel.[48] This coal-consumption figure could be further increased by including the coal used to power electric cars. Considered as a 'green technology', the electric car is above all a matter of energy sovereignty in China: half of the world's EVs are in China, where two-thirds of electricity is produced from coal.[49] For the time being, the electric car has had the effect of increasing coal's share in global mobility compared with oil. Orwell's comment is as true today as it was in 1937: coal and miners have never powered so many cars.

An ever-closer union

The symbiosis between oil and coal, unlike that between coal and wood, became stronger during the twentieth century. First, extracting and transporting oil requires more and more steel, and therefore more coal. In 1901, 300 metres of drill pipe were all that was needed for oil to flow from Spindletop in Texas; in 2009, by contrast, the Tiber Oil Field's deepwater discovery well in the Gulf of Mexico drilled 10 kilometres below the ocean basin's surface. The total length of pipelines has increased from 2,000 kilometres in 1900 to 2 million in 2020, and their diameter from around 20 centimetres to more than a metre on average.[50] The Second World War was an important milestone in this race to supersize with the construction of the Big Inch pipeline (2,000 km and 60 cm in diameter) linking Texas to the East Coast ports. The Bureau of Resources Allocation had long been opposed to the project because of the staggering amount of steel required: 600,000 tonnes, equivalent to the weight of a hundred Liberty ships.[51] But Big Inch would now seem rather modest: the gas pipeline that runs from Yamal in Russia to Western Europe is 4,800 kilometres long and 140 centimetres in diameter.

Oil Country Tubular Goods (OCTG) statistics provide a revealing though incomplete estimate of the mass of steel used by the oil industry.[52] The trend is clearly upwards: the United States consumed around 2 million tonnes of OCTG in 1950 and 7 million in 2010.[53] At that time, oil and gas extraction alone consumed as much steel as the entire US economy did at the end of the nineteenth century. When it is booming, the US oil industry can consume up to 10 per cent of the country's steel, almost as much as the car industry.[54] In Russia, the consumption of OCTG is around 5 million tonnes, or a tenth of its national steel consumption.[55] In China, 5 per cent of the steel stock is used to extract and refine oil.[56] Globally, in addition to the 2 million kilometres of oil and gas pipelines, there are 700 refineries – each with an average of 3,200 kilometres of pipes[57] – 3,500 supertankers, and tens of thousands of giant tanks storing 5 billion barrels of strategic oil reserves. To top it all off, this mass of steel is eaten away from the inside by the salt and sulphur compounds contained in the oil. In 1967, 7 per cent of the steel consumed by the US oil industry was used for maintenance. This proportion has probably increased with the ageing of refineries and the growing sulphur content of crude oil.[58] In total, it can be estimated that oil extraction consumes between 1 and 3 per cent of the world's steel, depending on the year.

Secondly, the symbiosis between oil and coal occurs mainly downstream, in the manufacture of all the machines that burn the oil.[59] The 1.5 billion cars and 100,000 commercial ships weighing over 100 tonnes in circulation around the world are made mainly (between 70 and 80 per cent) of steel.[60] Every year, 80 million new cars are built, the steel equivalent of more than 10,000 Eiffel Towers. In total, the automotive industry accounts for around 15 per cent of global steel flows, three-quarters of which is produced from coal – 1 billion tonnes in all.[61] In China, where almost a third of the world's cars are produced, life-cycle analyses indicate a consumption of around 2.5 tonnes of coal per car.[62]

Thirdly, burning oil in cars obviously requires road infrastructure, which also gobbles up gigantic quantities of steel, cement and, indirectly, coal. Cement works can use any fuel – oil, petroleum coke, gas, household waste; old tyres are very popular – but on a global scale they burn mainly coal (70 per cent of their fuel according to the IEA, 90 per cent according to cement manufacturers).[63] The fortunes of the cement industry are closely linked to road construction, and the countries that consume the most cement are those that are in the process of building modern infrastructure: China comes first, of course, and occupies the same position as the United States did a century ago, consuming around half the world's cement, half of which goes into its infrastructure.[64] India comes next, consuming seven times less cement than China but four times more than the United States.[65] Vietnam pours more cement than the United States, and five times more than France. The new frontier of the cement industry is now in Africa, in the immense megalopolis of 40 million inhabitants linking Lagos, Accra, Cotonou and Abidjan. The Nigerian Aliko Dangote has become the richest man on the African continent: his company produces more cement than Germany and Great Britain combined. The Dangote Group also owns coal mines to fuel its cement plants, and recently inaugurated the first oil refinery in sub-Saharan Africa.[66] Obviously, the fact that the cement industry is mainly located in developing countries casts doubt on the prospects for carbon capture and storage in this sector.

Finally, it should be noted that all this infrastructure generates a very long-term flow of materials, as the maintenance of existing infrastructure also requires a great deal of cement. In France, which is already well equipped in roads, public works consume 37 per cent of cement, with the remainder going to buildings. The orders of magnitude are similar for Europe as a whole, where roads account for 39 Gt and buildings for 35 Gt.[67] In short, from extraction to combustion, oil relies on heaps of steel and cement, and therefore coal.

Moving mountains

Conversely, during the twentieth century coal mining became increasingly dependent on oil. This was due to the expansion of opencast (also known as open-pit) mining. Encompassing tens of thousands of hectares, these spectacular mines regularly make the headlines, and as the memory of coal is associated with the underground, they might seem like a novelty.[68] In reality, the development of opencast mining goes back a long way.[69] In the first half of the twentieth century, thanks to draglines, dump trucks and bulldozers, removing the soil covering the coal became more economical in certain geological circumstances. At the time, up to 20 metres of 'overburden' could be removed to mine economically a vein 1 metre thick.[70] In the United States, opencast mining took off during the First World War, increasing from 1.2 million to 22 million tonnes between 1914 and 1929. By then, coal output per employee was already three times higher in opencast pits than in underground mines.[71] Despite its destructiveness, strip mining was irresistible: it accounted for 5 per cent of American coal in 1930, a third in 1960, half in 1970 and two-thirds since the 1980s.[72] In the USSR, the opencast mines of the Kuznetsk basin were already being worked by machines between the wars. Their share of Soviet coal production rose from 20 to 40 per cent between 1960 and 1980.[73]

Opencast mining was also making headway in Europe. In France, by 1918, 150 mines were producing 750,000 tonnes of coal using pick-axes and wagons. In the largest mine, the aptly named 'La Découverte' at Decazeville in Aveyron, mechanization began between the wars and was completed in the early 1950s.[74] In Great Britain, surface coal mining began during the Second World War: the lack of manpower and the availability of American bulldozers led to the opening of around a hundred opencast mines. By the early 1950s, these mines were producing 10 million tonnes of coal a year, and their share of British coal production continued to grow. Opencast mines became the last to close in the 2000s.[75]

But it was above all in Central Europe that strip mining took on great importance, in order to exploit lignite, a young, low-energy

The first rotary excavators were built in 1926 by the German company Lauchhammer-Rheinmetall. After the war, this East German company became part of a combine called TAKRAF. The GDR extracted a quarter of the world's brown coal in the 1980s.[76] After German reunification, TAKRAF benefited from the global coal boom. Its flagship product, the Bagger 293, the largest land machine of all time, can theoretically extract 70 million tonnes of earth a year with just five technicians. It can be found in action in mines in Russia, China, India and Australia. (Charles Berthelot, 'Du charbon aux essences de synthèse', *La Science et la vie*, vol. 54, no. 253, 1938, p. 3.)

and highly polluting coal. Germany produced 80 million tonnes of so-called 'brown coal' in 1918 and 250 million tonnes in 1940.[77] At the beginning of the twentieth century, German opencast mining outstripped French underground mining. And during the Second World War German lignite outweighed British coal by weight – but not by energy. In the course of the twentieth century, brown coal cost Germany 170,000 hectares, of which only 20 per cent could be converted back to agricultural use.[78]

In today's strip mines, the energy that literally moves mountains comes from oil. At its peak in the 2000s, American strip mining consumed 2.7 million tonnes of ANFO, a mixture of ammonium nitrate and petrol, every year – roughly as much explosive as all the Allied bombs in the Second World War. Then come the excavators to clear the ground and remove the coal. Finally, special mining dumpers bring the coal up from the pits. These machines burn 1,500 tonnes of diesel a year, or as much energy *per minute* as the daily consumption of an American household. In surface mines, it takes between 1 and 2.5 litres of diesel to extract one tonne of coal.[79] In Australia, South Africa and Canada, the mineral industry consumes around a tenth of the country's energy.[80] Thanks to this profligate use of energy, labour productivity in the mines has reached record levels. In Australia, mining salaries are higher than those in the banking sector.[81]

Oil also facilitated the transportation of coal over increasingly vast distances. Although steamships have disappeared, never before has so much coal sailed the oceans. As a new phenomenon, Australia in the 1970s and Indonesia more recently have developed mining industries geared primarily to export. Every year, hundreds of millions of tonnes of coal are transported over thousands of kilometres. Following oil, coal is the second most significant commodity by weight in seaborne trade, accounting for 1.4 Gt, compared to 1.8 Gt. Coal is also one of the leading rail freights, transported in huge convoys pulled by diesel locomotives. In China, spurred by the rise in coal production in Inner Mongolia, Ningxia and Xinjiang, far away from major consumption hubs, extensive dedicated rail lines for coal have recently been commissioned. Estimated to handle around 3 trillion tonne-kilometres per year in the 2020s, they likely rank among the largest mass transfer systems in history.[82] If world coal prices have remained stable despite soaring Asian consumption, it is thanks to a technical system that runs on oil.

The union of oil and coal is also the union of capital. Some of the investment that has enabled the extraordinary expansion of coal over the last four decades has come from oil companies seeking to diversify and anticipating, particularly in the United States, increasing extraction difficulties. In 1971, the energy economist Bruce Netschert described oil companies being transformed into 'total energy companies', active in hydrocarbons, coal and uranium, and far-sighted enough to invest in shale gas and oil shale.[83] After the 1970s oil crisis, this trend was reinforced: BP, Exxon and Shell invested in Wyoming and Australian coal mines, Amoco got involved in China, and Total acquired coal mines in South Africa.[84]

The scene is filmed in slow motion: detonations, the ground smoking, swelling, rising and then falling in a cloud of dust. Excavators move in. In a wide shot, a huge rail convoy stretches across the landscape. In 1969, the Ford company boasted about the quality of its cars with these striking images of an opencast coal mine. 'A Ford', commented the voice-over, 'is born of the brute force needed to make the car that people want.'[85] For a long time, entrepreneurs were proud of their material footprint. In the nineteenth century, they adorned their letterheads with images of factories and smoking chimneys; in the twentieth century, it was with film and cinema that they displayed their industrial grandeur. Henry Ford even owned one of the biggest studios of the early twentieth century. As early as 1910, Americans could admire the Highland Park factory on film, and then, between the wars, the immense Dearborn plant, on the side of the River Rouge, with its stockpile of coal, its blast furnaces and shining streams of molten steel.[86] Rather than being regarded as something to conceal, industrial consumption of raw materials was detailed and explained. In 1933, at the Chicago World's Fair, the Ford pavilion displayed a long list of materials used in the

Ford's Cycle of Production at the 1939 World's Fair in New York.

manufacture of cars. In 1939, visitors to the New York World's Fair marvelled at an immense globe spinning majestically on itself while thirty automaton miniature workers dug the earth to extract the materials necessary to build the Ford V8 sitting atop the globe.[87] Entitled 'The Cycle of Production', this attraction called on the bourgeoisie to play its part: millions of miners and farmers were waiting for orders. The carousel also demonstrated Ford's presence throughout the United States. 'A car', recalled an advertisement from the 1950s, 'is first and foremost labour and raw materials.'[88] Against a backdrop of American landscapes, the voice-over ran through a litany of materials: iron from Minnesota and Michigan, copper from Utah and Montana, cedar from the Pacific Coast, aluminium from Tennessee and Alabama, coal from Kentucky, gas from Texas, leather and wool from the Midwest, alkali from Louisiana . . .

Until the 1970s, material consumption was an important motif for advertising. Product quality and customer satisfaction depended on it. The consequence is paradoxical: the emergence of political ecology, the demonetization of the technological sublime and the rise of environmental scruples have played a negative role in the material understanding of production. The 1969 'A Car is Born' advert was probably one of the last of its kind. After the first Earth Day, Ford's advertisements shifted away from materials and factories to concentrate on the finished product: the car as a purveyor of power, domestic happiness, leisure and libido. Industrialists began to talk about environmental protection, while casting a discreet veil over the mines and plantations. The material footprint disappeared from advertising, only to reappear in Corporate Social Responsibility reporting and environmentalist literature, whose impact was obviously incommensurate with the power of advertising. Dematerialization was under way, at least in people's minds.

6.

The Carbon Fallacy

Carbon Democracy is probably the most significant work in the history of energy published since the beginning of the twenty-first century. It also serves as a perfect example of stagism. Its author, the British historian Timothy Mitchell, a specialist of the Middle East, proposed a new reading of the nature of political power in the light of a supposed transition from coal to oil. At the close of the nineteenth century, coal, solid and buried underground, bestowed European and American miners with newfound autonomy and economic power, which they wielded to secure social and democratic advancements. Conversely, in the twentieth century, oil – a fluid extracted from the surface and demanding significant capital with minimal labour – purportedly undermined the demands of the workers' movement in the Middle East and beyond. Mitchell's thesis deserves to be properly examined, as its enthusiastic reception in the academic world testifies to an appetite for materialist explanations of politics and a paradoxical lack of interest in the history of production.

The first problem with *Carbon Democracy* is that it compares oil and coal at different moments in their history. Implicitly, the modern oil industry of the 1960s is contrasted with a vision of coal mines frozen in 1900. In reality, when oil began to compete directly with coal at the very end of the 1950s, coal production was modern, mechanized and capital-intensive. Since the inter-war period, coal had been mechanically mined in most American and many European mines.[1] In the Lorraine coalfield, the most modern in France, 90 per cent of the coal was mined by coal-cutting machines, the jackhammer being confined to the thinnest veins.[2] In the 1950s and 1960s, the general electrification of the mines enabled the installation of coal shearers and loaders, conveyor belts for the removal of coal, and then hydraulic walking roof-support systems. Most of the coal was mined, loaded and transported using machines.[3] In 1960, a Russian apparatchik marvelled at modern mines where 'coal flows like a continuous stream without ever being touched by the hand of man'.[4] These comments, which are clearly exaggerated (especially where the mines of the Donbass are concerned), nevertheless reflect a major development: the mines changed more after 1950 than at any time in their history. Productivity gains meant that by the 1958 US Census, coal mines employed fewer people than oil fields: 200,000 miners compared with 313,000 oil workers. The refineries also employed a huge number of workers (200,000 in 1958), to which we could add the 180,000 pump attendants . . . The oil sector, from extraction to distribution, stood as one of the largest employers in the United States at the time, along with the automobile and textile industries.[5]

In the 1970s, it was the mines of Western Europe that set the standard for underground mining. For a long time, these mines had mainly used the longwall mining method. More complex to implement than the rooms-and-pillars method, its advantage was to maximize coal recovery, whereas in American mines blocks of intact ore were left to support the gallery ceilings. After 1950, thanks to the increased electrical power available at the bottom of the mines, the longwall method allowed for more advanced mechanization. In 1952, James Anderton, an engineer with the British National Coal Board, patented a particularly powerful electric cutter. British Coal placed an order for several hundred units with Anderson-Boyes, a mining equipment company. The 'Anderton Shearer Loader' was an international success.[6] In France, the armaments company SAGEM manufactured both the inertial measurement units for Exocet missiles and Mirage fighter planes and the Dressmatic cutters for Charbonnages de France. These powerful machines were integrated with removal systems using conveyor belts and, from the 1960s onwards, walking support systems, a key innovation that revolutionized roof support. As early as 1963, remote control mining (ROLF – Remotely Operated Longwall Faces[7]) was being tested in the Nottinghamshire mines. The impact of these methods was spectacular. In France, while productivity had stagnated at 200 tonnes per employee per year since the end of the nineteenth century, it rose to 300 tonnes in 1950, 400 in 1960, 600 in 1980 and over 1,000 in the 1990s.[8] The trend was similar in the UK, and slightly less marked in Germany. When, in the wake of the oil crises, American companies sought to modernize their mines, they sent their engineers to Europe to learn the new methods.[9]

These techniques have fallen into relative oblivion because they were developed by European collieries that were entering terminal decline. Charbonnages de France, British Coal and the National Coal Board, which were consigned to the scrap heap in the 1990s, actually played a key role in the economic history of the late twentieth century.[10] The machines and methods invented or subsidized by these state-owned companies had their greatest impact not in Europe or in the United States but in China's state mines, where 80 per cent of coal extraction was underground and where longwall mining was also practised.[11] From 1960, after the departure of Soviet engineers, China turned to European mining expertise, carrying out study trips and purchasing equipment. Between 1965 and 1973, Maoist China bought $100 million worth of European mining equipment, more than half of it from the UK.[12] When the Chinese market opened up in 1978, it was companies such as Anderson, SAGEM and Germany's Eickhoff Bergbautechnik that supplied the state mines with the latest generation of equipment.[13] And even though China has since developed new machines,[14] Europe remains the world's leading exporter in this field. Anderson, acquired by Bucyrus and subsequently by Caterpillar, has long since closed its Strathclyde plant in Scotland. Nevertheless, its flagship product of the 1990s, the Electra 2000 shearer and loader (1.2 megawatts in power), is still cutting coal in mines around the world.[15] And under its teeth, the solidity of the coal so central in Mitchell's narrative seems more than relative.

Mitchell's contrast between a solid and national coal and a fluid and global petroleum neglects the importance of the international coal trade, which, in the 1950s, still surpassed that of oil.[16] It also overlooks all the techniques for converting coal into various fluids. By the time Rockefeller's Standard Oil laid its first pipelines in the United States, gas lighting had been flowing through pipes for more than half a century. In 1926, the Ruhrgas company distributed coal gas produced in the Ruhr coking plants in Holland, Belgium and northern France. Until the 1970s, natural gas represented only a modest injection into pipelines built to transport coal gas.[17]

Of course, coal produces the most fluid and versatile form of energy there is: electricity. In the inter-war period, thanks to advances in high-voltage lines, thermal power stations could be built at the mouth of the mines to minimize coal transport. In the power stations, coal was also handled in large quantities. Machines capable of overturning several wagons simultaneously could unload thousands of tonnes of coal in a matter of minutes. The coal was then crushed, reduced to the consistency of talcum powder, which improved combustion and allowed it to circulate through pipes.[18] The boilers could burn heavy fuel oil, pulverized coal or a mixture of the two.[19] In 1931, the London socialist Fred Henderson, who worked in a thermal power station, described installations where loading and unloading operations had been entirely mechanized. Stokers had become 'combustion engineers' whose job consisted of watching dials and pressing buttons. All their work, he wrote, was like driving a car: skill and attention, but no muscular effort.[20] Between the wars, pulverized coal was also used in cement works, ships and steam locomotives – with crew conveyors feeding the boilers with coal. Nowadays, thermal power stations burn coal in a process known as 'fluidized bed' reactors. Reduced to fine particles and floating on a cushion of pressurized oxygen, the coal behaves much like a liquid, making combustion more efficient.[21] Finally, but more anecdotally, raw coal can also be transported in 'carboducts', where it is dragged along by water pressure. The United States inaugurated its first coal pipeline in 1957. As it eliminates the need for diesel locomotives, this technique is sometimes touted as 'green'. Recently, China unveiled a coal pipeline spanning nearly a thousand kilometres to further showcase this 'environmentally friendly' approach.[22]

Conversely, the fluidity of oil does not offer advantages only when it comes to manpower – and we will see in the next chapter that armies of coopers were employed to produce barrels to store petroleum. Pipelines do transport crude oil but relatively few refined products, which depend on more traditional logistics. In the United States during the 1950s, when considering both petroleum and refined products together, their transportation breakdown was approximately 40% by pipeline, 30% by ship, 25% by truck and 5% by rail tanker.[23] So oil does not bypass dockers, railway workers or truck drivers. In Europe, volumes were for a long time too limited to justify pipelines. Even on the major Le Havre–Paris route, a pipeline project did not seem profitable in the inter-war period: 'it is economic heresy', said one expert, 'to want to double a waterway as excellent as the Seine'.[24] The first pipelines were built for military reasons: PLUTO between England and the Normandy beaches, then the NATO pipeline linking Donges to Metz.[25] Finally, oil refining produces significant quantities of petroleum coke, or petcoke (currently 150 million tonnes a year), a solid residue similar to coke, which is highly prized in metallurgy, cement works and for producing graphite for electric batteries.

Based on an abstract rather than historical opposition between coal and oil, it is hardly surprising that the political history of energy proposed by Mitchell is just as problematic. First of all, oil has clearly not been the gravedigger of social movements: on the contrary, oil fields and refineries have been the site of major social movements, shaping history in profound ways. Between 1911 and 1938, Mexican oil workers in the Veracruz region organized more than 120 strikes that led to the nationalization law of 1938.[26] In Iran, strikes in 1946 and 1951 at the huge Abadan refinery, owned by the Anglo-Iranian Oil Company, contributed to the rise of Mohammad

Mosaddegh to power, and he hastened to nationalize the oil industry. In 1978, it was again the oil workers – 5 per cent of the country's workforce – who played a key role in the success of the Iranian Revolution.[27] In Saudi Arabia, in the autumn of 1953, 13,000 of the 15,000 workers employed by Aramco went on strike and won better working conditions. Three years later, during the Suez Crisis, strikes broke out in the oil fields of the Middle East. The oil workers became major supporters of Arab nationalism, the Palestinian cause, the Algerian FLN, Gaddafi's revolution and the Saudi National Reform Front, which was close to communism.[28]

In Europe, it was clearly not a non-existent transition from coal to oil that got the better of the miners and their unions. During the great strike of 1947–48 in the collieries of northern France, the miners were not defeated by oil but by the army, redundancies and foreign coal. During the strikes, the government brought in a million tonnes of coal *a month* from the United States.[29] Just like with coal – and perhaps even more than with coal – oil gave refinery workers, railway workers, dockers and lorry drivers considerable political power. For example, between the wars, the International Brotherhood of Teamsters, the powerful truckers' union common to the United States and Canada, had half a million members.[30] In May 1952, at the height of the Korean War, 90,000 oil workers went on strike in the United States, raising fears about the supply of fuel to the air force.[31]

The desire, understandable on the part of historians, to link 'energy transitions' to explanations of a political or geopolitical nature is evident in the pages Mitchell devotes to the Marshall Plan. The 'European Recovery Program' (ERP) is portrayed as the Trojan Horse of oil in Europe.[32] However, on this well-trodden topic, the conclusions drawn from the archives and statistics are clear: oil was a secondary issue compared to coal.[33] At the end of the war, the shortage of coal was the main bottleneck in the European economy. A senior American official explained that coal had to be supplied at all costs 'to avoid economic and political chaos . . . which might adversely affect our national interests'.[34] The architect of the

Marshall Plan was none other than George Kennan, the famous theorist of Soviet containment.[35] A few months before the ERP was revealed, Kennan had drawn up a 'Coal Plan for Europe' showing the crucial role of coal, particularly from the Ruhr, in the industrial revival of the continent. In retrospect, from the standpoint of the 1960s, it is rather the failure to take oil into account that seems surprising. Kennan's plan provided the matrix for other, more famous plans: Robert Schuman's in 1950, followed by the European Coal and Steel Community in 1952. Beyond the rosy stories of European integration, the common market in coal had the advantage of protecting governments from their miners, since it was possible, in the event of a strike, to obtain coal from neighbours at set prices. This is one of the reasons why the French trade union the Confédération Générale du Travail, close to the Communist Party, rejected European economic integration.[36]

To support his thesis, Mitchell, following David Painter, cites the figure that 10 per cent of Marshall Plan funds were used to buy oil, which implies that the remaining 90 per cent was spent on other things. In the case of France, after EDF – a major coal player – it was Charbonnages de France that received the most aid.[37] In the mid-twentieth century, capitalist countries did not particularly favour oil over coal. On the contrary, at the height of the Cold War, they invested massively to modernize their mines and develop electricity networks that depended on coal. In any case, the importance of the ERP in the rich countries of the continent should not be overestimated. In 1950 and 1951, it accounted for just 1 per cent of the UK's GNP and 2 per cent of France's, not enough to trigger a purported transition to oil.[38]

Mitchell also argues that Europe's oil supply ensured its anchorage in a Western bloc dominated by the United States. However, after 1947, the United States exported almost no oil, and crude from the Middle East was the subject of intense struggles between the various powers. Great Britain was fiercely opposed to US influence in the region.[39] In France, too, during the Algerian war, Prime Minister Guy Mollet was convinced that the CIA and American oil companies were plotting with the FLN in the hope of appropriating the oil that French geologists had just discovered in the Sahara.[40] In the 1950s, under the aegis of Enrico Mattei, the Italian national oil company ENI challenged Anglo-American oil interests by proposing more advantageous contracts to the oil-producing countries of the Middle East and North Africa, which aroused the anger of the US State Department and the British Foreign Office and, perhaps, provoked Mattei's death.[41]

Oil further fragmented the Western bloc by fostering economic co-operation between Western Europe and the USSR. In the mid-1950s, when Khrushchev sought to modernize the Soviet oil industry and export oil to the 'brother countries', he came up against the weakness of the national steel industry, which was unable to supply the large-diameter tubes needed for pipelines in sufficient quantity and quality. This bottleneck had been clearly identified by American strategists who, as early as 1947, were pushing for a strict embargo on steel pipes to the USSR. Despite pressure from the United States, between 1958 and 1962 Germany, Austria and Italy exported 1.3 million tonnes of pipeline to the USSR.[42] The history of *détente* and German *Ostpolitik* is partly linked to this highly lucrative exchange of capitalist pipes and Communist oil. With domestic consumption rising and production stagnating, the USSR desperately needed Western technology to exploit and transport Siberian oil and gas. In Western Europe, interest in this new energy frontier grew even stronger after the 1973 oil crisis: in response to American concerns about the danger of dependence on Russian gas, European leaders began to express their own anxieties about potential energy shortages and emphasized the importance of preserving jobs in their national steel industries.[43] From the point of view of the history of energy and material symbioses, it should be remembered that, during the Cold War, the fundamental affinity between oil, steel and coal was sufficiently powerful to pierce the Iron Curtain and lead, despite strong and constant opposition from the United States, to the construction of the largest gas and oil pipeline network in the world.

*

Finally, let's come back to the 'transition' from coal to oil. In the early 1960s, heavy fuels began to encroach on coal markets, particularly in electricity production.[44] But we must be wary of seeing any political malice in this. In 1959, the US government, urged on by Texan oil companies, imposed import quotas that led to a fall in the price of oil on the world market. It was against this backdrop that OPEC – the Organization of the Petroleum Exporting Countries – was founded the following year.[45] In Europe, car-fuel consumption was rising and, despite advances in cracking and hydrogenation, refineries were producing increasing quantities of heavy oil, which they sold cheaply to power stations. Between 1960 and 1974, a kilowatt-hour produced from heavy oil was cheaper than a kilowatt-hour produced from coal, which is enough to explain the spread of oil. This was a global phenomenon, with oil's share of world electricity production rising from 5 per cent in 1960 to 25 per cent in 1973.[46] In countries with large coal mines, the rise of oil in the electricity mix was slower. The French government, for example, obliged EDF to buy French coal, while the UK and Germany decided to tax fuel oil so as to protect their collieries.[47] With the Jeanneney Plan of 1960, France resigned itself to accepting the massive use of fuel oil in its power stations. But here again, the aim was not to circumvent the miners: De Gaulle was convinced that France would emerge as a major oil producer thanks to the discoveries in the Algerian Sahara. French engineers even contemplated liquefying Algerian methane and exporting it by ship to the UK.[48] It should also be noted that the Commissariat au Plan's forecasts never (to my knowledge) mention 'energy transition', despite the ongoing trend of fuel oil gradually displacing coal in many industries. The term used was 'energy coordination': managing the coexistence of the two fuels as effectively as possible, recognizing that coal would continue to serve markets in power stations or the steel industry.[49]

It is worth noting, without drawing any conclusion about its political effect, that the oil boom at the end of the 1960s also coincided with a period of social protest in Europe and the United States, leading to major wage increases in several countries. Conversely, in the

1980s, the neo-liberal revolution was perfectly compatible with the resurgence of the American coal industry. Indeed, the rise in inequality was more pronounced in the United States at the height of its coal production in the 2000s than it was in Western Europe, where mines were closing one after the other. Far more than oil, it was the technical evolution of coal that transformed the political culture of the American energy sector. In the 1970s, the heart of extraction migrated from the underground mines of Pennsylvania, where unionization was strong, to the opencast mines of Wyoming – where productivity was much higher, coal was less sulphurous and the political culture was individualistic and Republican.[50] Mitchell's book should perhaps be understood in the British context, as an echo of the role of oil during Thatcher's 1984 offensive against the miners, but it has to be said that his thesis does not work well elsewhere.

7.

The Roots of Growth

Oil and wood. Historians generally study these two subjects separately. The first is associated with speed, geopolitics and modernity; the second with tradition, environmental history and conservation. In the history of energy, oil and wood are kept at a distance by the coal of the industrial revolution. And yet, over the course of the twentieth century, wood and oil have had a relationship that is fundamental to understanding their respective histories and much more besides. From derricks to cardboard packaging, from eucalyptus plantations to construction panels, the symbioses of wood and oil played a central role in the world's energy and economic growth in the twentieth century.

There will be wood

Wood was first and foremost essential to the emergence of the oil industry. For more than half a century, oil extraction depended entirely on trees. Derricks were made of wood, tanks were made of wood, barrels were made of wood, as were the barges and boats that transported them. The much-vaunted fluidity of oil was for a long time a logistical nightmare, and considerable amounts of wood and labour were used to contain it. In 1864, at Oil Creek in Pennsylvania, crude oil gushed out in such abundance that the drillers erected dykes before letting it flow into the river. The price of a barrel was twenty times that of the oil it contained. The coopers were busy, and barrels from all over the eastern United States and even Europe converged on Pennsylvania. On the Allegheny river, the logistics of oil were identical to those of timber rafting: during the high waters of spring, dykes were opened to transport barges loaded with barrels.[1]

According to some historians, this anarchic, wooded phase of the oil industry was merely a parenthesis that was quickly closed by Rockefeller, innovation, steel and capital. In a recent book on the history of energy infrastructure in the United States, Christopher Jones writes as follows: 'by the 1860s oil had left the age of wood as steel tanks, steel pipelines and steel tank cars had replaced wooden barrels, wooden wagons and wooden boats'.[2] That appears to be somewhat precipitous. Until the 1880s, the railways transported oil in vertical wooden tanks. Until the 1930s, the majority of derricks were built primarily from wood. These sturdy structures had to withstand the impact of drilling equipment and typically weighed around 30 tonnes each. At least 810,000 wells were drilled in the United States before 1930.[3] Add to this the shacks that housed oil workers and the massive

Spindletop, Beaumont, Texas, April 1903. It was nicknamed 'the matchbox' because of the density of derricks and the risk of fire. (Texas Energy Museum.)

tanks, made of wood, it becomes evident how the presence of oil could induce a great flurry of activity in the logging, sawmill and cooperage sectors wherever its extraction was underway.

The first oil age marked the heyday of the wooden barrel. As a representative of the American cooperage industry explained to oil companies and refiners in 1918: 'you need us and we need you'.[4] It is no coincidence that the American cooperage union was founded in 1890 in Titusville, the capital of oil, or that the greatest cooper in history is called Rockefeller. In the 1880s, his Cleveland cooperage employed 3,000 workers and produced 10,000 barrels a month. This was more than all the cooperages in London's East End, which at the same time were supplying the docks with packaging.[5] During the early twentieth century, the consumption of oil entailed an immense demand for barrels, particularly in areas lacking pipelines or railways. Furthermore, barrels played a crucial role in the transportation of refined products, including kerosene, which had long been deemed excessively hazardous for bulk transportation. Given the vast quantities of petroleum products involved, even a modest proportion, when stored, transported or sold in barrels, generated substantial opportunities for the cooperage industry.

Until the 1890s, oil was brought to Europe in barrels.[6] The transatlantic trade alone used more than 30 million barrels.[7] A decade later, steam-powered oil tankers made of steel began traversing the Atlantic, enabling the pumping of crude oil into metal tanks. However, the advent of metal tanks did not mark the obsolescence of wooden oil barrels. In Bristol, in the year 1898, both large metal tanks and wooden barrels coexisted. The preference for wooden barrels persisted due to their lower cost, ease of handling and simpler reparability in comparison to their more expensive, less manageable and harder-to-repair metal counterparts.[8] At the beginning of the twentieth century in France, countless small distilleries distributed kerosene using a horse, cart and barrel.[9] In the United States in the 1900s, 10 million barrels a year were still produced to meet the needs of the oil industry, twice as many as were required for all alcoholic beverages, including beer.[10]

In 1903, Standard Oil created the Interstate Cooperage Company in Belhaven, North Carolina. Production exceeded 700,000 barrels a year.

The industrialization of the barrel was primarily driven by the demand from oil companies. 'The enormous quantities of crude oil supplied by America', noted one observer, 'were enough to revolutionise the cooperage industry there.'[11] French coopers complained about this unfair competition, as oil barrels were often reused for wine.[12] In 1903, Rockefeller's Standard Oil created a new gigacooperage, even bigger than the one in Cleveland, the Interstate Cooperage Company in Belhaven, North Carolina. Production exceeded 700,000 barrels a year.[13] These industrial cooperages used chamfering, stave-cutting, strapping and painting machines, some of which no longer exist. In Russia, too, the first industrial cooperages seem to have been created for the needs of oil logistics, in the 1870s in Baku and Chistopol.[14]

During the 1930s, the logistics of oil underwent a transition towards complete metallization. In the United States, the increased wages and escalating wood prices resulting from the First World War led to the growing competitiveness of metal oil drums. By 1934, the American oil industry utilized 535 million cans (for lamps), 6 million metal barrels and an additional 1.4 million wooden barrels.[15] By 1942, the transportation of oil by troops had entirely shifted to metal barrels and jerry cans.[16] Oil had ultimately emancipated itself from its reliance on wood, accomplishing this transformation much more rapidly than coal, albeit after nearly a century of dependence.

Does this mean that oil no longer consumes wood? No: in a perfect twist to the transitionist narrative, one of the world's largest producers of charcoal happens to be the French company Vallourec, a leader in steel tubes for the oil industry. Here, wood is used to produce the steel used to extract oil, which in turn is essential for forestry. In 2000, Vallourec acquired its German counterpart Mannesmann, which owned a 230,000-hectare forest in the Minas Gerais region of Brazil to supply charcoal to its steel-making facilities. Vallourec Florestal now produces and consumes 1.2 million cu. m of charcoal a year, roughly as much as the entire American steel industry at its peak and four times as much as the entire French steel industry at its peak in the 1860s.[17] The mass of wood harvested by Vallourec (around 3 million cu. m per year) probably exceeds the consumption of the world oil industry at the end of the nineteenth century, when derricks, barrels and tanks were all made of wood.[18] The history of energy symbioses is made up of loops; it is a story without direction, and re-embedding processes are always possible.

A war interlude

In April 1936, a notable international conference on wood took place in London. Among the twenty-two delegations, the German contingent caused quite a stir. They arrived in cars fuelled by wood gas, donned suits made of artificial wool derived from wood, and even distributed wooden sweets to their colleagues. The underlying message was clear: Germany was on the verge of ushering in a new 'Wood Age', a time of abundant resources based on the most readily available material on Earth. While the 'age of oil' cemented Anglo-American dominance, Germany sought to challenge this hegemony

by promoting an alternative material. Germany had the best foresters, the best chemists, and there were immense wood resources
within reach of conquest in Europe and Russia. The fact that the
forestry delegation was led by Friedrich Bergius, who had won a
Nobel Prize for his work on the hydrogenation of coal, lent some
credibility to these grandiose prospects.[19]

Ten years later, British and American experts dispatched to Germany to assess technological advances demolished the lofty claims
made by Nazi foresters. Apart from a few interesting adhesives, the
chemical transformation of wood had in fact made little progress.
As for its use as a source of liquid fuel, it had been marginal compared to the hydrogenation of coal. For 'economic reasons', noted
the experts, wood had not been used on a large scale as a raw material for chemicals.[20] Indeed, conscription had deprived forestry of its
main motor, namely human muscle: in the 1930s, Germany had
more than 130,000 professional woodcutters, and many more farmers regularly cut wood.[21]

In the other belligerent countries there was also a scarcity of
lumberjacks, and military demand for timber far from compensated for the collapse of the construction sector. The United States,
the world's leading forestry power, saw its wood consumption fall
by a quarter during the war.[22] In France, despite coal and oil shortages and the famous *gasogène* cars (wood-gas powered), wood
consumption fell under the occupation.[23] Britain, severed from its
European suppliers, was compelled to slash its consumption by
half and resort to intensive exploitation of its meagre forests. The
supply of wood to Britain relied primarily on the transatlantic tonnage allocated by the Admiralty – to such an extent that the concept
of floating rafts across the North Atlantic was even considered as a
potential solution.[24] In Finland and Sweden, the increase in firewood and gas-powered cars did not compensate for the loss of
export markets.[25]

Despite statistics all pointing in the same direction, the idea of
extraordinary wood consumption during the Second World War
continues to linger in historiography. For example, the chapter on

the environment in the recent *Cambridge History of the Second World War* states that the war 'modified forest ecology on a global scale', or that it 'exacerbated depletion from France to Fiji'. This vision is based on apparently impressive figures about wood removals which, when put into perspective, prove the opposite of what they were intended to demonstrate.[26] If military strategists were concerned about supply, it is not because war consumes more wood than peace, but because it disrupts the forestry industry. The heavy emphasis in environmental history on military requisitions or on wood as an ersatz material is just another aspect of the standard transitionist narrative. It shows that a massive and obvious phenomenon is perhaps not appreciated for what it is: in the twentieth century, wood consumption grew with modernization, with the size of an economy fuelled by coal and oil. The twentieth century was indeed an 'age of wood', not because it replaced oil as the Nazi foresters had hoped, but because it accompanied its rise.

Capital accumulation

Wood consumption increased in the twentieth century as it played an important part in the huge symbiosis of energy and materials that urbanization represents. Buildings are generally absent from the energy epics of humanity, which focus more on engines than on heat and materials. Yet they consume a third of all energy and produce a third of the world's CO_2 emissions. The share of energy consumption accounted for by buildings is increasing as economies become proportionally less industrial and more service-oriented.[27] Similarly, the history of capitalism in the twentieth century may not have adequately acknowledged the significance of the construction industry. According to figures provided by Thomas Piketty, housing alone represents a substantial portion of capital accumulation. In Europe, it accounts for over half of the total, while in the United States it comprises a slightly smaller share.[28] A large part of this capital accumulation occurred after 1945, with a substantial percentage of housing being constructed during this period. In the United States, approximately 90 per cent of the housing stock was built after the war, while in Europe, the figure stands at around 75 per cent. The trend is even more pronounced in poor or formerly poor countries. For instance, in China, eight out of ten dwellings were built after 1980.[29]

This massive transformation took place under the reign of concrete. Not for nothing has 'concrete jungle' become a synonym for urbanization. Concrete is by far the most consumed man-made material in the world: in the early 2000s, 10 gigatonnes of concrete were poured every year, and this figure has now already doubled. But when it comes to construction, as with energy, the new hasn't made the old disappear. The extraordinary rise of concrete between 1950 and 2000 (from 0.5 Gt to 10 Gt), far from eradicating other construction materials, has enabled them to grow: glass, of course (by a factor of 9), but also brick (by a factor of 8), even though it competes with it directly. Construction is the biggest consumer of steel (which has grown by a factor of 3) and wood (also by a factor of 3).

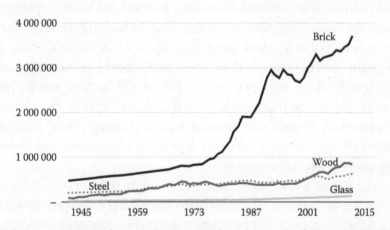

Global consumption of construction materials in thousands of tonnes. It should be noted that earth remains by far the most important building material, for earthworks and hydraulic structures, but its ubiquity and cost-free nature have made it invisible in statistics. (Data from Barbara Plank et al., 'From resource extraction to manufacturing and construction: flows of stock-building materials in 177 countries from 1900 to 2016', *Resources, Conservation & Recycling*, 179, 2022.)

The reason for this symbiosis is obvious: under the reign of concrete, every material has its purpose. Almost half of all concrete is used to build the infrastructure that serves the buildings and enables them to multiply. The other half is used to produce the slabs and shells on which the other materials, glass and bricks alike, can accumulate.

Urbanization since 1950 has also depended on wood. As a traditional material, well-suited to light, one- or two-storey buildings, timber has been key in the expansion of suburbs. The case of the United States, where 90 per cent of houses use timber as the main building material, shows that wood, touted for its 'green' virtues, is not in itself a guarantee of reduced emissions.[30] While in terms of mass, wood has little weight compared with concrete, the opposite is true in terms of value. In the United States, the construction timber industry is a much larger business than cement.[31] In Europe, timber experienced a significant increase in use starting from the 1960s, coinciding with the widespread adoption of private car ownership. The pursuit of the American model of single-family homes led to a surge in demand for timber, as it offered more opportunities for use compared to the collective-housing models that were favoured in the post-war period. Even if it is invisible, wood is omnipresent. In France, although 'wooden' houses are virtually non-existent (making up 4 per cent of the overall housing stock), per capita timber consumption is nevertheless half that of the United States. And French construction-timber consumption doubled between 1950 and 1980, precisely during the period when the country entered the 'concrete era'.[32]

The role of wood has become even more significant with its thorough modernization. Thanks to petrochemistry, wood provides the basis for some truly revolutionary construction materials. Available in sheets or rolls, these materials combine mass production with on-site adaptability. Coupled with the use of portable electric tools, they had a major impact on productivity in the building industry. Let us take, for example, plasterboard, which came into widespread use after 1945. This seemingly trivial invention, by an obscure American

In Paris in the 1946 Exhibition of American housing techniques, the new building materials were based on wood. They were much more modern than the iron and glass of the Grand Palais, which housed the show house from the United States. The company Placoplatre was founded the following year at the instigation of the Minister for Reconstruction, Raoul Dautry, and used US gypsum patents.[33]

papermaker, made it possible to cut construction times considerably: instead of applying several layers of plaster to panelling with a trowel and waiting for it to dry, large factory-made cardboard panels covered with a skim of plaster were simply nailed or placed on rods.[34] American production rose from 200 million to 1 billion square metres between 1945 and 1965, while the number of plasterers halved in the same period.[35]

Another example to consider is plywood, where the symbiosis between oil and wood takes place at a molecular level. In the 1930s, in relation to aircraft construction, new formaldehyde-based adhesives were developed. These resins, unlike traditional organic glues, have the ability to penetrate deep into the wood, making it waterproof, resistant to rot, and significantly more rigid. This innovation in plywood production allowed for the creation of stronger and more durable wooden panels that could be used in various construction applications. The combination of oil-derived adhesives and wood revolutionized the capabilities and performance of plywood as a versatile construction material.[36] Plywood opened the construction industry to the chemical industry. During the war, military barracks and workers' housing on the West Coast served as a testing ground for extensive experimentation in construction techniques. In the decades that followed, the expansion of housing in the United States made massive use of new plywood boards: 80 per cent of houses used them, mainly for interior partitions and roof underlays. In fact, a significant proportion of houses, the least expensive, around a quarter of them, even employed plywood on the exterior.[37] American plywood production rose from 1 million to 15 million cu. m per year between 1945 and 1965. During the 1960s, the decreasing cost of formaldehyde made it economically viable to use as a binder for sawdust. This development led to the creation of particleboard, a composite material made of plastic and wood. Particleboard gained significant popularity in Europe, where wood was more expensive: consumption rose from 5 million to 20 million cu. m in the 1960s.[38] Lastly, wood, in the form of kraft paper, was employed as a backing material for rolls of glass wool or polyurethane foam. These insulation materials played a significant role, particularly after the energy crisis of 1973, in reducing the energy intensity of affluent nations.[39]

Like many unrealized futures, the renowned 'plastic house' exhibited by Monsanto in 1957 at California's Tomorrowland amusement park may be tempting to dismiss with a smile. However, the reality is quite different. The plastics industry made early inroads into the realm of construction, and wood was its Trojan Horse. As early as 1942, Monsanto engaged the architect Marcel Breuer to develop its initial 'plastic house', which featured plywood extensively from the roof to the floor.[40] Today, despite their toxicity, the various composite wood panels are produced at a rate of 400 million cu. m per year, half of which is produced in China. As a sign of the triumph of alloys over raw products, their production has caught up with that of sawn solid wood.[41]

Finally, it should be noted that this modernization of wood by means of petroleum in turn enabled much more concrete to be poured. In the early stages of concrete construction, a substantial amount of timber was required, almost on a par with structures constructed solely from wood. The early editions of the journal *Cement Age* featured numerous articles on formwork and showcased photographs of wooden structures that were both spectacular and short-lived. The assembly of formwork, performed plank by plank by carpenters, often incurred higher costs than the actual cement itself.[42] Thanks to oiled plywood and the construction of reusable forms, the 'wood intensity' of concrete diminished in the 1930s. But even so, concrete infrastructures consume a lot of wood: between 1950 and 1970, the construction of American motorways required more than 1 million cu. m of wood every year.[43] In the 2010s, China was consuming 70 million cu. m of plywood a year (18 per cent of global production) to pour several billion tonnes of concrete.[44] It is regrettable that plywood has replaced plank formwork: one of the merits of the 'brutalist' textures favoured by architects in the 1960s was precisely that they fixed in the building the traces of this fundamental symbiosis between concrete and wood, between the modern and the supposedly ancient.

Packaging growth

Wood consumption increased in the 20th century for a second reason: the need to package products for an economy fuelled by oil and coal. The packaging industry is an essential component of the global economy, and its turnover was estimated at 1 trillion dollars in 2020, more than aviation or the mobile-phone sector.[45] Once again, new materials, in this case plastics, have been added to the old ones, whose flows continued to increase. Despite the 4.9

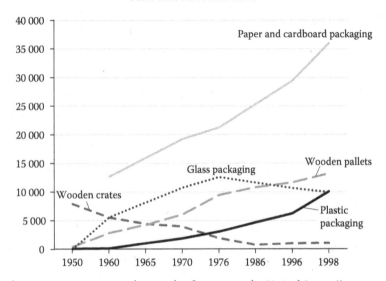

Packaging consumption in thousands of tonnes in the United States.[46]

billion tonnes of plastic that have accumulated in the biosphere since the 1960s, wood remains the first material for packaging.[47] By weight, Europeans and Americans throw away three times more cardboard packaging than plastic.[48] Torn-open cardboard boxes reign in our garbage bins. Rather than replacing it, plastic has joined forces with cardboard to make it waterproof and impact resistant. Similarly, one of the most important developments in contemporary logistics – palletizing, to which we will return – is based on a very cheap wooden object and uses plastic film to hold goods in place.

Let's take the case of the United States, for which precise packaging statistics are available. The American historian Susan Strasser speaks of a 'packaging revolution', beginning at the end of the nineteenth century, to describe the transition from a distribution system based on bulk to one based on individual packaging. Branding and advertising play a central role in her story: individual paper or cardboard packaging was chosen because it provided a good support for ink and therefore for commercial communication. With the advent of this new packaging, manufacturers were able to instil in

Americans the practice of requesting specific branded products from their grocers, such as a box of Ivory soap or two boxes of Uneeda biscuits, rather than simply asking for a pound or two pounds of generic items. This individual packaging bypassed the control of wholesalers who traditionally had governed the distribution chains. The rise of brand names empowered manufacturers to stabilize their markets, as their success became dependent on the choices made by numerous consumers rather than those of a select few intermediaries. At the end of the nineteenth century, a fundamental economic transformation was taking place in the United States on the six sides of packaging cartons.[49]

From a material standpoint, the 'packaging revolution' seems more modest, a transition from wood to wood, which had to be transformed and thinned to keep pace with the growing volume of goods. Take cement, for example: in 1895, in the United States, all cement was transported in a million wooden barrels. Twelve years later, cement factories were producing 35 times as much cement but using 'only' 5 million barrels, the rest being sold in paper bags. Finally, in 1937, the factories' production had tripled again, but they now used only paper bags and had begun to deliver their cement in bulk by rail or ready-to-use by truck – all America's cooperage would not have been enough to contain it.[50]

In contrast, the paper industry was able to match the extraordinary volumetric expansion of production. By the end of the nineteenth century, it had become a heavy chemical industry, using huge machines and huge amount of energy. The market for books and newspapers was showing signs of saturation, and the appetite for reading could no longer absorb paper production. Manufacturers in the sector were looking for new outlets. Kimberly-Clark, for example, introduced the use of paper in hygiene products.[51] But packaging provided a far more important market. Innovations followed in rapid succession: corrugated cardboard, which improved strength; folding cardboard, which drastically reduced costs; and multi-layer bags, which enabled paper to conquer heavy loads such as cement, seed or fertilizer.[52] Then there's cellophane, a transparent film manufactured

"HOW SELF-SERVICE
HELPS YOU BUY
BETTER MEATS..."

Self-service meats in DuPont Cellophane
save time, save work, save waste

The 'plastic age' began with wood. In 1958, the year of its peak, American cellophane production reached 200,000 tonnes, employing around 10,000 people of whom 1,000 were researchers and engineers.[55]

in the 1920s by the Franco-Swiss company of the same name. It enabled supermarkets to extend self-service to fresh produce.[53] Between the wars, packaging was the driving force behind the growth of the paper industry: consumption of newspapers stagnated, that of hygiene products increased but was of little importance, while that of packaging soared. In 1937, the United States consumed 16 million tonnes of paper and cardboard (half the world's production), of which 8 million tonnes were used to package goods.[54]

The development of cardboard as a packaging material coincided with the rise of road freight and the automobile, and these two processes are interconnected. For a long time, railway companies' pricing policies favoured wooden barrels and crates, which were reputed to be sturdier. Behind this official reason they were also safeguarding their own interests, as crates and barrels ensured higher turnover. Additionally, railway companies had often made investments in sawmills and crate factories to help get the most value from their forest estates.[56] Lighter, cardboard boxes, on the other hand, were well suited to being transported by lorry. Less robust, they benefited from the fact that road freight did not break the load. The car, for its part, made repeat purchases easier: rather than making occasional trips to the market to buy in bulk and stock up at home, the motorized rural family could now shop more frequently, buying food in smaller quantities, packed in cardboard.[57] Finally, individual packaging made self-service possible, a commercial practice first introduced in the United States in 1917. The tempting availability of packaging necessitated vast shelves and larger sales areas, ushering in the reign of the car-accessible supermarket.

More surprisingly, as goods transport has increasingly relied on petroleum and cardboard, it has also led to a growing demand for solid wood. This phenomenon can be attributed to the forklift truck, a seemingly modest yet transformative innovation that has revolutionized load handling over the past half-century. The first models appeared in the United States in the 1910s and arrived in Europe with the American Expeditionary Force in 1917.[58] During the Second World War, the American army laid the foundations for a new practice: palletizing loads. The wooden pallet ceased to be merely an accessory for local handling, limited to ports or depots, and instead became the primary method of bulk packaging for long-distance shipments. The initiative seems to have fallen to the Quartermaster Corps – one of the three corps in charge of the American army's military logistics – whose operations expanded considerably during the conflict: it distributed food to 8 million soldiers, stored and distributed a fifth of American industrial production, employed 75,000 people and managed 60 million square feet of hangars – a third of the total area of private warehouses in the United States.[59] In 1942, the Quartermaster General placed an order for 13,500 forklift trucks, equivalent to seven years' US production, and 60 million pallets.[60] Palletization, which was relatively unknown or in its early stages in the industrial sector, gained momentum due to military demands. The transformation required significant adjustments, from factories to ports. Forklift trucks were ill-suited for multi-storey warehouses or the uneven surfaces of quaysides. They were obstructed by rails, and pallets were not easily stowed in the cargo holds of ships.[61] It was only at the end of the war that US army logisticians managed to ensure continuous palletization from suppliers to bases in the Pacific. In the following decade, palletization was pushed forward by experts who had often trained in the military. Such was the case of Norman Cahners, a former Navy logistician, who founded the magazine *Modern Materials Handling*, which was essential in the post-war spread of the pallet.

Palletizing encouraged a new type of industrial architecture: horizontal, without storeys, and with more space to facilitate the movement of forklifts. In order to find the land they needed, manufacturers set up operations far from the cities, on sites served by cars and lorries rather than trams or railways. The wooden pallet was one of the many factors contributing to post-war industrial and urban sprawl.

In material terms, cardboard boxes and pallets represent an extraordinary gain in efficiency: a cardboard box weighs one-twentieth of a wooden crate, while a pallet can support up to fifty times its own weight. The history of packaging provides another example of the rebound effect: individual lightening leads to overall weight increase. Even though the production of crates and barrels collapsed after 1950, logistics consumed more and more sawn wood. In the United States, pallet production rose from 62 million to 450 million units between 1960 and 2000. At that time, it consumed 13 million cu. m of wood, four times more than cooperage at its peak in 1909 and twice as much as crates at their peak in 1950. In addition to pallets, there are packaging cardboard boxes (40 million cu. m at the beginning of the twenty-first century), double the amount of raw wood and far more than all the wood used by all modes of transportation in the United States a century earlier. As logistics increasingly relied on metal, petroleum and plastic, it continued to consume more and more wood. If packaging were included in freight statistics, it would

The 'National Supply Depot' in Clearfield, Utah (1944). During the war, the US Navy built 12 million sq. m of warehouses, ten times the surface area it had in 1940. In particular, it built four huge logistics areas designed entirely for forklifts and pallets: a single level, a flat cemented surface and a height defined according to the vertical reach of the forklift. The Clearfield site totals 800,000 sq. m spread over more than 50 warehouses. By way of comparison, Amazon's largest logistics site is 330,000 sq. m.[62]

likely reveal that wood is one of the most transported materials in the world.

The same rebound effect has occurred on a global scale: cardboard consumption quadrupled between 1960 and 2000. In recent decades, thanks to digitalization, global consumption of printing paper eventually declined, but the demand for cardboard packaging skyrocketed, partially due to the rise of the internet. With over 200 million tonnes, packaging accounts for half of the world's paper and cardboard production and consumes approximately 8 per cent of the world's harvested wood.[63]

Black liquors and green energy

The growing consumption of wood for packaging or construction has had the unexpected consequence of increasing the use of wood in the energy mix of rich countries. This phenomenon went relatively unnoticed because it took place in sawmills, wood-panel factories and paper mills, while at the same time the consumption of firewood in households was falling. In the 1960s, sawmills expanded, modernized and equipped themselves with steam turbines, some of which had a capacity of several megawatts. To make better use of waste, a new fuel appeared in the 1970s: wood pellets. When subjected to high pressure, the lignin contained in wood shavings and sawdust is transformed into a plastic film that simplifies the storage and transport of wood energy. Cheaper than gas or oil, wood-pellet consumption in Europe has tripled between 2010 and 2020, reaching more than 60 million cu. m for heat and power generation.[64]

Another wood residue played an even more important role: black liquors from the paper industry. Until the 1950s, these lignin-rich liquids were generally poured into rivers, causing major pollution. With the development of environmental standards and the rise in oil prices, paper manufacturers have invested in systems to recover black liquors for heat and electricity. The impact of this seemingly modest technological transformation has been tremendous. Paper ranks as the fourth-largest industrial energy consumer, following cement works, the steel industry and the chemical industry. Since black liquors contain half of the energy found in the wood used for paper production, their recovery has resulted in a threefold increase in wood energy in the United States between 1950 and 2000. By 2020, black liquors from American paper mills alone accounted for twice the amount of energy produced by the country's solar-generated electricity.[65] The classification of black liquor as green energy is the subject of debate, since it comes from an industry that still relies on fossil fuels for a third of its energy consumption.[66]

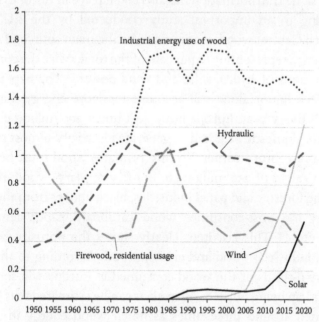

US

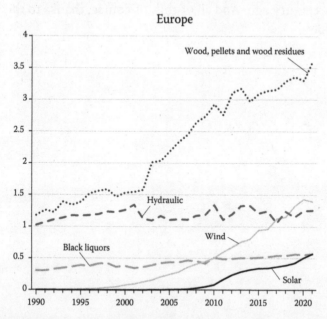

Europe

Renewable energies in millions of terajoules in the US and in Europe. (Data from IEA and Eurostat, primary energy.)

The same transformation has also taken place in Europe. In 2018, according to an important study conducted by the EU's Joint Research Centre, wood continued to be the main source of renewable energy, representing 64 per cent of the total, twice the combined contributions of hydro, solar and wind power.[67] The paper industry's black liquor alone still accounts for more energy than solar power.[68] Every year, Europe burns just under 200 million cu. m of wood for domestic heat and to generate electricity, almost twice as much as a century earlier. To this 'primary' wood must be added the equivalent of 250 million cu. m of 'secondary' wood: residues from the forestry and panel industries, black liquors from the paper industry and 'post-consumer' wood (cardboard, paper, demolition wood, etc.).[69] This last item clearly shows the porosity between timber, industrial wood and energy wood. According to the same study, two-thirds of the wood consumed in Europe will sooner or later end up being burned. All in all, it can be estimated that Europe consumed around three times as much wood energy in 2020 as it did a century ago. And all of this, of course, thanks to the rise of fossil fuels.

8.

The Pétrolization *of Wood*

One of the paradoxes of twentieth-century environmental history is that rich countries, while consuming ever more wood, have seen the surface area of their forests increase. Much has been written about this apparently encouraging phenomenon. This is yet another 'transition', in this case 'a forest transition', with a scientific literature to describe it. According to the geographer Alexander Mather, every country in the course of its history would see its forest regain ground once a certain threshold of economic development had been passed. This theory bore a striking resemblance to that of the (liberal) economists of the 1970s who refuted the neo-Malthusian forecasts of resource depletion.[1] Some of the theory's shortcomings have already been highlighted, in particular the fact that reforestation in rich countries was, in part, based on deforestation in tropical countries. The globalization of biomass – meat, soya, paper, oilseeds, etc. – has enabled importing countries to free up large areas of agricultural land for their forests. A recent study estimates that a third of reforestation in northern countries can be attributed to international trade.[2] But the problem with the 'forest transition' goes deeper than that: it obscures the absolutely fundamental role of fossil fuels – oil and gas – in this phenomenon by using such a vague term and multi-causal explanations.

The brutality of oil

Since 1950, forest equipment and harvesting methods, fertilization techniques and productivity per hectare, have all been radically transformed by fossil fuels. First, it is clear that trees are felled and transported by new machines whose 'brutal' nature, to use historian Paul Josephson's expression, is linked to oil.[3] In this field, coal had always been handicapped by the weight of boilers. In 1878, a 150-kilogram steam saw powered by a 750-kilogram boiler was presented as a feat of portability.[4] Faced with this failure, a form of expeditious mechanization – dynamite felling – was even used for a time.[5] Between the wars, oil began to make a timid inroad on forestry, initially with the use of trucks to drag logs away from felling areas ('skidding').[6] During the First World War, to make up for the shortage of lumberjacks, there were also trial fellings using horizontal circular saws powered by generators.[7] The chainsaw, patented in 1929 by the Bavarian engineer Andreas Stihl, met with little success: weighing 46 kilos, it required two workers to operate and was prohibitively expensive.[8] Until 1950, wood production remained largely dependent on muscle power, on the horses and oxen used for skidding, and on the woodcutters' ability to handle the axe, saw and wedge. In the United States, the number of loggers increased until 1950.[9]

The forestry revolution really began in the second half of the twentieth century. The reduction in the weight and price of chainsaws changed the situation, as they could now be bought by the loggers themselves, who were generally self-employed. They abandoned the axe and saw in the 1950s in North America, and in the following decade in Europe.[10] Another innovation of almost equal importance concerned skidding: forwarders, i.e. vehicles equipped with hydraulic arms or forks, mechanized the stacking of logs, which represented a third of the work of loggers.[11] Finally, in the early 1970s, multi-functional tree harvesters appeared: these sophisticated machines, produced by a handful of companies, were capable of felling, delimbing and cutting a tree into useable lengths in less than a minute, i.e. three times faster than with a chainsaw and in much safer conditions.[12] These machines are still being rolled out. Thanks to all these improvements, the forestry industry became more productive and timber cheaper, despite rising demand. In the United States, the price of wood, which rose sharply between 1945 and 1950, remained stable thereafter.[13] It goes without saying that all these machines depended on oil to produce this wood. A tree harvester burns 10 to 15 litres of diesel per hour. Recent studies show that 2 to 3 litres of diesel are consumed per cubic metre of wood extracted, meaning that wood has become, in part, a fossil fuel.[14]

Secondly, the mechanization of forestry has required roads and therefore other machines, bulldozers and scrapers, which also run on diesel. As transport accounts for a significant proportion of the price of wood, access to the forest is key to its economic value. Since the Second World War, the construction of tens of millions of kilometres of roads worldwide has made hundreds of millions of hectares of forest accessible and exploitable. The history of this immensely significant environmental transformation is largely understudied and poorly documented, primarily due to its nature as an informal, privately driven and frequently transient network. Data on American national forests show that there were 120,000 kilometres of forest roads in 1939 and 610,000 kilometres by the end of the twentieth century.[15] In Finland, the rate of forest-road construction experienced a tenfold increase after 1950 with the introduction of bulldozers.[16] In this heavily forested country, the total length of forest roads (350,000 km) exceeds that of conventional roads (100,000 km).[17] In France, after 1945, to lay out their forest roads, local authorities could take out a thirty-year loan at 0.25 per cent interest from the National Forestry Fund, which they repaid with the proceeds of the felling.[18] Even in mountainous regions, the bulldozer carried out its tasks, despite the recognized issues of erosion and landslides. In some cases, roads replaced the remarkable forest-cable systems that had been installed in Europe and the United States between the wars.[19] In the Brazilian Amazon rainforest, the construction of logging roads (many of them illegal) reached a massive scale, starting in the 1970s. Recent satellite-imagery analysis has unveiled their full extent. The Amazon rainforest now encompasses approximately 3.5 million kilometres of dirt roads, ten times the extent of the entire British road network. These logging roads are particularly concentrated in the

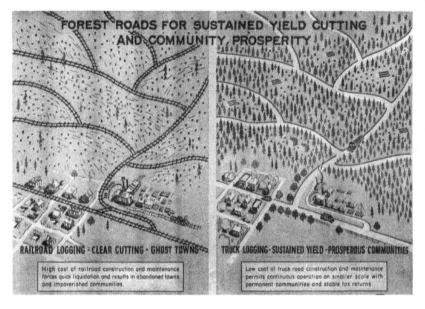

FOREST ROADS FOR SUSTAINED YIELD CUTTING AND COMMUNITY PROSPERITY

RAILROAD LOGGING - CLEAR CUTTING - GHOST TOWNS — High cost of railroad construction and maintenance forces quick liquidation and results in abandoned towns and impoverished communities.

TRUCK LOGGING - SUSTAINED YIELD - PROSPEROUS COMMUNITIES — Low cost of truck road construction and maintenance permits continuous operation on smaller scale with permanent communities and stable tax returns.

In the 1930s, the US Forest Service extolled the merits of roads for timber harvesting. Unlike railways, which would encourage clear-cutting, forest roads would form a network that was both denser and more extensive, making it possible to distribute harvesting more evenly and prevent deforestation. In the 1950s, forestry economists began to calculate the 'optimal density' of roads. This was regularly revised upwards to between 2 and 4 km of road per sq. km of forest.[20] By way of comparison, road density in French national forests is 1.8 km/sq. km, 1 km/sq. km in Finland and 0.9 km/sq. km in the Amazon rainforest – remarkably close to Scandinavian standards. With only 0.15 km of road per sq. km of forest in Russia, according to these calculations, the number of kilometres of logging road in this country should be multiplied by ten.[21] (Hearle Clapp, 'Report to Committee on Roads', US Forest Service, 1939, p. 11.)

southern and eastern regions of the Amazon rainforest.[22] Since the 1930s, bulldozers have profoundly transformed the forests, and if we are to believe the calculations of forestry economists on the 'optimal density of roads', their task is far from complete.

Thirdly, oil and gas have increased forest productivity through the use of synthetic fertilizers. From the 1960s until the 1990s, hundreds of thousands of metric tonnes of nitrogen fertilizers were applied, often using methods such as aerial spraying by planes or helicopters, across tens of millions of hectares of coniferous forests.[23] After the oil shocks of the 1970s, some considered this practice as a solution to the energy crisis: yield calculations showed that 1 unit of energy invested in fertilizer production could result in the recovery of 6 units of firewood from the increased forest growth.[24] Whatever their value, these calculations still bear witness to the hybrid nature of contemporary wood energy.

But it was mainly in industrial plantations that fertilizers played a fundamental role. In the early 1960s, the paper industry chose eucalyptus, a tree native to Australia, as a major source of cellulose. As its fibres are shorter than those of softwoods, eucalyptus is mainly used to produce packaging board. The expansion of the paperboard industry mentioned in the previous chapter is correlated with the extraordinary expansion of industrial plantations, first in the Iberian Peninsula, then in Latin America – mainly Brazil, Argentina and Chile – and finally in China in the 1990s.[25]

These plantations, sometimes referred to as 'fibre farms', represent a milestone in the history of wood when its production has become a branch of intensive agriculture.[26] Clones, some of which are genetically modified, are grown densely and in rapid rotations (four to seven years). Consequently, the fertilizer requirements for these plantations can reach those of cereal cultivation.[27] After felling, the plots are cleaned with herbicide before being replanted, enabling them to receive international sustainability certification. In terms of yield, the effect of oil and chemicals on wood is spectacular. In south-east Brazil, Aracruz Celulose (now Fibria Celulose) has 213,000 hectares of eucalyptus harvested by clear-cutting at a rate of 53 hectares *per day*.[28] Eucalyptus plantations in Brazil produce an average of 39 cu. m per hectare per year, and some plantations used for bioenergy even reach 80 cu. m per hectare per year.[29] By way of comparison, French forests at the beginning of the twentieth century produced little more than 2 cu. m per hectare per year.[30] At the beginning of the twenty-first century, industrial plantations of eucalyptus and pine produce a third of the wood harvested in the world from barely 3 per cent of the forested area.[31] The irony lies in the fact that industrial forestry upholds the concept of wood as a renewable resource, yet it increasingly relies on non-renewable agricultural practices and materials, such as oil, natural gas and phosphorus.[32] As early as the 1960s, in Portugal and Spain, the depletion and drying out of soils and the decline in biodiversity had been denounced, especially as eucalyptus was then associated with the ruling dictatorships and also with paper companies from northern Europe. In the wake of the oil crisis, foresters became concerned about the dependence of forestry on chemical fertilizers and machinery.[33] Nevertheless, since 1990, the area of forest plantation worldwide has increased by 55 per cent to 130 million hectares,[34] and that devoted to eucalyptus has doubled to 24 million hectares.[35]

Lastly, oil has played an indirect role in fostering the growth of wood production. With the introduction of tractors and automobiles, substantial areas of land once used for cultivating crops to feed horses and mules have been freed up. At the beginning of the twentieth century, 35 million hectares in the United States were used to feed beasts of burden for agriculture, and 6 million for horse-drawn transport in cities: in total, more than a quarter of the country's agricultural land was devoted to animal power. 'The first merit of tractors,' commented an American agronomist in 1949, 'is that they don't eat oats.'[36] Furthermore, the introduction of tractors resulted in the abandonment of marginal lands, especially sloping terrain that was not well-suited for tractor operations and became economically unviable. The use of fertilizers and pesticides, by enhancing crop yields, has also played a role in reducing the amount of farmland required for cultivation. Additionally, the emergence of synthetic fibres derived from petroleum contributed to a decline of around one-third in global wool production since the 1960s. Consequently, many countries have witnessed a substantial decrease in their sheep populations, which also freed up land for forests.[37]

Let us return to the forest transition. Recent studies, looking not at the surface area of forests but at the stock of wood they contain, have refined its chronology. The rebound of forest wood did not take place at the end of the nineteenth century, as previously thought, but later, in the 1950s and 1960s. From that date onwards, in rich countries, the volume of standing timber increased sharply, much faster than the surface area of forests.[38] It is obviously no coincidence that these decades also coincided with the influx of oil and fertilizers into the economies of rich countries: by intensifying both agriculture and forestry and facilitating international transfers of biomass, oil was the main cause of reforestation. The 'forest transition' may have dispelled fears about forest exhaustion, but it is not good news for the climate: based on oil, it reflects the multiple symbioses that have been forged between fossil fuels and wood since the 1950s. This historical observation is not without consequences for the viability of carbon-neutrality scenarios, which often include huge amounts of captured emissions from the forest 'carbon sink' – the European Union, for instance, expects to store 450 Mt of CO_2 per year by 2050. The problem is that this redeeming forest, the wooden leg of the net-zero scenarios, is growing, in part, thanks to the use of fossil fuels.[39]

Charcoal: a new energy

From the 1960s onwards, chainsaws, forestry tractors and lorries were at work in the tropical forests. Thanks to oil, many more trees – bigger, heavier, further from rivers and ports – could be transported over much greater distances. It was at this point that the international market for tropical wood really took off, with exports to industrial countries increasing sixfold between 1960 and 1980.[40] This had unexpected consequences for the energy mix of exporting countries. In the Philippines, for example, bundles of dipterocarp bark appeared on market stalls as firewood in the 1960s. These gigantic hardwood trees are highly prized for furniture, and timber companies transported them by lorry to the ports or to local plywood factories. Taking advantage of the drivers' breaks – and in return for payment – men climbed onto the trailers and debarked the trunks with machetes. The bark was then dried in the sun before women and children tied them in bundles using wire salvaged from old tyres. An FAO expert described an industry that flourished in the 1970s, as it was both profitable for the families who practised it and had the advantage of offering manufacturers logs that had already been debarked.[41]

This example from the Philippines illustrates a general phenomenon: by increasing the production and availability of wood, oil has made it possible to increase its energy uses. Since 1960, the amount of firewood in the world has risen from around 1 billion cu. m to 2 billion cu. m. To regard this as the persistence of old technology would be to misunderstand its novelty and scale. This is the first time in history that megacities of more than 10 million inhabitants depend on wood for energy: Lagos, Kinshasa, Dakar and Dar-es-Salaam alone consume more wood than large European countries did a century ago. Kinshasa, for example, with a population of 11 million, consumes 2.15 million tonnes of charcoal every year.[42] By way of comparison, Paris, one of the biggest consumers in the nineteenth century, burned just 100,000 tonnes of charcoal in the 1860s.[43] Given the poor yields of traditional charcoal kilns, it is estimated that Kinshasa burns the equivalent of 17 million tonnes of wood a year, more than France consumed in the mid-nineteenth century. This is a continental phenomenon: in the 1950s, no city in sub-Saharan Africa had more than 500,000 inhabitants, and the use of charcoal was limited.[44] In 2020, more than fifty cities have more than a million inhabitants, and most of their populations use charcoal to cook their food. Charcoal consumption in Africa has increased sevenfold since 1960.[45]

This new energy system is based on a combination of wood, muscle power and oil. Two to three times more energy dense than wood, charcoal is easier to transport in sacks loaded onto trucks, which offsets the costs caused by carbonization.[46] Trucks link an expanding urban world to distant forest resources. Farmers take the charcoal to a main road, where it is collected by lorries, buses or pick-ups. In town, motorbikes, bicycles or porters take over. The key role of the truck often enables the merchants who organize the transport to capture most of the added value.[47] Charcoal is also dependent on the bulldozers that open up the forests for exploitation. The supply of charcoal to Kinshasa, for example, depends on the tracks that are cutting ever deeper into the forest of the Congo Basin.[48]

It is easy to understand why the earliest and most serious criticism of the 'energy transition' came from Africa. In the 1970s, after the oil crisis, the gap between the rhetoric condemning firewood as an atavism and the reality of its expansion underlined the teleological illusion of the transition. Contrary to the idea of an 'energy ladder' running from wood to electricity, a ladder that households and nations would conscientiously climb as they became richer, it appeared that charcoal consumption was not decreasing with electrification – in Kinshasa, for example, 70 per cent of households use both charcoal and electricity – and that, on the contrary, it was increasing with economic growth and urbanization. What's more, the fact that charcoal provides millions of people with an income, and that farmers and traders have managed to set up supply circuits amounting to hundreds of thousands of tonnes, partly protecting urban populations from the erratic prices of oil, butane and the dollar, has helped to change the way international institutions look at wood energy.[49]

From the 1980s onwards the focus shifted, not only towards promoting a transition away from wood usage but primarily towards enhancing the existing energy system by disseminating more efficient stoves, cookers and charcoal kilns. Governments and international organizations also set out to limit the impact on forests by financing plantations and agroforestry projects. Rwanda, where most charcoal is produced from eucalyptus plantations, became the example to follow.[50] The FAO's publication of a report in 2017 titled *The Charcoal Transition* can be seen as a somewhat ironic reflection on the energy transition.[51]

Let us face it: there has never been an energy transition out of wood. Neither in the nineteenth nor twentieth centuries, neither in poor countries nor rich ones. The perfect symbol of this non-transition is to be found in the heart of the region that is supposed to be its birthplace: between Leeds and Sheffield, in the middle of the English countryside, stand the seven cooling towers of the Drax power station. When it was inaugurated in 1974, this power station was designed to burn coal from the Yorkshire mines. In the 1990s, after it was privatized, Drax imported its fuel from Australia, Russia and South Africa, a total of 9 million tonnes a year, making it one of the largest thermal power stations in the world. In the mid-2000s, with the help of generous subsidies and under the guise of climate change, the plant was gradually converted to 'biomass': a euphemism for wood, which it imports in the form of pellets, mainly from the United States and Canada. Drax claims to produce carbon-free electricity, which is doubly false: on the one hand, it contributes to the degradation of forests, and on the other, its operation depends from start to finish on oil, which fuels the forestry machines, lorries, crushers and ships that cross the Atlantic. In 2021, Drax burned more than 8 million tonnes of wood pellets, more than the UK's entire forestry production, to meet around 1.5 per cent of the country's energy needs.[52] That also represents four times more wood than was burned in England in the mid-eighteenth century: a fine result after two hundred years of energy transitions. Drax demonstrates the impasse represented by a transition running backwards, with a fossil-fuel economy claiming to become organic again, without shrinking in size – and the same could be said of the biofuels that are supposed to decarbonize air and sea transport.

The example of the Drax power station and, more generally, the tripling of wood-energy use in rich countries in the twentieth century, the explosion of charcoal use in Africa since 1960, the tripling of coal worldwide since 1980, oil use that continues to grow year after year despite or thanks to repeated oil crises, and the crucial fact that these phenomena are interlinked – all these factors should have led us to abandon the 'energy transition' as an analytical tool a long time ago, or to use it very cautiously as a normative (or even downright utopian) concept. Now that we are two-thirds of the way through this book, one question remains unanswered: how has the stagist vision of energy history been able to endure? How was 'transition' able to take hold at the end of the twentieth century, when the whole energy dynamic of the time contradicted it? How did this notion become, from the 1970s onwards, the normal, consensual future, that of governments, companies and experts who claim to be guiding us towards a carbon-free future?

9.

Technocracy Inc.

An energy transition gone wrong: for many intellectuals, this was the profound nature of the 1929 crisis and the Depression that followed. The question of technological unemployment was naturally on everyone's mind, but some people took the argument a step further: machines were merely the transmission belts of a more profound upheaval in the nature of energy.[1] The abundance, ubiquity and availability of energy made possible by electricity caused archaic economic structures to break down. For an American engineer, the crisis signalled the entry of the United States into the 'Power Age', the social effects of which were entirely different from those of the 'Machine Age' which had preceded it.[2] Whereas in the nineteenth century machines had increased human labour, in the twentieth century electricity was causing the obsolescence of the human muscle and consequently mass unemployment. To curb social chaos, it was imperative to tame 'the billion wild horses',[3] an expression coined by the economist Stuart Chase, referring to the power of the engines installed on the Earth at that time.

This interpretation of the Great Depression was based on statistics of a new kind, showing the enormous growth in energy since the beginning of the twentieth century. In the United States, thanks to electrification, the power of industrial machinery had increased twentyfold between 1902 and 1927.[4] This brutal transformation would have made human muscle obsolete, and with it an entire economic system organized around scarcity. Electricity nourished crude stage-theory thinking. It also fuelled a discourse, widespread at the time, of the technological obsolescence of the political system.[5] It was in this particular context of the 1930s that original political proposals based on energy emerged, such as Social Credit in England and Technocracy in North America.

These two movements are already familiar to historians, the latter more than the former,[6] and their social theories are simplistic to say the least. What interests me is that in the early 1930s, faced with the combined threat of entropy and unemployment, new ways of thinking about and visualizing energy dynamics emerged; representations that have stayed with us to this day.

Energy radicalism

Energy radicalism is an ideology of scientists and engineers struck by the second law of thermodynamics, impressed by economic planning during the First World War and shocked by the irrationality of an economic system capable of generating both overproduction and poverty.

One of its sources of inspiration was the Nobel Prize-winning chemist Frederick Soddy. In *Cartesian Economics* (1921), a short, hard-hitting work that has been widely read, Soddy proposes a complete overhaul of the economy on 'rational' bases, i.e. energy. The fatal flaw of capitalism, he explains, is that it runs counter to the laws of thermodynamics. Why can capital demand interest and grow when its physical foundations – machines, buildings, factories – are inexorably deteriorating? How can we even accept that its unequal accumulation is taking place at the expense of fossil fuel, that irreplaceable national treasure? By exchanging manufactured goods or, worse still, coal for agricultural goods, Britain had squandered a stock in exchange for flows. And because of global demographic growth, this vital trade between carbon and food was reaching its limits, hence the resurgence of imperialism, the First World War and other, even more terrible crises to come.[7]

At the same time, the engineer Clifford Hugh Douglas, or Major Douglas – he had served in the Royal Flying Corps during the war – was also proposing to rebuild the economy by fixing the price of goods on the basis of productive effort measured in 'time-energy'. The equalization of supply and demand would be based on the payment of a universal wage: the 'social dividend' or 'social credit'. In 1922, Douglas predicted 'the imminence of an economic crisis' which would lead to the emergence of 'a new system based on the principles of the conservation of energy'.[8] After 1929, the ideas of Soddy and Douglas were in vogue. In New Zealand, Australia and Canada, political parties based on them emerged. In Alberta in 1935, a Social Credit Party even won an election. In England, the artist John Hargrave, who had previously founded the Kibbo Kift, a movement derived from scouting, became the promoter of Douglas's theories.[9] He swapped his Saxon garb for well-ironed green shirts and founded the Green Shirts for Social Credit party. In Hargrave's mind, the two movements were in fact linked: the universal wage, made possible by energy abundance, would give the urban masses the time they needed to recharge their batteries in the forest. A former member of the Green Shirts recalls the evenings spent around the fire singing: 'Energy, energy, ceaseless energy, / The fearful and wonderful energy of the electron . . . All is energy. The Energy of One.'[10]

In the United States, energy radicalism was driven by a group of intellectuals and engineers who had also been marked by the experience of the First World War, when, in their view, the economy was managed in watts rather than dollars.[11] They came together under the banner of 'Technocracy', a new word that had appeared in 1919 in the columns of the journal *Industrial Management*. In a series of articles, the engineer William Smyth celebrated the planning that made American intervention in the Great War possible as a true revolution, the advent of rational government which applied the precepts of industrial management to the whole nation.[12] These articles, reprinted in leaflet form, aroused the enthusiasm of a group of intellectuals led by the famous Thorstein Veblen. In 1919, they founded the first Technical Alliance.[13] Scientists from Columbia University, such as Walter Rautenstrauch, Lelan Olds, Marion K. Hubbert and Richard Tolman, economists like Stuart Chase, intellectuals such as Upton Sinclair, Walter Lippmann, Herbert Croly, Harold Loeb and Lewis Mumford were associated, directly or indirectly, with Veblen and the Technical Alliance.

The political project of this group was rather simplistic. In the manifesto book of the technocratic movement, *The Engineers and the Price System* (1921), Thorstein Veblen schematically contrasted the new world of technicians with the old world of businessmen, who acted as parasites on the former without understanding anything about it. Electrification, automation, mass production, standardization and cartelization would render capitalism obsolete. Veblen placed on an equal footing workers and capitalists as they each, in their own way, constrained or even sabotaged the means of production.[14] Veblen was merely applying F. W. Taylor's accusation against the workers to the employers as well. Only the engineers found favour in his eyes, because they defended the efficiency of the industrial system and therefore the common good. The 'price system' artificially generated scarcity in order to create rents. For Veblen, the problem with capitalism was not that it exploited man and nature, but rather that it was incapable of properly harnessing modern technology. Engineers already held the reins of industry; now they had to take control of the country and run it like a big business.

Alongside Veblen, Charles Proteus Steinmetz was the other mentor of the Technical Alliance. Although forgotten now, Steinmetz was a true celebrity in his own lifetime, the third electric wizard after Edison and Tesla.[15] The son of a Breslau railway worker, suffering from dwarfism, a socialist student hunted down by Bismarck's police, a refugee in the United States, he revolutionized electrical theory and eventually became head of R&D at General Electric. His political ideas were less original. In his eminently stagist book *America and the New Epoch*, Steinmetz explained that the complexity of the industrial system signalled the end of capitalism – a source of inefficiency – and the advent of a rational regime modelled on the workings of the big modern company.[16] In 1919, a journalist chose to interview 'the world's greatest electrical genius' to find out 'whether the United States will become Bolshevik'.[17] The country's political destiny seemed closely correlated with its electrical system.

To designate this political transformation driven by technology, the American technocrats, following the British Fabians, readily used the term 'transition', the indeterminacy of which made it possible to reassure the middle classes. Just as, for Veblen, 'the price system' was a disguise for 'capitalism', 'transition' acted as a euphemism for 'revolution' at a time when the latter was not an entirely abstract prospect. The 'Soviet of Technocrats' that Veblen called for should not frighten anyone. Technocracy had nothing to do with Bolshevism: in an advanced capitalist country like the United States, socialism would not be born of class struggle, but of a painless 'transition' guided by experts and flowing naturally from the modernization of the industrial system.[18] According to the left-wing technocrat James MacKaye, the transition to socialism would not bother anyone, 'just as a good civil engineer can displace an old railroad bridge by a new one without disturbing the operation of the road'.[19] In short a simple maintenance operation of the social order.

In 1932, with 12 million people unemployed in the United States, the ideas of the technocracy movement were gaining a large following. The Technical Alliance split and one of its branches, Technocracy Inc., grew into a mass movement with up to 250,000 members, organized into local branches scattered across the United States and Canada.[20] The movement's organizer was Howard Scott, a rather enigmatic figure, a salesman who briefly became a media darling thanks to a series of popular lectures predicting the collapse of capitalism.[21] The cause of this collapse? Energy. Not because energy was running out, but because it had made the American economy too productive for businessmen and democratic institutions to contain mass unemployment and social war. Howard Scott, who embellished his professional career, liked to compare himself to Galileo: his doctrine of 'energy determinants' (a theory à la Soddy, basing the value of goods on embodied energy) would enable economic science to be entirely rebuilt on secure foundations.[22]

In August 1932, Scott revealed to the press the existence of a titanic survey that the Technocrats had carried out, a historical survey tracing the evolution of the energy and labour required to manufacture 3,000 goods between 1830 and 1930.[23] This enigmatic 'Energy Survey of North America' would show categorically that the economic crisis was not a mere downturn in the economy but the result of an immense transition from man-hours to watt-hours. Electricity, by destroying industrial employment, reduced demand. This forced companies to reduce their selling prices and therefore their production costs, encouraging them to equip themselves with ever more productive machines, reducing employment and therefore demand, etc., etc. The bankers were the only winners in this race to the bottom, which they financed. The process, Scott added, was only just beginning, because in every branch of industry the mass of companies had not yet reached the productivity of the leaders. The crisis of 1929 was different from all those that had preceded it: it did not correspond to a cycle, but to a peak: that of American industrial employment.[24]

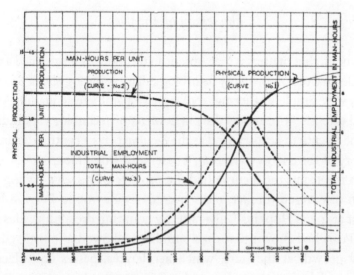

'Peak employment', *Technocracy Study Course*, 1934, p. 87.

The 'transition' as seen by the technocrats: the electric golem is a threat, but in their hands it will rid America of the plutocrats of Washington and Wall Street. (*Technocrats' Magazine*, 1933.)

The lesson of the flies

The point that matters is that American technocrats introduced a new intellectual tool into energy futurology, namely the logistic or S-curve. This very simple intellectual tool – a two-parameter equation – was used extensively to model the phenomena of technological diffusion in the twentieth century. And as the S-curve plays a central role in the theory of the energy transition, it deserves a closer look.

In the 1920s, the S-curve had the prestige of novelty, having just been discovered (in fact, rediscovered) by Raymond Pearl, a biologist at Johns Hopkins University. By counting drosophila flies in a jar, Pearl had shown that their numbers followed a logistic curve: slow growth at the start, which accelerates, passes an inflection point and then converges towards an asymptote. According to Pearl,

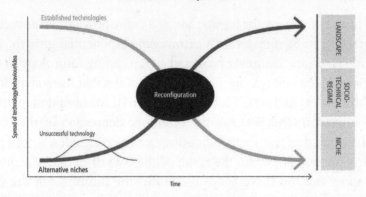

General diagram of 'transition dynamics' according to Frank Geels, and used by Group III of the IPCC. The study of the logistical diffusion of innovation has profoundly influenced thinking on the energy transition. (IPCC, *Mitigation of Climate Change* (Geneva, 2022), p. 139.)

this law is universal. It applies just as much to bacteria in a petri dish as to humans in a given territory. Strikingly, in *The Biology of Population Growth* (1925), Pearl followed his study of drosophila with a second on Algerian demography.[25] The verdict of the logistic curve was that the population would peak at 5.5 million. And Pearl didn't stop there: armed with the S-curve, he predicted world agricultural production, the size of the American rail network and coal extraction. All these phenomena and many others obeyed the iron law of the logistic function.[26] Exponential or linear growth was not sustainable. As far as coal was concerned, 'the volume of the planet is strictly limited . . . and there is no need to project coal consumption far into the future before it reaches a point where its tonnage would correspond to a globe entirely composed of coal'.[27] For Pearl, one of the most eminent neo-Malthusians of the inter-war period,[28] the situation of human beings on earth was analogous to that of the flies trapped in his jars, and it was hardly a cause for rejoicing: for the last dozen years or so, the curve of agricultural production had been bending and could no longer keep pace with population growth. This scissor effect was synonymous with immense chaos, of which the First World War gave a foretaste.[29]

At the beginning of the twentieth century, for anyone interested in the future of energy, the logistic law or S-curve provided an attractive alternative to Stanley Jevons's extravagant exponential growth. For example, in 1918 Steinmetz proposed an interesting futurology in the General Electric magazine. First of all, he noted that the convulsions of history had had no effect on American coal consumption: neither the American Civil War nor the economic depression of the 1890s had disrupted its rise. Energy consumption, he concludes, is not a historical phenomenon but 'the result of the laws of nature'. Secondly, he notes that the curve bends over time: the future is not the one predicted by Jevons.[30] Finally, he estimated that the maximum hydroelectric potential of the United States was roughly equal to the country's total energy consumption in 1918. This forecast pointed to a form of transition, with hydroelectricity replacing coal little by little, albeit insufficiently, as the latter became depleted. When asked by journalists about the electrical wonders of the future, Steinmetz replied that hydroelectricity could more modestly prevent Americans from shivering in the cold once their coal reserves were exhausted.[31]

At the same time, the logistics curve was used to study market saturation. In 1921, the Detroit consultant Raymond B. Prescott used an S-curve to estimate the future size of the American car market. He justified his choice by referring to the sociology of Gabriel Tarde. Initially, a new industry has to contend with habit and resistance from existing interests. But if it manages to overcome the 'spirit of routine', it will spread faster and faster according to the laws of imitation, until it reaches saturation point.[32] In 1925, the American Petroleum Institute similarly employed the S-curve model to project the trajectory of American oil consumption. Their analysis indicated a stabilization in consumption, attributed to the saturation of the automobile market and advancements in engine technology. Consequently, concerns regarding the rapid depletion of American oil reserves were deemed unfounded.[33]

In 1932, this approach was taken up again by a young geologist from Columbia University, Marion K. Hubbert, a key figure in the technocratic movement. Hubbert had met Howard Scott at a club in Greenwich Village. As he would tell the historian Ron Doel sixty years later, he was literally fascinated by the man.[34] Hubbert had read Pearl and admired his quantitative methods and the predictive power of the logistic curve. As with Steinmetz, energy seemed to him to be a matter for the biological sciences. In the *Technocracy Study Course*, Hubbert modelled a number of material consumptions in the United States with an S-curve, and this seemed to work perfectly: 'the drosophila curve', Hubbert wrote, 'is exactly the same as those for coal or iron production'.[35]

How to interpret this success? What was the causality behind the concomitant inflexion in most American material consumptions? Hubbert put forward three reasons. First: the peak in employment described above, with all its repercussions on the fall in demand. Second: increasing material efficiency. Engines were turning faster and becoming smaller, reducing demand for metals to such an extent that the United States could in the near future meet its needs by recycling its old machines – a kind of 'circular economy'. Third: geological limits. Hubbert, who was familiar with modern oil-exploration methods with electrical instruments, was convinced that the Earth's surface had been explored from top to bottom. No major oil discovery had been made in Europe since 1850 and in the United States since 1910, so major discoveries were unlikely. The limits of the Earth further reinforced the idea of peak employment: it was physically impossible to reduce unemployment because labour productivity was such that full employment would require staggering quantities of raw materials and energy. The crisis of 1929 was therefore neither financial nor economic: instead, it was both technological and Malthusian, corresponding with the peak of an ultra-productive economy in a finite world. 'The era of the great industrial expansion in America is over', Hubbert wrote in 1934.[36]

So what could be done? How to manage the finiteness of the world without causing economic collapse or social war? In practical terms, the technocrats proposed to reduce working hours and standardize goods to curb conspicuous consumption and planned obsolescence. Secondly, they formulated a reform for the monetary system with one striking proposal: to replace the dollar with a non-transferable energy currency that expired after one year and could not be accumulated. 'Energy certificates' would be distributed on an egalitarian basis in exchange for sixteen hours' work a week.[37] Issuing this currency in the correct quantity would resolve the crisis of overproduction. Finally, to steer the economy scientifically through energy, a bureaucracy of engineers was to be installed, a North American Technate, stretching from Canada to Panama, in order to be self-sufficient in all its resources. The main interest of this continental superstate would be to offer the United States the possibility of exploiting the enormous hydroelectric potential of its northern neighbour. From 1936 onwards, technocratic literature was full of 'continental hydrology' plans showing an America streaked with canals, dams and high-voltage lines: energy again and again.[38]

It would be simple to mock the Technocrats, who were often out of sync with the prevailing trends. In the 1920s and 1930s, when they dreamed of putting engineers in positions of power, those very engineers were already occupying prominent roles in Washington. Herbert Hoover, a former mining engineer, proudly referred to himself as the 'chief engineer' of the USA. Additionally, the New Deal implemented during that time brought forth a prosperous period for the American engineering community. Leland Olds, a member of the Technical Alliance, became close to Franklin Roosevelt, who appointed him to head the Federal Power Commission.

In 1942, the isolationist stance of the Technocrats,[39] their military parades, their grey uniforms and the cult of the leader organized by Howard Scott contributed to the political discrediting of the movement – which nevertheless continues to this day. In 1939, Scott explained that the North American Technate would be invulnerable to a European attack because it could, at will, stop the Gulf Stream and provoke a new ice age on the other side of the Atlantic: 'It is cheaper to kill on a continental scale,' he boldly asserted.[40] Finally, given their proclamations of empiricism, it is astonishing to note the extent to which the Technocrats confused the part with the whole: the few technological giants like General Electric, Ford or Westinghouse with American industry as a whole, which, as the historian Philip Scranton pointed out, was then two-thirds made up of small businesses, manufacturing non-standardized products.[41]

And yet it is in the ideological cauldron of American technocracy, mixing unemployment, reformism, neo-Malthusianism and entropy, that a new vision of the energy transition emerged. In his 1934 *Technocracy Study Course*, Hubbert summed up his thoughts on growth in graphic forms destined for a very bright future. The solid line represents the past. The dotted line shows the future, branching out into four trajectories. Curve I, from which humanity has already deviated, represents the impossible dream of economists: growth at a constant rate; Curve IV, Jevons's nightmare: a peak in fossil fuels followed by a collapse; Curve III: an economy reduced to the sustainable exploitation of biomass; and finally Curve II, the one we should be aiming for: a stationary state at a high-level of production, made possible by hydroelectricity. Over the course of his long career, Hubbert would revise this graph several times and, above all, adapt it to the advent of atomic energy. The essential elements were already present: an abstract, concise and effective portrayal of the past and future of energy, which now serves as a foundation in all presentations of

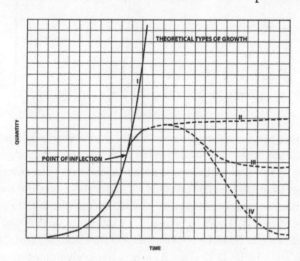

Technocracy Study Course, 1934, p. 74.

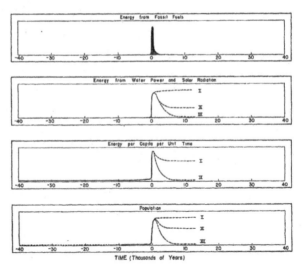

FIG. 8.   Human affairs in time perspective.

Marion K. Hubbert, 'Energy from fossil fuels', *Science*, 109, 1949, pp. 103–9.

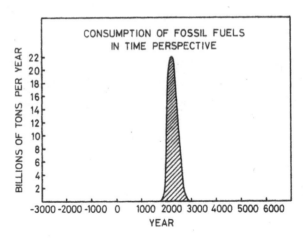

Hubbert's 1949 curve presenting 'human affairs' from a very long-term perspective and the exhaustion of all fossil fuels has haunted energy thinking ever since. It was taken up by Harrison Brown, an atomic scientist who also coined the term 'energy transition', and by his student Charles D. Keeling, the author of the eponymous and fundamental curve plotting the increase in CO_2 in the atmosphere since 1958. (Harrison Brown, *The Challenge of Man's Future: An Inquiry Concerning the Condition of Man during the Years that Lie Ahead* (New York, 1954), p. 169, and Charles D. Keeling, 'A chemist thinks about the future', *Archives of Environmental Health: An International Journal*, 20, 6, 1970, pp. 764–77.)

scenarios related to energy or emissions. In 1949, in an article in *Science*, he proposed another even more dramatic curve: considered over 80,000 years, the irruption of fossil fuels into 'human affairs' appears as a narrow, frail peak. This striking image, a powerful *memento mori* of industrial civilization, would be pondered by a long line of futurologists. In particular, it was taken up by Harrison Brown, an American atomic scientist and figurehead of the neo-Malthusian movement, who also invented the expression 'energy transition'.

The graphical forms utilized to illustrate energy dynamics were developed nearly a century ago in the crucible of American technocracy, as engineers chose to apply the same tools used by biologists studying flies in a jar to contemplate the future of energy. However, the issue we face with the current climate catastrophe is not a simple exhaustion problem. On the contrary, it stems from an excess: our metaphorical jar contains an overwhelming abundance of coal, oil and gas, with no natural limit preventing us from rapidly transforming the whole lot into a furnace. Passing through a peak – the conventional oil peak in 2008, the current coal peak (?) – does not preclude subsequent upswings or undulating plateaus that are ultimately even more perilous than the steep descents of Malthusian collapse.

10.

Atomic Malthusians

In 1970, to commemorate the twenty-fifth anniversary of the first 'Trinity' nuclear explosion, the head of the Atomic Energy Commission (AEC), Glen Seaborg, imagined the world in 1995. Breeder reactors by the thousands, the first steps in nuclear fusion and an atomic lunar colony: the road travelled since Los Alamos gave cause for optimism. Nuclear satellites topped it all off: forming a global communications network, they would enable the birth-control campaign dear to the American neo-Malthusians to be broadcast throughout the world.[1] Seaborg's utopia reflects the meeting of two imaginaries: that of Malthus and that of the 'atomic age'. Malthusian collapse and nuclear technophilia are not contradictory: they have fed off each other and given rise to the theory of the energy transition.

The origin of this concept is closely linked to the atom: 'energy transition' began as a concept in atomic physics – the change of state of an electron around its nucleus – before becoming a key word of nuclear futurology. Opening up an energy horizon measured in thousands of years, in the early 1950s the atom gave rise to thinking about the very long term. What will the world's energy consumption be in 2000, 2050 or 2100? Will there still be coal in the twenty-first or twenty-second century? Or what might be the effects on the climate of burning most of the fossil-fuel reserves of the world? Because the early promoters of atomic energy in the United States defended a very long-term technological option, they created a new kind of energy futurology, a futurology that looked both at the end of fossil fuels and at climate change.

The future as an expanded present

Until the 1970s, economists, geologists and engineers hardly ever talked about energy transition. Their projections typically foresaw a stabilization of energy consumption over the following decades and changes in the composition of the energy mix, but not a transformative shift caused by innovation or exhaustion. The post-war economic boom and the oil fields in the Middle East had refuted the Malthusian alarms of the 1930s. This absence of transition in energy futurology was based in part on extrapolating historical experience: since the late nineteenth century, both in the United States and in most industrialized nations, the consumption of coal, oil and hydroelectricity had consistently increased in tandem. Admittedly, coal had experienced bouts of weakness in the 1930s and at the end of the 1950s, but these were temporary phenomena obeying economic conditions that did not foreshadow its future demise. Coal would always be needed, if only for making steel. This permanence of fossil fuels explains why conservationists were concerned with the very long term, for instance with coal stocks three centuries from now – a sign that the idea of a medium-term transition to another energy source was alien to them.[2]

Nuclear power, despite all the media hype about the 'atomic age', did not change this perspective. Contrary to the condescending clichés about the 1950s that our 'reflexive modernity' likes to maintain, neither the experts nor the public were fooled. As early as 1947, even before the Soviet bomb, opinion polls showed that almost half of Americans did not expect any wonders from the atom and even regretted that nuclear fission had been discovered.[3] In France, a year after Hiroshima, there were already sarcastic articles about the fantastic predictions of an 'atomic age' made in the relief of the summer of 1945.[4]

In 1950, the Cowles Commission of the University of Chicago, known for its role in the birth of econometrics, published a comprehensive report on the economic impact of the atom. The report was led by the economist and historian Sam Schurr, assisted by the future

Nobel Prize-winners Herbert Simon and Tjalling Koopmans. The desirability of the atom was assessed sector by sector and compared with existing alternatives. Conclusion: the use of atomic energy would only marginally increase US GDP (by 2 per cent) in the long term.[5] And even this conclusion seemed to some to be too optimistic. Using the Leontieff matrix method, Walter Isard, an economist at MIT, considered nuclear power to be 'non-revolutionary'.[6] Reports confirming this diagnosis accumulated over the following years.

Industrialists were also hesitant and cautious regarding the economic risks associated with the development of nuclear power. Since the cost of electricity also came from distribution and not just from production, the atom did not seem to make such a difference. As John McCone, the director of the Atomic Energy Commission, himself acknowledged in 1959: 'in economic terms, we don't need nuclear power'.[7] In any case, if nuclear electricity were to be developed, it would probably simply be *added* to that produced by fossil fuels.[8] The commission headed by Senator William Paley charged with assessing the future of American natural resources, considered the atom to be 'a valuable addition to other energy sources'.[9] Admittedly, the energy mix would change over the rest of the century, but 'each of the energy sources would continue to grow considerably'.[10] Even within Atom for Peace, an international organization created on the initiative of President Eisenhower to promote civil nuclear energy,[11] the Electricity Committee concluded that nuclear power 'will have no disruptive effect on conventional fuels'.[12]

In the 1960s, advocates of renewable energies were equally cautious: solar and wind power could not, even in the distant future, compete with coal in the steel industry, fertilizer plants, cement works or replace oil for transport. The physicist Farrington Daniels, a former high-ranking official in the Manhattan Project who later became a solar-energy pioneer, acknowledged that 'we should not expect too much too soon' from this energy source.[13] A book with an emphatic title, *The Coming Age of Solar Energy* (1963), actually took a measured approach to the future significance of solar energy.[14]

Renewable energies were primarily depicted as supplementary

or backup sources, primarily catering to domestic needs such as heating, or as technologies deemed 'appropriate' for developing nations. This was the conclusion drawn by the five hundred scientists who were invited to Rome by the United Nations in August 1961 to discuss the future of renewable energy. According to their forecasts, solar and wind power would prove useful in rural areas of impoverished countries for purposes like irrigation or telecommunications.[15] In their forecasts, solar-energy advocates such as Leon P. Gaucher did not anticipate any major substitution; rather, renewables were seen as additions to the existing array of primary energy sources. In essence, prior to the 1970s, energy specialists envisioned the future of energy as an expanded version of the present.

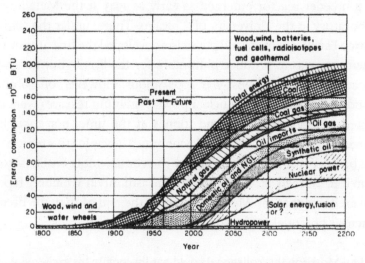

The energy future as an expanded present. The perception of energy as a generally stable system is reflected in the graphs showing the evolution of energy mixes. Most show curves in absolute values which, stacked one on top of the other, show the cumulative nature of the history of energy. When Sam Schurr and Bruce Netschert proposed a diagram showing the evolution of the relative shares of the different energies, they immediately warned their readers: wood energy seems to be disappearing, crushed by oil and coal, but its consumption in the United States in 1960 was still very important.[16] Other authors use a logarithmic scale to represent the rise of coal and the stagnation of fuelwood.[17] (Leon P. Gaucher, 'Energy requirements of the future', *Solar Energy*, 14, 1972, pp. 5–10.)

Peak oil and atomic plateau

The petty calculations of economists exasperated the atomic scientists. According to them, the issue of nuclear power was not merely an economic one; it was existential. Its purpose was not to compete with coal when it was still abundant, but to ensure its replacement for when it would become scarce. This very different future, both Malthusian about fossil fuels and utopian about nuclear power, was obviously born of the atom, but not just any atom. It was used to defend a very specific technological option, namely nuclear breeder reactors. Although it has in practice produced very little electricity, this technique has been of major ideological importance. The idea of a breeder reactor emerged as early as 1943 at the Metallurgical Laboratory at the University of Chicago. There, under the aegis of Enrico Fermi, chemists and physicists developed the first atomic pile. Their role was to produce plutonium for the bomb, but they were already dreaming of post-war applications. However, one obstacle stood in the way of civil nuclear power: uranium reserves were estimated at just a few thousand tonnes at the time, not enough to provide energy for an industrial economy.[18] It was for this reason that the breeder reactor, with its ability to produce more fissile isotopes than it consumed, aroused such enthusiasm. Alvin Weinberg reports the excitement at the Met Lab when, at the end of 1943, the breeder reactor's potential appeared in all its splendour:

> Phil Morrison [his colleague] could hardly contain his excitement as he showed me his calculations: if uranium was burned in a breeder, the energy released through fission exceeded the energy required to extract the 4 ppm of uranium from the granitic rocks. The breeder reactor therefore represented an essentially inexhaustible source of energy!'[19]

Breeder reactors gave a different meaning to the Manhattan Project: the scientists involved had not only contributed to making the bomb – many of them would later campaign for disarmament – they had opened the way to an endless-energy future. As Alvin Weinberg would later confess in his autobiography: 'I became obsessed with the idea that the entire future of humanity depended on the breeder reactor.'[20]

In 1949, Carroll Wilson, the first executive director of the Atomic Energy Commission, commissioned a prospective study to determine the potential market for nuclear energy fifty and one hundred years ahead, in the United States and worldwide.[21] The AEC had just launched two breeder reactor projects, the EBR-1 reactor in Idaho, under the direction of Walter Zinn, and another at Oak Ridge, Tennessee, under the direction of Alvin Weinberg, both former Met Lab staff. It was important to demonstrate to the supervisory body of the AEC (the Joint Committee of the House of Representatives and the Senate) the significance of investing in research that was not expected to have industrial applications for several decades.[22] Wilson asked two questions: to estimate global energy demand up to 2050, and to assess the maximum that fossil fuels could supply. The subtraction would give an approximate idea of the market reserved for atomic energy. To carry out this work, he recruited Palmer Cosslett Putnam as a consultant to the AEC.[23] Heir to a major publishing house and trained in geology at MIT, Putnam had made a name for himself by developing a 1.2 MW wind turbine, a record at the time, which had aroused the interest of the great science administrator Vannevar Bush. During the war, Putnam worked for the Office of Scientific Research and Development headed by Bush, with whom he became friends.[24] Carroll Wilson, who had been Bush's assistant at the OSRD, knew Putnam as well. After the war, Putnam worked for Senator Paley's commission, which asked him to study the potential of renewables. His conclusion: they absolutely had to be developed in order to save coal. 'Now is the time for aggressive research in the field of solar energy', he wrote, but he did not expect wonders. By 2050, the solution to the rising cost of fossil fuels would rely mainly on nuclear power (60 per cent) and secondarily on renewables (15 per cent), with the remainder corresponding to residual fossil fuels.[25] At the same time, Putnam was writing a major report for the AEC: *Energy in the Future*. Published in 1953, its scientific importance cannot be overstated: as Alvin Weinberg points out in his autobiography, it was Putnam who introduced energy futurology to the nuclear field.[26]

Putnam developed three arguments in favour of atomic energy: the increase in American and global energy consumption, the inevitable rise in the cost of fossil fuels, and, already, the issue of global warming – to which we will return at the end of this chapter. The Putnam report is innovative from every point of view, starting with its approach to the history of energy. Its aim, as we said, was to forecast world energy demand in 2000 and 2050. To avoid overestimating the past growth rate, which, extrapolated, would result in high demand in the future, the report takes into account the utilization of so-called traditional energy sources (such as wood, water and agricultural residues) throughout history. Putnam provided, to the best of my knowledge, the first comprehensive global estimate of energy consumption since 1850. And the result was very different indeed from the standard accounts of historians of the time, which focused on coal and oil. It is India that emerges as the leading energy producer until 1830, before giving way not to England with its coal, but to the United States with its firewood. Similarly, Putnam takes into account efficiency gains and changes in the energy intensity of the global economy. With the help of the economist Colin Clark, one of the pioneers of GNP calculations, Putnam studied the now famous question of 'decoupling'. He showed that in mature industrial countries the energy intensity of the economy had been declining since the end of the nineteenth century, in contrast to the USSR, whose economy was particularly inefficient at converting calories into roubles.[27] Armed with these historical rates of rising energy demand and efficiency and forecasts of GNP and population growth, Putnam ventured to predict the future: in the year 2000, the world would consume 10 times more energy than it did in 1950, and 28 times more in 2050 – an estimate that proved about twice the actual figure for the year 2000, partly due to the assumption that poor countries would catch up economically. At this rate, fossil-fuel reserves would not last beyond the middle of the twenty-first century. A 'transition to nuclear power', he explained, would be costly and difficult, but inevitable.[28]

While the idea of a nuclear transition appeared very early on, the more precise expression 'energy transition' came later. It was coined by Harrison Brown, a chemist and Met Lab veteran during the Manhattan project, who joined Caltech in 1951. There he played an important role in the field of geochemistry and the determination of the age of the Earth. Brown was also an important figure in the American neo-Malthusian movement. After the war, neo-Malthusianism remained influential in the United States, and the energy question played a growing role. As a result of improvements in agricultural yields (corn yields doubled between 1930 and 1950), concerns had shifted: the limit in rich countries was less about surface area and food than about energy reserves. Energy was presented as the 'ultimate natural resource', the only one 'for which there is no substitute'.[29]

In 1955, Brown took part in the conference on Man's Role in Changing the Face of the Earth; the following year, together with Aldous Huxley and Kinglsey Davis, he founded the think tank Population Limited; he was also a member of the Population Council, another neo-Malthusian group richly endowed by the billionaire John D. Rockefeller III.[30] Brown was also the author of an important neo-Malthusian book, *The Challenge of Man's Future* (1954), which received the endorsement of Albert Einstein. This book gives an impressive overview of mineral resources that extends Marion K. Hubbert's theory. Their increasing scarcity could lead, according to Brown, to a third world war, a war from which civilization would not recover because of the lack of good quality resources still available. But there was a way out: a transition to nuclear power.[31] If humanity succeeded in this task, energy would no longer be a limiting factor. In 1955, at the inaugural conference of the Atom for Peace programme in Geneva, Brown spoke about the depletion of fossil fuels and the need to develop atomic energy. He presented striking calculations, typical of the neo-Malthusians of the inter-war period, of the planet's carrying capacity revised for the atomic age. His conclusion: 7 billion people could live 'American-style' for thousands of years thanks to 17,000 breeder reactors burning the uranium contained in granite or dissolved in the water of the oceans.[32] The Earth could even support 200 billion people, but then it would look like 'a dead cow covered with a pulsating mass of maggots'.[33]

In the 1960s, Brown was in charge of international scientific cooperation at the US National Academy of Sciences. Under President

In the early 1970s, fast-breeder reactors absorbed a substantial proportion of public R&D in the energy sector (30% in France and Germany, 40% in the United States and the United Kingdom).[34] The nuclear breeder reactor also played a central role in the energy futurologies of the 1970s. Because it could increase the planet's carrying capacity, the breeder reactor represented the essential way out of the Malthusian trap. An abundance of energy would make it possible to desalinate ocean water, manufacture nitrogen fertilizers and transform vast arid expanses into farmland; it would also make it possible to extract and refine minerals, recycle metals ad infinitum and protect the environment.[35] (Alvin M. Weinberg and R. Philip Hammond, 'The limit to population set by energy is extremely large, provided that the breeder reactor is developed', *American Scientist*, 58, 4, 1970, pp. 412–18.)

Johnson, the 'demographic transition' had become a strategic objective, one of the keys to winning the Cold War. With subsidies from
the State Department, Brown set up a programme at Caltech which,
for a decade, would send its experts to the Third World to make the
case for birth control. And it was in November 1967, at a conference
attended by the neo-Malthusian elite, that he coined the expression
'energy transition'.[36] The inspiration came from Kingsley Davis's
famous 1945 article on the 'demographic transition'. Just as the first
'energy transition', that of the industrial revolution and fossil fuels,
had increased the planet's carrying capacity, the second transition,
that of nuclear power, would also change the parameters of the
demographic question. Brown had in mind the Water for Peace programme once dreamed up by the Johnson administration: solving
the Middle East question by making the desert bloom with nuclear-
powered desalination and fertilizer plants.[37] Brown borrowed a
term from nuclear physics – his first area of expertise – and set it up
as an analogue for the demographic transition, making it the key to
the future of humanity.

After Putnam and Brown, the third key scientist in atomic Mal-
thusianism was a geologist at Shell, the famous peak-oil theorist and
ex-technocrat Marion K. Hubbert.[38] His links with nuclear power
dated back to 1955, when the AEC was exploring various options for
disposing of its waste. One of them was to pour radioactive liquid
residues into abandoned oil wells.[39] It was for this reason that the
AEC recruited Hubbert.[40] His geological expertise justified his
appointment, but Hubbert was of interest to the AEC in another
capacity: since 1949, he had become known for his estimates of oil
reserves that were lower than those of the industry. From then on,
all his publications on peak oil were in fact linked to the promotion
of nuclear energy. In 1956, at the annual conference of the American
Petroleum Institute, he took up Brown's work and updated Putnam's
to weigh up the radically different quantities of energy contained in
fossil fuels, on the one hand, and uranium on the other.[41] Considered
on the scale of human history, coal and oil would appear to be 'no
more than an ephemeral event', writes Hubbert. Uranium, on the

other hand, opens up an endless energy future for humankind – on one crucial condition: developing fast-breeder reactors before the two disasters of atomic war and demographic explosion (and these were precisely the arguments put forward by Brown).[42] The idea of a 'peak' also appeared with Hubbert and stems from the original graphic form he had invented in 1949: fossil fuels (and not just oil) form a frail peak, but this is because they are considered on the scale of several millennia and set against the unlimited energy plateau to which breeder reactors provide access. While the end of oil might be near (2060 in the United States), Hubbert does not venture to

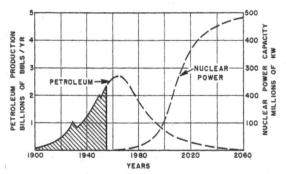

Figure 29 – Concurrent decline of petroleum production and rise of production of nuclear power in the United States. Growth rate of 10 percent per year for nuclear power is assumed; actual rate may be twice this amount.

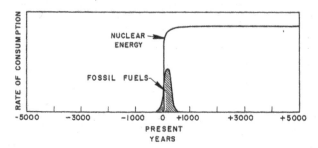

According to Brown and Hubbert, the atomic transition will be driven by the increasing scarcity of fossil fuels (including coal). It is therefore a long-term process: the end of oil is near (2060 in the United States) but the end of coal in the world is much further away – this graph shows the 24th or 25th century. (M. K. Hubbert, 'Nuclear Energy and the Fossil Fuels', Shell Development Company report, 95, 1956.)

give a date for end of coal use in the world, which should neverthe-less occur before 2500.

Hubbert became a key figure in the AEC's scientific lobbying. In 1962, he wrote a more detailed estimate of peak oil for the National Academy of Sciences, using the classic neo-Malthusian prediction tool: the logistic curve.[43] The sum of cumulative oil discoveries on American soil since 1865 follows such an S-shaped curve: rapid growth, an inflection point (already passed) and a trend towards the asymptote. Since production follows discoveries by a few years, Hubbert deduced that peak oil in the US would occur around 1970. This report formed the basis of the official report that the AEC submitted to President Kennedy that same year: the government absolutely had to fund the fast-breeder reactor programme to cope with the depletion of fossil fuels and to ensure that the 'transition did not take place suddenly'.[44] The following year, Hubbert was invited to develop his theory before the Joint Committee on Atomic Energy.[45] Finally, in 1969, he wrote the chapter on energy in an influ-ential report by the Academy of Sciences entitled *Resources and Man*. At the time, the AEC was in the midst of a lobbying operation to finance its costly and controversial fast-breeder reactor programme, and Hubbert demonstrated the vital need, in order to preserve uranium in the long term, to make the 'transition to fast-breeder reactors' as soon as possible. 'Failure to make this transition would constitute one of the major disasters in human history.'[46] The peak-oil theorist has certainly served the nuclear cause well.

Global warming: an atomic alert

The history of warnings about climate warming is closely linked to that of the atomic Malthusians. As we have seen, the proponents of the atom in the 1950s took a very long-term view of energy: will there still be oil in 2000, coal in 2050 or even 2100? The passage of such masses of carbon from the lithosphere to the atmosphere raises questions. What could be the climatic consequences of burning most of the world's fossil fuels? Because the nuclear lobby was defending a very long-term technological option – the fast-breeder reactor – it produced a dystopian and innovative futurology, focusing not only on the end of fossil fuels, but also, as early as 1953, on global warming. The historiography about climate knowledge has generally left the role of the nuclear lobby in the shadows and turned towards a more general account, that of the 'Cold War', military funding and its structuring effects on scientific equipment – aircraft, sounding balloons, satellites, super-calculators, etc. – the 'vast machine' well described by Paul Edwards that made it possible to confirm the problem of global warming.[47] Yet, while the confirmation process did indeed involve a very large community of researchers from a variety of disciplines, the greenhouse effect in the early 1950s was studied by a much smaller and much more homogeneous group of scientists, all linked to the atom.

Take the Putnam Report commissioned by Carroll Wilson, the first chairman of the Atomic Energy Commission. It concluded with what was probably one of the first research programmes on global warming. Putnam's starting point was the US Geodetic Survey's observation that sea levels had been rising since the end of the nineteenth century. This phenomenon has been measured in all American ports, both in the Pacific and the Atlantic.

For Putnam, the only possible explanation for such a global phenomenon was the melting of glaciers, itself due to the increase in the greenhouse effect. He links this observation to his historical work on energy: humanity is pumping carbon dioxide into the atmosphere at an accelerating rate – 170 Gt between 1800 and 1849 versus 560 Gt between 1900 and 1949. Measurements of the concentration of atmospheric CO_2 show an increase from 290 ppm to 320 ppm between 1900 and 1935, which appears to be greater than natural variability. According to Putnam, the real problem of global warming lies in the future. In a century's time, humanity will have burned at least ten times more carbon than in the previous century, and the concentration of CO_2 could reach staggering levels: 'Perhaps such a derangement of [the] CO_2 cycle [could] affect the

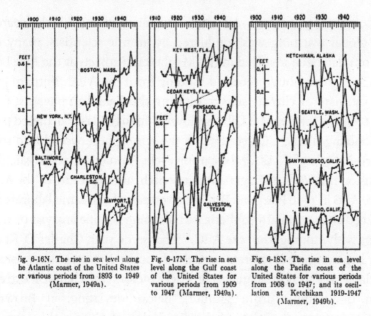

Fig. 6-16N. The rise in sea level along the Atlantic coast of the United States for various periods from 1893 to 1949 (Marmer, 1949a).

Fig. 6-17N. The rise in sea level along the Gulf coast of the United States for various periods from 1909 to 1947 (Marmer, 1949a).

Fig. 6-18N. The rise in sea level along the Pacific coast of the United States for various periods from 1908 to 1947; and its oscillation at Ketchikan 1919-1947 (Marmer, 1949b).

P. C. Putnam, *Energy in the Future* (New York, 1953), p. 455.

climate and cause a further rise of sea level. We do not know this. We ought to know it.'[48]

Putnam was not the only one with an interest in climate change. In 1947, for instance, the Swedish geographer and glaciologist Hans Wilhelmsson Ahlmann delivered a lecture at the University of California on Arctic warming, which even garnered attention in the *New York Times*. The journalist summarized the lecture by stating that 'oceanic surfaces would rise to catastrophic proportions'.[49] The Pentagon also took an interest in this phenomenon, as it could potentially alter the Arctic, which was seen as a likely theatre for future conflicts with the USSR.[50] During the hot summer of 1953, the American press covered global warming on several occasions, presenting it as an ongoing phenomenon. Some articles even used it to absolve atomic tests from the meteorological effects that the public occasionally attributed to them.[51]

The fact remains that Putnam's climate warning was issued at an early stage. That it originated from an Atomic Energy Commission document is significant. After the war, much of the initial research on global warming was conducted by atomic scientists, many of whom had been involved in the Manhattan Project, at the Met Lab in Chicago and often received funding from the AEC. Putnam got his estimate of climate sensitivity from the Canadian physicist Gilbert Plass, a former Met Lab employee.[52] In 1953, Plass calculated that a doubling of the CO_2 content of the atmosphere would lead to a warming of 2.3°C. As for the carbon cycle, Putnam based his calculations on the work of Eugene Rabinowitch, also formerly of the Met Lab. Also in 1953, Harrison Brown, a veteran of the same laboratory, studied changes in atmospheric carbon using isotope analysis of tree rings with funding from the AEC.[53] That same year, Charles D. Keeling began a post-doctorate at Caltech under Brown's supervision: initially on a subject related to breeder reactors (the chemical extraction of uranium from granite), before deviating, at Brown's instigation, into the study of the dissolution of CO_2 in the ocean.[54] A few years later, Keeling would be the author of the famous curve that now bears his name, which traces the increase in the concentration of CO_2 in the atmosphere. It was also Harrison Brown who invited physicist Hans Suess to the US from Austria. In 1953, Suess began studying the exchange of CO_2 between the atmosphere and the oceans before publishing, with Roger Revelle, the key article on the subject, demonstrating the limit of oceanic absorption.[55] 'Human beings are now carrying out a large scale geophysical experiment of a kind that could not have happened in the past nor be reproduced in the future', wrote the authors, and that's why scientists had to study it carefully. This work was funded by the AEC, which hoped to find an outlet in the oceans for its liquid nuclear waste.[56]

Naturally, if atomic scientists were able to revolutionize the history of climate and the study of the carbon cycle, it was above all for instrumental reasons: they had access to state-of-the-art mass spectrometers that allowed for precise measurements of various carbon and oxygen isotopes. This breakthrough transformed the study of the carbon cycle and paleotemperatures. The main difficulty was technological: detecting a difference of 1°C meant measuring the

O-18 concentration to an accuracy of 1:25 million. In this regard, atomic energy remains crucial, as the precision of mass spectrometers experienced a leap forward thanks to the advances made during the Manhattan Project. The American chemist Harold Urey, one of the founders of isotope analysis, insists on this point. To carry out his pioneering work, he had received the help of Alfred O. Nier, an experienced mass-spectrographer who, during the Manhattan Project, had worked at General Electric to perfect the instrument.[57] Until the 1970s, mass spectrometers with sufficient accuracy were rare and expensive. In Denmark, one of the founders of ice-core science, Willi Dansgaard, financed the purchase of his mass spectrometer through the International Atomic Energy Agency.[58] In France, it was at the Commissariat à l'Énergie Atomique that Étienne Roth carried out the first isotope analyses of ice cores – after training in the use of spectrometers in America. In the 1960s, he was one of the few people in Europe to have such a precise spectrometer.[59]

While instrumentation therefore played a key role, more self-interested motives linked to the promotion of the atom should not be overlooked. In the 1950s and 1960s, the rare warnings about global warming, such as those issued by Putnam, Brown and Plass, served the cause of nuclear energy. In 1959, Edward Teller, the 'father of the H-bomb', warned representatives of the oil industry about the greenhouse effect. His lecture at Columbia University gained a certain celebrity due to its discomforting implications for oil companies, who were evidently aware of the issue. In reality, however, the lecture made only a brief mention of climate change and focused mainly on the merits of fast-breeder nuclear reactors.[60] Two years later, Hans Suess used global warming to argue the case for nuclear power in the *Bulletin of Atomic Scientists*.[61] In the 1960s, during the hearings of the Joint Committee overseeing the AEC, the issue of climate change was raised several times in defence of public investment in atomic energy.[62] In 1967, Alvin Weinberg and Lewis Strauss explained to senators that 'nuclear power will have the last word: the limit to the fossil fuels that can be burned is the one that would turn the earth into a huge greenhouse'.[63]

The role of the nuclear lobby does not end there. Even more interesting is the fact that Carroll Wilson, the first director of the AEC, was also a key player in the internationalization of climate warning. After a spell in industry, Wilson joined MIT as a professor of management at the Sloan School. In 1970, he set up an international working group of around thirty researchers: the Study of Man's Impact on Climate (SMIC). The following year he organized the very first international conference on climate change, in Stockholm.[64] The famous report *Limits to Growth* is also indirectly tied to Wilson, as he introduced Jay Forrester, another MIT professor at the Sloan School and founder of system dynamics, to Aurelio Peccei and the Club of Rome. Forrester's work formed the basis of the report's model.

It was also Wilson who passed on the SMIC report to his friend Maurice Strong, an oil-company director who happened to chair the UN Environmental Programme (UNEP) at that time. It was thanks to this link between Wilson and Strong that the 1972 United Nations Conference on the Human Environment addressed the dangers of the greenhouse effect. The issue of climate change became global at this very precise moment in history, and Carroll Wilson, who in 1949 had commissioned the Putnam Report, was the linchpin of this process.

The climate activism stemming from the atomic milieu proved to be a double-edged sword. In the mid-1970s, while climate scientists were confirming that global warming was occurring, it was sometimes dismissed as a pretext for defending nuclear power. The case of Alvin Weinberg is a perfect illustration of this misunderstanding. In 1974, after being dismissed as director of Oak Ridge National Laboratory, Weinberg set up the Institute for Energy Analysis, a modelling think tank that would also become one of the best sources of information on historical CO_2 emissions. As orders for nuclear power plants dwindled in the 1970s, Weinberg embarked on a career as a whistleblower on climate, writing articles, testifying before Congress and participating in various expert bodies. A US 'nuclear moratorium', he argued, could lead to a climate catastrophe.[65] After the 1973 oil crisis, Weinberg fought against the American coal revival, which he compared to the dangers of nuclear proliferation.[66] 'Suppose,' he explained to the National Academy of Sciences in 1977, 'that in ten years' time the world's leading climatologists meet at the United Nations, in Geneva or New York, and solemnly declare that the world is on the road to a climate catastrophe. What will we do then?'[67] For some, the trick seemed too obvious, especially after the Three Mile Island accident in 1979: 'carbon dioxide seems to be the last defense of nuclear proponents' scoffed an energy specialist at the UN.[68] Weinberg's image as a paladin of the atom stuck to him. In October 1977, he even invited a representative from Exxon to think about the best way to raise the US administration's awareness of the issue.[69] It would be better, he explained in substance, if other lobbies were at work: otherwise President Carter could think that CO_2 was just a new ploy to promote nuclear power.[70]

Atomic scientists had discovered a problem infinitely more vast than the solution they were proposing. Even today, nuclear power plays only a marginal role in the world's energy supply, half that of firewood, and after serious incidents and financial problems, fast-breeder reactor programmes have been abandoned in most countries. France and Japan, the most nuclear-powered countries on the planet, have not seen their CO_2 emissions fall drastically, if imported emissions are taken into account. Three-quarters of a century after Putnam, the world is up against the wall: climatologists and then common experience have confirmed the climate risks identified by the Chicago atomic scientists as early as the 1950s. The problem is that energy debates are replaying their futurology based on the idea of 'transition', with a lot of coal still under our feet and fading nuclear dreams.

The Invention of the Energy Crisis

In the 1970s, the energy crisis brought transition out of its nuclear cradle and into public discourse and official expertise. This chapter therefore takes a brief detour to examine the history of this other crucial semantic invention. Oil is generally at the heart of stories about this crisis. Historians link it to the OPEC oil embargo of 1973, to the monopoly of the major producers seeking to increase their margins, or to the peak of conventional oil in the US.[1] However, on closer examination, the term appeared in the American energy debate as early as 1969, and at that time it concerned neither oil production nor imports, but electricity production. Here again, nuclear power plays a key role in the creation of the energy lexicon.

Environmental backlash

In the United States, the 1960s were marked by a series of 'black-outs', the most famous being the one in New York in November 1965.[2] In the press, the neo-Malthusian interpretation centred on resource exhaustion was either absent or quickly dismissed. The causes of the supply challenges were clearly identified: mining companies prioritized exporting the more profitable coke used in steelmaking to Japan and Europe; stricter environmental standards, particularly regarding sulphur dioxide, had led to the abandonment of certain deposits until desulphurization units could be installed; health regulations in mines regarding dust necessitated investments that reduced profitability; the construction of atomic power plants had experienced delays; oil majors, which had acquired mining companies, sought to increase their profit margins; and lastly, in the case of gas, producers were reluctant to exploit it at the price set by the Federal Power Commission.

The nuclear lobby tried to exploit the situation to its advantage: the power cuts were a sign of a deeper, Malthusian problem, that of an 'energy crisis'. And this crisis called for a radical solution that only nuclear power could provide. In the summer of 1969, the expression appeared in the Atomic Energy Commission's internal documents. Initially, it was used in talking points against the anti-nuclear movement, whose guerrilla legal warfare was slowing down the authorization procedures for power plants.[3] One memo, for example, explained that it was necessary to 'educate the public' about the risks of radiation and, above all, to weigh them up against the real risk of an 'energy crisis'.[4] On 15 October 1969, James Ramey, a senior AEC official, gave a speech to the Federal Bar Association: legal action against nuclear power plants was threatening the nation with an 'energy crisis', and lawyers had to take their responsibilities seriously.[5] The journal *Science* peddled this argument: environmentalists were responsible for the energy crisis, but they would also be its first victims, because 'when the air conditioning and televisions stop, the public will say "to hell with the environment, give me abundance" '.[6] Talk of the energy crisis was part of the 'ecological backlash' that the *New York Times* noted since the day after the first Earth Day in 1970. For example, Philip Handler, the president of the National Academy of Sciences and an acquaintance of Brown and Hubbert, emphasized the discrepancy between the two crises: the environmental crisis, which was far away but which the media feasted on, and the energy crisis, which was invisible but which was already knocking on the US door. More directly, the *Oil and Gas Journal* explained that it was high time 'to blow the whistle on the environmentalists' delusions', because they 'risk plunging the United States into an energy shortage'.[7]

In addition to the anti-anti-nuclear campaign, the AEC launched a lobbying campaign in 1969 for its breeder reactor programme. Industry remained sceptical, and it was necessary to persuade Congress to once again loosen the purse strings.[8] In June 1970, the journal *Nuclear Industry* spoke of a 'fossil fuel crisis'.[9] In August, John Nassikas, chairman of the Federal Power Commission, introduced the term 'energy crisis' to the National Press Club in Washington. While he mentioned the price of gas, the bulk of his speech focused on nuclear power and called on electricity companies to support the AEC's fast-breeder reactor programme.[10] A few months later, Ralph E. Lapp, a former member of the Manhattan Project, organized another seminar on the same subject for journalists.[11] The results of these efforts were not long in coming, as several articles appeared in the *New York Times* and elsewhere about the 'energy crisis' and the need to develop fast-breeder reactors.[12] Congressman Chet

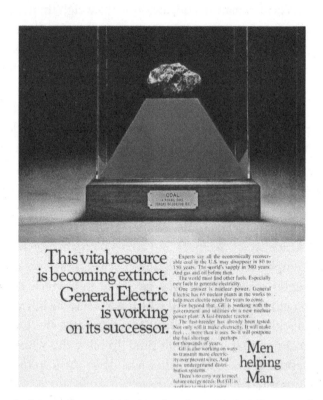

The spread of the 'energy crisis' before the oil crisis. Advertising campaign for General Electric and fast-breeder reactors, April 1972, in *Life*, *Time*, *Forbes*, the *New Yorker*, etc.

Holifield, chairman of the Joint Committee on Atomic Energy and a great advocate of nuclear power, also hammered home this idea: 'this country is facing an energy crisis' and those who doubted it, 'bankers and industrialists', had 'little understanding of the problem'.[13] It should also be noted that the first books on 'the energy crisis' (before 1973) were *all* written by atomic energy advocates and devoted long pages to breeder reactors.[14]

Shock and transition

The oil shock of 1973 gave a whole new dimension to the theme of the energy crisis launched four years earlier by the AEC. The term was now on everyone's lips, invading reports, parliamentary debates and television programmes. In its wake, the expression 'energy transition' spread and evolved, becoming a patchwork of disparate futurologies.[15]

Used without an adjective, 'transition' was inherited from debates on growth: transition from exponential to equilibrium (Jay Forrester, the Club of Rome), transition 'from infinite space' to the 'closed sphere' or from the 'cowboy economy' to that of the 'spaceship earth' (Kenneth Boulding), transition to a stationary state (Herman Daly).[16] This understanding of transition as a change in the trajectory of a complex system spread into the energy debate. It is at the heart of the Ford Foundation's remarkable *A Time to Choose* report (1974). Faced with the crisis, the solution, argued the report, was not to chase after more energy, but to decouple growth from it, to aim for the 'ZEG' scenario (Zero Energy Growth).[17] This meant changing lifestyles, shifting from the consumption of material goods to the consumption of services, leisure, health and culture. The most original part of the report dealt with energy taxation, its economic effects and the compensation to be introduced for low-income households. As far as the energy system itself was concerned, it was more modestly a question of 'renovating' it, because, as the slow spread of nuclear power demonstrated, betting on its rapid transformation was illusory.[18]

The 'energy transition' also became a watchword of the environmental movement. In 1976 and 1977, Friends of the Earth, the World
Watch Institute and the Club of Rome each took their turn to publish
a plea for a 'solar transition' – which at the time also included wind
and biomass.[19] The most influential text was that published by Amory
Lovins in October 1976 in *Foreign Affairs*. Lovins was a twenty-nine-
year-old physicist employed by Friends of the Earth. His aim was to
show that the United States could cope with the energy crisis without
nuclear power – the association that employed him had split from the
American environmental organization the Sierra Club on this issue.[20]
Contrary to what the AEC, General Electric and Westinghouse all
claimed, 'another path' was possible without the risk of nuclear proliferation or atomic technocracy, a 'soft energy path' based on
decentralized, small-scale, 'resilient', 'sustainable' and 'harmless' technologies. Lovins popularized the idea of the convivial technologies of
Illich and Schumacher in a highly influential magazine. In particular,
he emphasized the counter-productivity of the atom: what sense does
it make to use reactions reaching a thousand degrees to heat homes?
Why centralize production and then devour half the capital and a
third of the energy in distribution? Far from being a handicap, the diffuse nature of renewables would, on the contrary, save on network
costs. Released in the middle of an election campaign, the article
shook up the energy debate. Dozens of articles and several books
were published to refute it. Even the Nobel Prize-winner Hans Bethe
took the trouble to discuss the young physicist's arguments. Lovins
became a coveted expert, was heard by a congressional committee,
met President Carter and embarked on a brilliant career as an energy
consultant to the UN, various governments and major companies,
including oil companies. As for Denis Hayes, his counterpart at the
World Watch Institute, already known for having organized the first
Earth Day, Carter appointed him to head the new Solar Energy
Research Institute. By investing in the 'energy transition', the anti-
nuclear movement gained notoriety in Washington and became a
(secondary but paid) player in President Carter's energy policy.[21]

Defined in opposition to nuclear power, this 'energy transition' of environmental NGOs led to a very optimistic vision of *other* energies. Lovins claimed, for example, that biomass could replace petrol, that renewable energy could be easily stored, and even that coal could be made clean through innovation.[22] Roger Naill, a doctoral student of Dennis Meadows and one of the contributors to *Limits to Growth*, used the tools of system dynamics to demonstrate that coal use would have to grow very strongly until the year 2000.[23] In 1981, he became vice-president of Applied Energy Services, an important company operating a large contingent of thermal power stations worldwide. According to Lovins, unlike nuclear power – the fruit of a monstrous distortion of competition known as the Cold War – renewables would prosper in the market economy. Less esoteric, less dangerous, less regulated, they would offer thousands of inventor-entrepreneurs the chance to experiment and improve the technologies without being hindered by 'centralized bureaucracies'. Lovins and

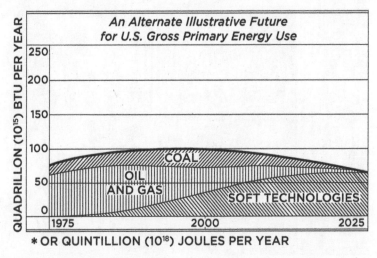

An Alternate Illustrative Future for U.S. Gross Primary Energy Use

QUADRILLON (10^{15}) BTU PER YEAR

250 / 200 / 150 / 100 / 50 / 0

COAL

OIL AND GAS

SOFT TECHNOLOGIES

1975 — 2000 — 2025

✳ OR QUINTILLION (10^{18}) JOULES PER YEAR

Despite his vehement criticism of the atomic lobby, Lovins adopts its futurology style, with rapid technological substitution but less energy consumption and 'soft technologies' instead of nuclear power. Coal would provide the 'transitional energy' until an economy powered entirely by renewables arrived in three to five decades' time. Today presented as the great 'precursor' of renewables, Lovins has largely underestimated the inertia of energy systems. (Amory Lovins, 'Energy strategy: the road not taken', *Foreign Affairs*, 1976.)

Wary of the long queues at gas stations and schools closing due to lack of heating during the winter of 1973–74, municipalities and states encouraged initiatives for 'energy preparedness'. In Oregon, in 1974, Joel Schatz drafted a Transition Plan at the request of the governor to 'prepare' the state for a rapid energy descent. His wife, the artist Diane Schatz, created a series of posters titled 'transition graphics', brimming with details such as solar panels and wind

turbines, bicycles and gardens, building insulation, candles for blackouts, energy fasts and discussion forums on the end of oil. ('Community Alert: Preparing for Energy Emergencies', *The Energy Consumer, Community Alert, Preparing for Energy Emergencies*, 1980, and Joel Schatz, *Transition: A Report to the Oregon Energy Council* (Portland, OR, 1975).)

Denis Hayes envisaged very rapid changes to the energy mix: an 'all-solar society' could be built 'in thirty years': all we had to do was trust American ingenuity spurred on by the search for profit.

The other issue was that the environmental movement had adopted the concept of the 'energy crisis', which was originally invented to oppose the environmentalists. The notion of an imminent collapse caused by energy exhaustion became a widely anticipated future, thereby naturalizing the transition as an inevitable fate.[24] The neo-Malthusian agronomist Lester Brown, founder of the World Watch Institute, put the problem in these terms: 'The question is not whether we make the transition or not. We will make it. The only question is whether it will be a smooth one.'[25]

By the end of the 1970s, the idea of the energy transition was becoming commonplace, a discursive umbrella encompassing all possible futures. Promoters of decoupling, of the stationary state, of fast-breeder reactors, of coal or solar power, environmentalists and neo-Malthusians: everyone could find their place in the highly inclusive lexicon of transition. For institutions, the expression was convenient in that it allowed sometimes contradictory strategies to be lumped together under the same heading. It was used extensively by the Energy Research and Development Administration, an avatar of the AEC created in 1975, responsible for fast-breeder reactors, solar energy and energy conservation. In 1979, the National Academy of Sciences chose the ecumenical title *Energy in Transition 1985–2010* for a major report bringing together the divergent opinions of more than 350 experts.[26] In the official documentation, the 'energy transition' often referred to all sorts of possible measures to make the USA less dependent on Middle Eastern oil: energy efficiency *and* nuclear power *and* energy taxes *and* pipelines in Alaska *and* offshore oil *and* coal . . . In 1977, Robert W. Fri, a close friend of President Nixon and former vice-president of the Environmental Protection Agency, set up a synthetic fuels company (coal liquefaction) called, not without irony, The Energy Transition Corporation. More comically, in 1981, President Reagan's energy programme to deregulate and pump more oil was drafted by an 'Energy Transition Task Force' headed by Michael Halbouty, an oilman from Houston.[27]

The energy transition was above all a discourse of national sovereignty, and it was for this reason that it featured in the energy programmes of the Nixon ('Project Independence') and Carter administrations ('National Energy Plan'). In terms of communication, it gave a futuristic flavour to programmes which, mainly based on the revival of domestic coal, were hardly futuristic at all.[28] And in this respect at least, the goal seems to have been achieved: after the presentation of Carter's energy plan – which provided for a doubling of coal extraction – the *New York Times* wrote: 'The United States and the world are at the beginning of a new energy transition.'[29]

Waves of the future

On 18 April 1977 in the Oval Office of the White House, in front of the television cameras, President Jimmy Carter delivered a curious history lesson to his fellow citizens:

> Over the last few centuries we have experienced two transitions in the way we use energy. The first was about two hundred years ago, when we switched from wood to coal . . . This change led to the Industrial Revolution. The second took place this century, with the use of oil and natural gas.[30]

With oil becoming increasingly scarce, it was time for a third transition – to energy saving and solar power. As the historian Duccio Basosi has recently shown, this speech played a major role in the subsequent fortune of the expression: after that date, reports on the 'energy transition' proliferated. The following year, the UN passed a resolution encouraging an 'energy transition away from fossil fuels'. In 1979, the OECD president Jacques Lesourne discussed the energy transition.[31] In 1981, a conference on 'renewable energies' was held in Nairobi, bringing together 4,000 delegates from 125 different countries. Energy transition was the key word in the discussions. Although the conference came to nothing, it did help to globalize the term.[32]

President Carter's speech raises another question: what was the basis of this very strange energy history? Three months earlier,

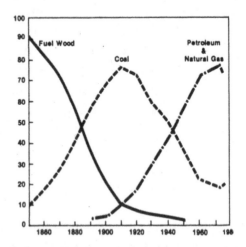

Executive Office of the President, *National Energy Plan*, 1977 (Cambridge, MA, 1978).

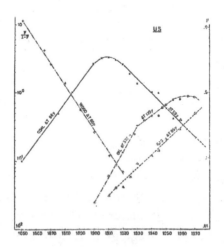

Cesare Marchetti, 'Primary Energy Substitution Models', IIASA Working Paper, 75–88, June 1975.

Carter had commissioned a report, the 'National Energy Plan', which included an extraordinary graph: three curves representing three energy systems in harmonious succession. Wood, then coal, then oil and gas. It was this graph that Carter commented on in front of the cameras. It is worth highlighting its novelty: at the end of the 1970s, as before, the energy system was usually represented by stacked curves showing the *cumulative* evolution of primary energies; here, on the contrary, the energies are presented in *relative shares* in order to show a historical dynamic of *substitution*.[33]

These curves are borrowed from an Italian atomic physicist, Cesare Marchetti, on whom I'm going to focus because I believe he played a very important role in the intellectual construction of the energy transition. Marchetti is best known for having been the great promoter of the 'hydrogen economy'. This project was based on the following observation: in order to become a major energy source, nuclear power had to conquer markets other than the electricity market, and therefore to produce some form of liquid fuel that could replace oil – hence hydrogen. From the 1960s onwards, Marchetti

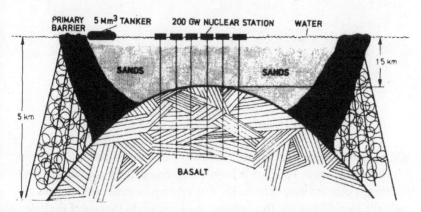

Cesare Marchetti's concept of the 'energy island'. Nuclear reactors would be installed on giant barges. The dotted vertical lines indicate the trajectory of the self-sinking capsules containing nuclear waste. (Cesare Marchetti, 'Geoengineering and the energy island', in W. Häfele et al., 'Second Status Report on the IIASA Project on Energy Systems, 1975', IIASA Research Report 76–1, 1976, pp. 220–44.)

was a tireless promoter of this vision, first within the EURATOM programme, where he held senior positions, and then within General Electric, and above all through his numerous articles and conferences – his colleagues eventually dubbed him 'Mr Hydrogen'.[34] After the oil crisis, Marchetti was invited to Japan to present his projects at the highest level. The proposals were grandiose: floating atomic power stations built near atolls in the Pacific would produce hydrogen, which a fleet of H2-tankers would export to the four corners of the world. Japan would become the Saudi Arabia of the twenty-first century. As for radioactive waste, while waiting for nuclear fusion,

In 1974, when the first international conference on hydrogen was held in Miami, Marchetti was seen as a pioneer. A *Journal of Hydrogen Energy* was founded, and Marchetti published its manifesto. The first volumes covered developments in fuel cells, electrolysers and hydrogen-powered aircraft. In the case of the latter, engineers imagined new fuselages that could accommodate their bulky tanks. Fifty years on, hydrogen-powered aircraft are still at the project stage. While Airbus is persevering, Boeing has given up: liquid hydrogen takes up three times more volume than aviation fuel and must be kept at −253°C. (G. D. Brewer, 'Aviation usage of liquid hydrogen fuel – prospects and problems', *International Journal of Hydrogen Energy*, 1, 1, 1976, pp. 65–88.)

we would get rid of it by self-burial: by its own heat it would melt the ocean floor and sink into the basaltic base of the atolls.[35]

But the focus of Marchetti's work lay elsewhere: he was interested in the time it might take to complete such a transformation. In 1974, he left EURATOM and the shores of Lake Maggiore for the International Institute of Advanced System Analysis (IIASA), founded two years earlier in Laxenburg, not far from Vienna. The special feature of this institute was that it was a 'détente' initiative: experts from East and West were to work together on modelling 'global problems' such as the environment, population and energy. In doing so, IIASA played a fundamental role in bringing together experts and disseminating ideas on an international scale.[36] Its energy programme focused on nuclear energy. It was headed by Wolf Häfele, an atomic scientist from the *Kernforschungszentrum* (Nuclear Research Centre) in Karlsruhe, who had previously led Germany's fast-breeder reactor programme. This technology, he wrote, should 'make it possible for industrial civilisation to survive on an overpopulated and limited planet'.[37] Harrison Brown was directly involved in the creation of IIASA and sat on its energy project committee.

As its name testifies, IIASA's methods were inspired by those of the Club of Rome. They were based on the use of computer models to explore how the energy system behaved under different constraints linked to technologies, investment and raw-material reserves. Regarding energy, the aim was to identify the scenario or scenarios 'that would ensure a *smooth* transition away from oil and towards an inexhaustible energy system [a category that included both renewables and nuclear power] within 50 years'.[38] Even if nuclear was predominant, among the 140 scientists from 20 different countries taking part in the project, visions of the future differed widely. Dennis Meadows, who was invited to the IIASA, reports on the lively debates between Amory Lovins and Wolf Häfele.[39] More interestingly, methods themselves were controversial. A former modeller of the energy project confided that the IIASA simulations were very sensitive to small variations in parameters (raw material prices, for example), so any conclusion in favour of a particular technology (fast-breeder reactors, for example) was risky.[40] Brian Wynne, a future major figure in Science and Technology Studies, spent a year at IIASA and criticized the rhetoric of the models, which masked an implicit choice in favour of nuclear power.[41]

Marchetti was also sceptical, but for different reasons: by generating multiple scenarios, computer models gave the impression that the global energy system was malleable and therefore governable. The Italian physicist was convinced of the opposite: because of its enormous inertia, the future of the global energy system was already written, and it was much more sensible to forecast its future in historical statistics than with lines of computer code.[42] With the help of the young economist Nebojsa Nakicenovic, Marchetti set about compiling a massive amount of historical energy data. The aim: to grasp the pace of change in the global energy system over the last two centuries and deduce how long the major transition away from fossil fuels could take.

Marchetti presented this approach as iconoclastic, but in fact it represented a return to the roots of futurology, a return to the logistic function. Since the Second World War, the logistic function had spread from neo-Malthusian demography to technological forecasting. At RAND, for example, it was routinely used to anticipate the spread of weapons systems and changes in their performance: aircraft speed, instrument accuracy, satellite weight, etc.[43] The S-curve is the starting point for the field of innovation economics, with the work of economists such as Zvi Griliches, James Coleman, Elihu Katz and Edwin Mansfield. It was also used at TEMPO, General Electric's forecasting department, where in the 1960s two physicists, John C. Fisher and Henry Pry, studied the dynamics of technological substitution using logistic functions. New technologies replaced old ones following an S-shaped curve: this applied to weapons systems, certain industrial processes and could also work for primary energy sources.[44] The IIASA was closely linked to the TEMPO programme, which gave it two directors, including Henry Pry himself. Marchetti was a consultant for GE. He knew John C. Fisher, who was then leading a major historical project at TEMPO: using industrial censuses as a starting point, he set up the best database on the history of energy in the USA.[45] Marchetti and Nakicenovic took over this programme and extended it worldwide.

Marchetti's dynamic vision of energy systems was original in several respects. Unlike Malthusian atomic scientists, he suggested that energy sources faded away not due to depletion but due to obsolescence. For instance, wood remained abundant in the United States when coal became dominant. Furthermore, the world would not

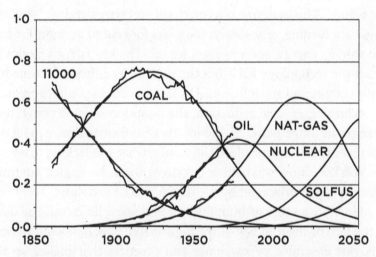

Cesare Marchetti's originality lies in applying a technological diffusion model to the global energy mix. More specifically, he used the Lotka-Volterra equations (named after two founders of population ecology), derived from the S-curve, which modelled populations of species competing for the same resource. In Marchetti's method, old techniques disappear through obsolescence as innovations spread. With the benefit of historical hindsight, we can see that his forecast anticipated (and exaggerated) the rise of natural gas but underestimated the importance of coal and wood at the start of the 21st century. In his books, Vaclav Smil points out the errors of the Italian scholar but nevertheless follows him in adopting his logistic curve method.[46] Beyond Smil, Marchetti popularized the view of energy systems in relative terms and influenced a number of historians such as Richard Rhodes, Arnulf Grubler and Paolo Malanima.
(C. Marchetti and N. Nakicenovic, 'The Dynamics of Energy Systems and the Logistic Substitution Model', IIASA Research Report 79–13, December 1979, p. 13.)

transition directly from oil to nuclear power. Nuclear power was starting from too far behind to play a predominant role before 2050. The logistical substitution model pointed to natural gas as the successor to oil, which had the advantage of preparing the infrastructure for the future development of nuclear hydrogen.[47] Compared with the scenario method used at IIASA, the approach is strictly deterministic: 'the entire destiny of an energy seems to be completely decided from its infancy. These trends emerge unscathed from wars, huge price swings and depressions.' The congruence of the data with the logistic curve reveals the 'domination of the system over the actors'. The 'system has its own will, its own calendar'.[48] And the pages are turning very slowly: 160 years for coal to account for half the world's energy, and 100 years for oil. The key factor was not so much the technology itself but the pace of its diffusion, a time not easily compressed and influenced by factors such as the improvement of technologies, cost reduction, the adoption of new converters, changes in usage patterns, the inertia of infrastructure, capital displacement and amortization. Ultimately, what was lacking to ensure the 'soft transition' was neither resources nor technologies, but time. The fifty-year horizon set by the IIASA was far too short. According to Marchetti, a sense of humility was necessary: little could be done in the face of the iron law of the logistic function; nobody governed this vast ensemble of machines and practices that makes up the global energy system. Governments are merely optimisers: 'don't forget the system, because the system won't forget you',[49] concluded Marchetti.

Today, Marchetti's work is generally criticized for its determinism and incorrect forecasts. As Vaclav Smil points out, far from disappearing, coal increased its weight in the global energy mix after 1980, and wood energy obviously did not disappear in the year 2000.[50] These criticisms are partly unfair: Marchetti's aim was to convince his colleagues at IIASA of the enormous inertia of the global energy system. And, from this point of view, subsequent events proved him entirely right, even more so than he had envisaged. The worrying moral of this story is that the pessimistic forecaster of fifty years ago turned out to be far too optimistic.

The real problem with Marchetti's work lies less in his errors than in his influence: after him, many experts chose to study energy dynamics as processes of technological diffusion, thus introducing a damaging confusion. Marchetti's work also contributed to popularizing the relative view of energy dynamics. Smil highlights the errors of the Italian scientist in his own work, while making extensive use of the logistic curve. Like Marchetti, Smil defines transition in relative terms (the time taken for a new energy to occupy between 25 and 50 per cent of a mix).[51]

This influence stems from the more general intellectual context of the 1980s, a period during which innovation became, in the political and economic discourse, the core ingredient of growth, to such an extent that innovation came to be confused with technological

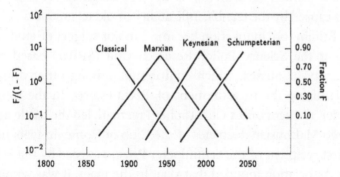

Within the IIASA, the study of logistic diffusion was pursued by several authors, including Arnulf Grubler and Nebojsa Nakicenovic. Nakicenovic went on to hold important positions within the IPCC. Jesse Ausubel, an American economist working at the National Academy of Sciences and IIASA, applied the substitution model to growth theories themselves, with Schumpeter having the final word. Ausubel played an important role in organizing the first World Climate Conference in 1979. He also coined the word 'decarbonization', understood as the intrinsic tendency of the energy system to evolve from carbon to hydrogen. (Jesse Ausubel, 'Rat race dynamics and crazy companies: the diffusion of technologies and social behavior', in Nebojsa Nakicenovic and Arnulf Grubler (eds), *Diffusion of Technologies and Social Behavior* (Berlin and New York, 1991), p. 16.)

phenomena in general. The substitution curves attracted attention because they seemed to give Schumpeter's 'creative destruction' a solid empirical foundation. In the United States, this led to Paul Romer's theory of endogenous growth, followed by Clayton Christensen's theory of 'disruptive innovation'. In France in the 1980s, Bruno Latour – who worked in the Centre de Sociologie de l' Innovation – began to describe the ability of innovators (such as Pasteur) to completely reconfigure society. The so-called 'actor-network theory' grew out of this vision of the innovator as a kind of demiurge. The Science and Technology Studies of the 1980s–2000s (in which I was trained) were certainly critical of diffusionism, but were still mainly devoted to the study of innovations, the risk and uncertainties they entailed, the scientific controversies they fostered, and the way they were 'socially constructed' – all these approaches did little to help us understand the nature of the climate challenge, which is characterized, on the contrary, by a high degree of certainty and is caused by the terrible inflexibility of old techniques.

In Britain too, innovation became a major subject of study especially at the Science Policy Research Unit (SPRU) based at the University of Sussex, which contributed, among other things, to standardizing the measurement of R&D efforts. In the 1970s, its founder, the economist Christopher Freeman, led the battle against the neo-Malthusian doctrines of the Club of Rome. In 1986, he was the first recipient of the Schumpeter Prize, awarded by the Schumpeter Association founded that year. In the 1990s, it was within this institute that the 'transition theories' emerged, which, as I mentioned in the Introduction, flourished in the wake of climate change thanks to the confusion between the diffusion of 'green' innovation and decarbonization.

Even today, the many studies of technological diffusion hinder our understanding of the climate challenge. On the one hand, as the historian Svante Lindqvist pointed out a long time ago, they say nothing about the disappearance of the old, making the assumption – implicit or explicit and in any case unjustified – that this would be symmetrical with diffusion of the new.[52] On the other hand, and this will come as no surprise to the reader of this book, since energies and materials are in symbiosis as much as in competition, we simply cannot use a technological substitution model to understand their dynamics. Nonetheless, the experts are still comforted by the upturn in the diffusion curve for wind and solar power, as if it were equivalent to the disappearance of fossil fuels. Marchetti's hypothesis is still there, explicitly or implicitly.

12.

'Play the technology card'

How did the energy transition move from debates about the energy crisis to debates about climate change? The improbability of such a shift must be emphasized: the leap was indeed gigantic. Let us recall that the energy transition, as conceived by the Malthusian atomists of the 1950s and 1970s, was a gradual evolution, taking place over the span of a century or more, primarily affecting wealthy countries and dictated by the rising cost of fossil fuels and technological progress. The climate challenge radically changed the nature of the transformation to be undertaken: fossil fuels were not only to decline but now had to disappear, the time frame was considerably shorter and the process was to take place in a context of abundance, without the sting of scarcity. The climate challenge was therefore entirely different from, if not orthogonal to, the 'energy crisis', and yet it was viewed through the same 'transitionist' lens. A neo-Malthusian technological futurology for rich countries had suddenly become a safeguard plan for the entire planet . . . How was this scientific and political scandal possible?

Fifty years for the transition

At the end of the 1970s, when climate change entered the American political arena, the main issue was not oil, which was thought to be on its last legs, but coal. The climate was used to question the planned expansion of the coal industry and to burnish the image of nuclear power, tarnished by the Three Mile Island accident. It was a particular project, based on coal, that launched the debate: the Synthetic Fuel Corporation, a public company, promoted by President Carter, endowed with $20 billion and charged with launching the American liquefaction industry on the South African model.[1] The Senate then began to take an interest in climate change and organized its first hearings on the subject in July 1979 and April 1980. 'Part of the reason for these hearings', explained Democratic Senator Paul Tsongas, 'is that we now find ourselves in a strange embrace of coal and synthetic fuels [whose dangers] are insidious and difficult to handle.'[2]

At the time, there was no doubt among American climate experts that global warming was real. The 'Charney Report' – named after the meteorologist who steered it – submitted to the White House in 1979, predicted that a doubling of the CO_2 content of the atmosphere would lead to a $3°C$ rise in temperature. The margin of error was large ($1.5°C$) but the trend was certain and no one was questioning it.[3] At the time, Exxon was co-operating with climatologists in earnest and published solid articles, even though some of its employees feared that this work would backfire on the company in the popular news media.[4]

What was being debated was not the reality of global warming, but its timing. As the National Academy of Sciences explained in 1980: 'The largest uncertainties connected with the CO_2 problem pertain to the timing rather than to the existence of the problem.'[5] Some climatologists believed that immediate action was needed. The Charney Report warned that because of the inertia of the climate system, 'A wait-and-see policy may mean waiting until it is too late.'[6] James Gustave Speth, director of the Council on Environmental Quality – Carter's environmental advisor – also highlighted this time trap: once detected, global warming would take centuries to subside. Procrastination was not an option, which is why Speth referred to it as the 'ultimate environmental problem'.[7]

But many climatologists, at least those that were called before the Senate hearings, seemed to differ on the urgency of action. As the date of the climate catastrophe remained uncertain – when exactly will the ice caps melt? – the prospect of an energy transition completed in the meantime alleviated their fears. The same scientists who had brought the climate issue into the public arena defused it by invoking a rather hypothetical future. For example, during the Senate hearings of July 1979, the scientist Roger Revelle was questioned about the opportunities of synthetic fuels. Surprisingly, he did not oppose them. When a senator raised concerns about the enormous investments required to develop the synthetic oil industry, which would commit the United States to a long-term reliance on coal, Revelle, who had played a major role in raising the status of the climate problem with his key 1956 article on oceanic CO_2 absorption and then with his involvement in Charney's report, responded in a singularly casual way:

> As we look at the history of energy in this country and in the world, we have made a major transition in the last 50 years from one major kind of energy to another. That is from coal to oil. This suggests that it is possible to make a transition in a time which is not long compared to our CO_2 problem.[8]

This was not simply an off-the-cuff answer from an oceanographer: since 1963 Revelle had been working at Harvard on issues of demography and development.[9]

Stephen Schneider, editor-in-chief of the magazine *Climatic Change* (founded in 1977) regretted the return of coal, but even 'for an environmentalist like him', *synfuels* were acceptable during the energy transition.[10] The climatologist William Kellogg painted a frightening picture before the senators of the consequences of global warming – the melting of the ice caps, the submergence of coastal areas, the virtual disappearance of Louisiana – which he immediately tempered with the prospect of a transition. The catastrophe would arrive by the middle of the twentieth-first century and fortunately 'the lead time for implementing a transition is approximately fifty years'.[11] The fifty-year time frame was thrown around by climatologists without any substantiation. It corresponds to the lifespan of a power station, but phasing out fossil fuels on a global scale is obviously more complicated than closing down a single coal-power station, or even closing down all coal-power stations. The work of Cesare Marchetti was sometimes cited in support of the fifty-year time frame, even though the Italian scientist had insisted on the inertia of the global energy system. When climatologists set out the course of the coming catastrophe, its occurrence seemed further away than the duration of the transition. At a symposium held at the IIASA in 1978, John Laurmann of Stanford University gave the following dates: the change would become noticeable in 2000 (+1°C), it would have serious economic consequences in 2038 (+2°C) and would become a global catastrophe in 2078 (+5°C). Fortunately, as the IIASA would have shown, a 'global reorientation of energy resource utilization', 'a smooth transition to a new energy source', would take around fifty years.[12]

This statement was not just made by a few climatologists venturing outside their field of expertise. The first world conference on climate change, held in Geneva in 1979, concluded as follows: 'It is possible that some effects on a regional and global scale . . . become significant before the middle of the next century. This time scale is similar to that required to redirect, if necessary, the operation of the world economy, including agriculture and the production of energy.'[13] In 1985, a conference in Villach in Austria, which foreshadowed the creation of the IPCC, took up this delaying tactic. The final report defined three warning levels – green, yellow and red. In 1985, the climate indicator was still green: global warming needed to be studied, but nothing more. Even at the 'yellow' stage, the experts felt that there would still be time, as 'many instruments are available to governments to stimulate a smooth transition'.[14] No evidence was given to support these peremptory assertions: neither history nor forecasting suggested that fifty years, or even more, would be enough to get the world off fossil fuels.

'We have to think of the climate as a resource'

One of the main reasons for the success of the idea of transition is the intellectual background of the experts who first tackled the thorny issue of 'solutions'. In the early 1980s, these experts were generally energy economists who had cut their teeth during the 'energy crisis'. The same institutions, the same experts and the same lines of reasoning moved seamlessly from the study of the energy crisis to that of global warming. In the United States, the Department of Energy, created in 1977, is in charge of what was then called 'the CO_2 problem'.[15] At the US National Academy of Sciences, the report *Energy in Transition 1985–2010* had barely been published (1980) and its authors were already working on the report *Changing Climate* (1983)[16] – and they would use a similar modelling method. At the IIASA, the issue of global warming was studied by the energy group set up in 1972 around Wolfgang Häfele, who took part in the 1979 World Climate Conference.[17] The IIASA was considered by the first IPCC reports to be the leading authority on energy modelling.[18] The organization of the IPCC into three groups (Group I: climatology, Group II: impacts and Group III: solutions) was based on that of a symposium held at the IIASA in 1978.[19] In the early 1990s, the first Integrated Assessment Models studied by Group III were based on computer programmes (MESSAGE, MEDEE and so on) developed in the mid-1970s for Häfele's energy project.[20] The continuity of expertise between the energy crisis and the climate crisis can be seen elsewhere. In France, the Centre International de Recherche pour l'Environnement et le Développement (CIRED), set up in 1973 partly as an answer to the Club of Rome, became an important energy-modelling centre in the following decade. In India, the TATA Energy Institute, which began work in 1977, gave the IPCC its third chairman. It was the Energy Research Institute, founded in Beijing in 1980, that provided the IPCC with its main contingent of Chinese experts.

The tools developed to think about a possible scarcity of fossil fuels were used to think about the problem of their overabundance. Take the case of William Nordhaus, winner of the 2018 Nobel Prize for Economics. The fact that he devoted part of his career to climate may seem surprising, given his clear lack of interest in environmental issues and his stance against the Club of Rome. In fact, it is easily

---

explained when Nordhaus is placed in his milieu of atomic futurologists. Like them, Nordhaus had been convinced that fast-breeder reactors would provide inexhaustible and cheap energy around the year 2000. In a 1973 article, he argued that efforts to conserve oil and coal might prove excessive because they neglected technological progress: there was no need to tighten energy belts, because by 2000 fast-breeder reactors would provide the real solution to the energy crisis. By the end of the twenty-first century, 'all fossil fuels will have been exhausted', writes Nordhaus, 'and the economy will then run solely on hydrogen and electricity from infinite resources'.[21] This will be 'the final stage of the transition'. Nordhaus's future corresponded exactly to that of the atomic Malthusians studied above. In 1974–75, Nordhaus joined Wolfgang Häfele's team at IIASA, where he was introduced to the issue of climate change by Cesare Marchetti, aka 'Mr Hydrogen'. During his stay in Austria, Nordhaus sketched out a very simple mathematical model designed to maximize GNP under a climate constraint – avoiding a doubling of the CO_2 content of the atmosphere. Unsurprisingly, this model justified the IIASA's strategy: to make up for the growing scarcity of oil, initially, we would have to draw massively on coal resources, then make a rapid transition to other energy sources at the end of the twentieth century. According to Nordhaus, waiting before taking action would allow time to develop the necessary technologies, in particular fast-breeder reactors. 'We have a comfortable amount of time', he wrote, 'to carry out research and draw up plans to reduce CO_2 should this prove necessary.'[22] 'The most surprising point is that the optimal path does not differ from the "out of control" trajectory, at least for the initial period.'[23] The transition remained essential; it was only to be postponed until technologies became available.

The influence of the energy crisis is obvious here: Nordhaus applied to the climate problem a reasoning derived from the economics of non-renewable resources. In 1973, he was thinking about the optimal time allocation of American oil and coal; two years later, he reasoned in the same way about CO_2 emissions and world

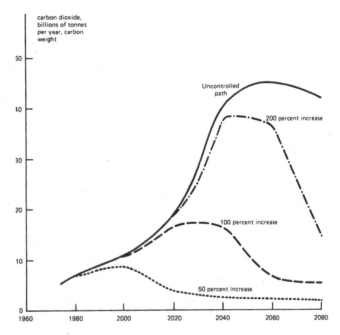

The doubling of CO2 in the atmosphere (optimal path) follows the same curve as the 'out of control' path until the year 2000. (William Nordhaus, 'Strategies for the Control of Carbon Dioxide', 1977, in *The Efficient Use of Energy Resources* (New Haven, CT, 1979), p. 145.)

GNP, the climate constraint having replaced the mineral constraint. In 1973, Nordhaus described fast-breeder reactors as a 'backstop technology' in the face of fossil-fuel depletion, the very same expression he would use later in his work on climate change. Other experts who have also exerted influence within the IPCC Working Group III have followed a similar trajectory. For example, Alan S. Manne, before becoming a pioneer in integrated modelling did research on the economics of fast-breeder reactors. In the mid-1970s, he collaborated with Wolfgang Häfele on the concept of the 'nuclear transition', which involved determining the optimal allocation of uranium reserves between fission and fast-breeder reactors. Their view was that the best strategy was to 'wait for the breeder'[24] in order to avoid wasting uranium in conventional nuclear power plants.

The representation of the climate as a sort of mine in the sky spread well beyond the discipline of economics. In 1979, the American meteorologist Robert White gave the inaugural lecture at the first World Climate Conference in Geneva. His speech concluded with this strange exhortation: 'We must therefore begin to think of the climate itself as a resource to be allocated wisely.'[25] This way of defining the climate problem directed the 'solutions' towards innovation, which had until then, at least in the rich countries, dealt successfully with the problems of resource scarcity. Similarly, the choice of a 2100 time horizon, inherited from the work on fossil-fuel depletion, galvanized technological confidence: it is always easier to imagine major changes when the time horizon is distant. Finally, as the economist Antonin Pottier has shown, the work on climate change published in the most prestigious economic journals deals with abstract questions that lend themselves well to mathematical treatment. For example, what are the optimal emissions pathways? Or, given a damage function, what temperature maximizes global well-being? The problem is that these stylized theories sidestep concrete technological problems – can we really decarbonize steel and cement on a global scale? Since these theories are based on the Pareto optimum, they neglect the questions of distribution: how can we allocate the remaining CO_2 quota fairly and/or efficiently? How can we take into account the extraordinarily diverse utility of carbon?[26]

Exxon invents the future

A second reason for the success of the transition idea lies in the discourse of industrialists, who immediately understood the advantage they could draw from this dubious futurology to postpone the climate constraint into the future and into technological progress. If we had to put a date on the birth of this crude but effective form of climate denial, it would be 16 October 1982. On that day, Exxon's R&D boss, Edward David, an influential figure as a former head of Bell Labs and former scientific advisor to President Nixon, gave a major speech to an audience of climatologists.[27] This text, entitled 'Inventing the Future', is an early example of the use of the notion of transition as a delaying tactic. David does not question global warming (he will do so in the following decade). The greenhouse effect is a well-established physical phenomenon that has been recognized since the nineteenth century. The interesting question is about chronology: which will come first, the climate catastrophe or the 'energy transition'? The latter was the key theme of his speech: 'Few people doubt,' said the Exxon executive, 'that we have entered an energy transition away from dependence upon fossil fuels.' It's a slow process, but it's inexorable. David pointed to history: the United States underwent two energy transitions in the nineteenth and twentieth centuries, one from wood to coal, the second from coal to oil. In 1860, Exxon contributed to save the whales, and a hundred years later, his company will participate in the third transition, the one that will save the climate, by installing 'a mix of renewable energies that will not pose a CO_2 problem'. David presented Exxon's investments in solar panels and electric cars but explained that, in the meantime, the company had to develop oil extraction and coal-hydrogenation plants to satisfy demand. Anyway, in the past, American capitalism had managed to produce two energy transitions: let's not stand in its way. The most revealing aspect of this affair is the reaction of the conference organizer, the renowned climate scientist James Hansen, who published David's speech in the first place in the conference proceedings. A misleading history of energy fuelled a form of climate denial and yet, in his preface, Hansen thanked the chairman of Exxon R&D for his 'thoughtful discourse'.[28]

Was Edward David sincere when he described an energy transition that was under way and would be completed in time to avoid catastrophe? Was this simply an echo of flawed energy forecasting – and so much the better if it suited Exxon's business? The reality is quite different. Edward David was well aware of the immense difficulty, to say the least, the world economy would have in moving away from fossil fuels. Two years before the conference, a major seminar was held in St Petersburg in Florida. Twenty-four men and three women were invited by the US House of Representatives to spend two days freely discussing the 'CO2 problem'. Among the meteorologists and climatologists was Henry Shaw, an Exxon engineer in charge of the climate programme of the company. He was silent and only spoke on one occasion, when the discussion became animated around the Synthetic Fuels Corporation. Climatologists were truly worried, because coal represents a much larger carbon stock than oil and gas. Exxon already had pilot plants and, with subsidies from the US government, it intended to put these investments to good use. Shaw therefore tried to justify the SFC to the other seminar participants: 'synfuels', he argued, 'make sense during the transition period, between 1990 and 2010 . . . We are not going to stop burning fossil fuels and start looking toward solar or nuclear fusion and so on. We are going to have a very orderly transition from fossil fuels to renewable resources.'[29] Moving away from fossil fuels was a necessity in the long term, but it had to be done in an 'orderly' way, in a 'smooth transition' – the key words of the IIASA.

At this point in the discussion, David Rose, a nuclear physicist from MIT, intervened and offered an implacable critique of the transition. For him, the strategies of Shaw, the IIASA and Nordhaus were all the same, and were quite simply unrealistic because they ignored the way industrial capitalism worked. When talking about energy transition, explained Rose, 'People make this kind of curve and then they stop. But they don't ask: what does it imply in terms of installing this kind of technology? . . . What does that imply for the world's productive capability to shift?' 'Nordhaus didn't really calculate how much – how fast you were really going to have to develop the new production facilities for these energy things. He didn't really take those derivatives.'

With the help of a few slides Rose made the problem crystal clear. If the energy transition were to start as late as 2010, we would need to install 1600 GW per year (nuclear power stations, solar panels, etc.) over the next two decades to avoid exceeding the

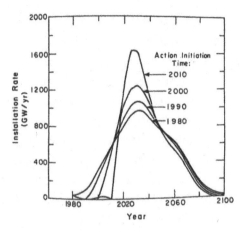

Rate of installation of decarbonized energy production as a function of the starting date of the energy transition. The curves plotted make it possible to stay below 600 ppm. (Slide by David Rose in 'Proceedings of the National Commission on Air Quality. Carbon Dioxide Workshop', St Petersburg, Florida, 29–31 October 1980.)

600 ppm CO_2 threshold that was considered dangerous. By way of comparison, in 1980 all the US energy companies together had an installation capacity of 30 GW per year. Making the transition would mean creating companies fifty times bigger than General Electric and Westinghouse combined. Not to mention the mines that had to be opened, the miners to be trained, the machines to be built, and so on. Furthermore, as the transition would have to be completed within twenty years, these investments would be useless as soon as they were made. For David Rose, capitalism would never tolerate such a jolt. The strategy defended by Nordhaus – namely, to postpone the transition until new technologies and new capital make it less painful – was the perfect recipe for climate disaster.

Rose's demonstration changed the tone of the seminar: 'we don't believe we can wait', 'the rapidity of change exceeds historical technological shifts', 'we have to fundamentally change the nature of economic and political systems'. Rose had the occasion to warn against the simplistic energy-transition discourse on other occasions, in July 1979 before the Tsongas Senate Committee and in a major report published by MIT in 1983.[30] Shaw was of course aware of this work but turned a deaf ear. In a memo he wrote to Edward David on 'Exxon's position if the issue [of climate change] comes up', he proposed three talking points: first, to explain that 'there is sufficient time to study the problem before corrective action is required'. Secondly, 'the increase in temperature will not be measurable before 2000'. Thirdly, 'this permits time for an orderly transition to non-fossil fuel technologies'.[31]

In November 1982, a few weeks after the Lamont–Doherty climate symposium, Edward David was in Beijing for the first Sino-American conference on energy. The inaugural address was on climate change. It was given by the Nobel Prize-winner Melvin Calvin, a specialist in photosynthesis. Calvin explained the basic principles of global warming and projected the Keeling curve. His message was unambiguous: 'I doubt that humanity can adapt to such macroscopic changes in two generations . . . we have to stop burning coal and shale oil.'[32] Edward David was the next speaker. His talk focused on the uncertainty in which energy companies operate. One thing he was certain of, however, was that 'even in the distant future, fossil fuels will dominate the global energy system'.[33] This prediction, which contradicted the discourse he had held before climatologists, would prove to be accurate, even more so than he had imagined: over the following three decades, gas consumption would triple, coal consumption would double, and oil consumption would increase by 60 per cent. By 2010, China alone was burning as much coal as the entire world did in 1980. As a result, the share of fossil fuels in the global energy mix would remain stable, at around 80 per cent, up to the present day.[34]

In the uncertain timelines of the transition and climate catastrophe, all dilatory manoeuvres and justificatory speeches would find their way to thrive. The end of the career of Carroll Wilson perfectly exemplifies the power of procrastination inherent in invoking the future. Let us recall who Wilson was. Assistant to Vannevar Bush, he was the first director of the Atomic Energy Commission, he ordered the Putnam Report, he also organized the first international conference on global warming in Stockholm in 1970 (Chapter 10). However, by the end of the same decade, disillusioned with nuclear energy, Wilson became convinced that coal would have to expand tremendously to meet the global energy demand.[35] As he had done for the climate in the late 1960s, he organized an international group of experts to prepare the revival of coal. The conclusion of the 'WOCOL' World Coal Report, which was much quoted at the time, was based on two figures: to meet global energy demand in 2000, coal production would have to triple, and the international coal trade would have to increase tenfold – objectives that would indeed finally be achieved in 2010.

This report followed a global trend. In 1979, the G7 countries meeting in Tokyo undertook to 'increase the use of coal as much as possible and to replace oil with coal, without damage to the environment'[36] – the end of the sentence was naturally hypocritical. Within WOCOL, the Chinese representative estimated that his country would consume 2 gigatonnes of coal by the year 2000, i.e. two-thirds of the world consumption in 1980.[37] Faced with such forecasts from Asia, the issue of synfuels, which had inflamed spirits in the United States, seemed almost secondary. As in Edward David's speech, there is no trace of climate scepticism in the WOCOL report, which also recognizes that capturing carbon dioxide from chimneys is economically unfeasible. The only way to reconcile the revival of the coal industry and the preservation of climate lies in the prospect of a transition, simply postponed. Based on the conclusion of the 1979 Geneva Climate Conference, Wilson explained that there was still ample time to avert disaster. Coal would only be a transitional energy, the 'bridge to the future', a stopgap for the next fifty years, pending the arrival of 'the energy sources of the next century – whatever they may be'.[38] World coal consumption would triple between 1980 and 2000 and then suddenly disappear, to be replaced by indeterminate techniques. This strange plan was also that of the *Energy in a Finite World* report published by IIASA in 1982. Here again, there was no doubt about global warming. The transition to solar and/or nuclear power was essential in the long term, but out of reach in the immediate future. Just as in the WOCOL report, coal was a 'transitional energy', the 'bridge to a renewable future'.[39] The IIASA's only recommendation on climate change was to continue research into solar energy and fast-breeder reactors so that a transition could be made quickly (around 2000–2020) if disaster loomed.

For excellent reasons, mainly judicial, historians have taken a great interest in climate scepticism. As shocking as it is, the strategy of doubt is perhaps not as important as the media make it out to be.[40] For more than twenty years now, industrial lobbies have been moving on to other delaying tactics, making contrite declarations about climate change with little or no change to their activities. As the scientific consensus – and then the common experience of global warming – made the strategy of doubt untenable, corporations have adopted en masse the far more astute rhetoric of energy transition. Already in 2000, British Petroleum changed its name to 'Beyond Petroleum' – with little effect on its core business.[41] More recently, the French oil giant Total adopted the ecumenical name of 'TotalEnergies'. The message, repeated everywhere, is that the oil companies are acting for the energy transition, but as this is a long process, they are obliged, in the meantime, to pump, drill and even explore, almost reluctantly. Beyond oil companies, Vinci promotes 'zero-carbon highways', Airbus advocates sustainable aviation, and Aramco promises to become 'net-zero' by 2050. The alignment of these inherently polluting industries under the banner of energy transition has at least one merit: it clarifies the ideological function of this notion. Energy transition has become the politically correct future for the industrial world.

'Living with climate change'

At a time when the first climate experts, followed by Exxon, were making the somewhat daring assumption that a transition was

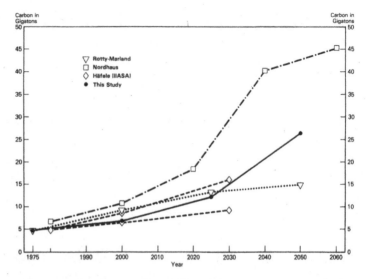

In 2023, it appears that the world has followed the high emissions path. (Jae Edmonds and John Reilly, 'Global energy and CO2 to the year 2050', *The Energy Journal*, 4, 3, 1983, pp. 21–47.)

under way and arriving in time to avoid catastrophe, the first models of the global energy system were leading to the opposite conclusion. Whether it was the linear optimization methods employed by Nordhaus, the system analysis carried out by Häfele at the IIASA or the logistical projections of Ralph Rotty at the Oak Ridge laboratory, all envisaged rising emissions in the first half of the twenty-first century.

Even Alvin Weinberg, the ardent promoter of nuclear power and inventor of the expression 'techno-fix', admitted that climate change would happen well before the general spread of atomic energy: 'a fossil-fuel-free world in the relatively near future is so bizarre an idea it is hard even to talk about it seriously'.[42] Climate change was bound to happen. In 1979, JASON, a group of scientists advising the White House on technology and defence issues, gave President Carter a report along these lines. If emissions continued to rise at the same rate as in the 1970s, the CO2 content of the atmosphere would double by 2035. And if, in 2000, we succeeded in

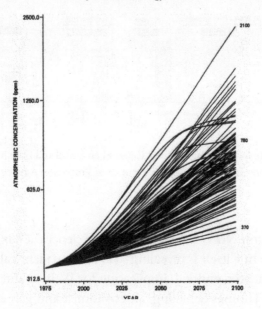

CO2 concentration of 100 random 'runs' of the energy model by William Nordhaus and Gary Yoe, in *Changing Climate*, National Academy of Sciences, 1983.

reducing the rate rise to 1 per cent (which happened in 2022), the doubling would only be postponed until 2060.[43]

In 1982, the Environmental Protection Agency confirmed this pessimistic scenario. Using the Oak Ridge Laboratory energy model, the authors tested the effect of various measures on global CO2 emissions. Even the most radical would only postpone the date on which the +2°C limit would be passed. For example, a global tax on energies according to their carbon intensity (up to 300 per cent for coal) would put it back by barely five years. Only a complete ban on coal and shale oil from the year 2000 would give a substantial additional delay of twenty-five years (from 2040 to 2065). But the report also underlined its consequences: nothing less than 'economic dislocation'.[44] The conclusion was clear: the +2°C limit would be reached by the middle of the twenty-first century. Therefore, it was necessary to prepare for relocating populations from areas of the planet that would become uninhabitable.

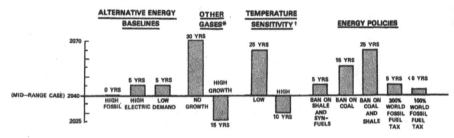

Change of date for a warming of +2°C. (Stephen Siedel and Dale Kayes, 'Can We Delay a Greenhouse Warming?', Environmental Protection Agency, 1983, p. vi.)

In the same year, the Academy of Sciences' *Changing Climate* report – the title itself is revealing – came to an identical conclusion. The final chapter, entitled 'Implication for Welfare and Policy', was written by Thomas Schelling, an economist and game theory and nuclear war theorist. He described the climate issue as the classic 'prisoner's dilemma'. With the bulk of carbon stocks distributed between the USA, the USSR and China – in other words, between two rival superpowers and a developing country – it was perfectly illusory to think that any of these players could give them up. Moreover, the recent experience of oil shocks would dissuade any government from opting for a voluntary increase in energy prices. Rather than climate scepticism, Schelling was expressing a form of resignation, coupled with an unfailing confidence in the ability of rich countries to adapt.[45]

This is a key point. As Romain Felli has shown, in the United States, earlier than elsewhere, global warming was understood primarily as a problem of adaptation, with economic costs but also opportunities.[46] As early as November 1976, the MITRE organization, a think tank close to JASON and the White House, organized a symposium entitled 'Living with Climate Change: Phase II'.[47] The climate was certainly going to change, but what could be expected? What would be the consequences for the US economy? To answer this question, MITRE wanted to open 'a dialogue with leaders in industry, science and government'. Almost half a century later, the results of the conference are impressive in their prescience and in their blindness. Prescient when the report tackles the problem of the contraction of clay soils and its effects on the solidity of buildings, an already costly consequence of global warming. Blind when nothing is said about the drying up of the Colorado river, the mega-fires or the storms in Louisiana. Agriculture was identified as vulnerable, but, on the scale of the United States, there would always be the possibility of moving production areas, modifying seeds and, if necessary, reducing the huge proportion of grains destined for animal feed. The conclusion was reassuring: the United States of America had great capacity to adapt, given its size, technology and capital.

In 1979, the US Department of Energy (DOE) organized an international conference in Annapolis, Maryland, on the impacts of climate change. Adaptation dominated the debates, presented as the only seriously conceivable strategy. The panel on economic consequences (including Henry Shaw of Exxon, Alvin Weinberg and Kenneth Boulding) considered that preventing global warming would be much more costly than managing its impacts. The panel on agriculture once again put the danger into perspective:

> The prospects of climatic change from increasing atmospheric levels of carbon dioxide do not terrify U.S. agriculturalists and foresters . . . The history of the past century, fortunately, provides evidence that U.S. agriculture and its research establishment can cope with – and even improve – during climatic change.[48]

One of the new features of the conference was the involvement of the social sciences, and history in particular: 'retrospective climate impact assessments' provided reassuring examples of successful past adaptations. Unlike 'prevention', which conjured up images of planning, centralization and inefficiency, adaptation corresponded perfectly to the prevailing neo-liberal ideology, that of flexible, rational and *resilient* individuals – the term is already omnipresent – modifying their behaviour rationally according to circumstances.

For less fortunate countries, migration was presented as another form of adaptation.[49]

In 1983, the Academy of Sciences' *Changing Climate* report also endorsed the adaptation strategy. In the final chapter, Schelling acknowledged the impact of global warming on agriculture, but, as its weight in GNP was small, this was of little importance: 'a rise of 10% or even 20% in the cost of producing food would be a few percent of world income . . . the living standards that might have been achieved by 2083 in the absence of climate change would be achieved instead in the late 2080s.'[50] As for the 'catastrophically affected areas', their sacrifice was necessary so as not to hamper growth for everyone, even if they would probably have to be compensated. Under the pretext of economic realism, this 'calm assessment' condemned whole swathes of the globe to disaster. It is worth noting that these reports were written, and these conferences held, at the end of a decade marked by drought in the Sahel and devastating cyclones in Bangladesh and Burma.

Exxon executives, who naturally followed all these debates, were reassured. An internal document provides a concise but basically accurate summary of the strategy explicitly chosen by the American elites at the turn of the 1970s and 1980s: 'We can either adapt our civilisation to a warmer planet or avoid the problem by sharply curtailing the use of fossil fuels. The general consensus is that society has sufficient time to technologically adapt to a CO_2 greenhouse effect.'[51]

Ronald Reagan's presidential election dispelled the last remaining illusions. Kellogg, who in 1980 explained that it would take only fifty years to make a transition, acknowledged in 1987 that 'it is unlikely that we will take measures to avoid climate change, and in fact the opposite is true. It is therefore prudent to prepare for it.'[52] Shortly before his death, Carroll Wilson was awarded the Tyler Prize, considered to be the Nobel Prize for the environment. His speech focused on genetic engineering: with climate change inexorable, it was time to create new seeds for a warmer world.[53]

Third group or fifth column?

Initially, the existence of the IPCC did not alter this climate strategy, combining transition claims and resignation to adaptation. It should be pointed out that when it was set up in 1988, this institution had nothing to do with the image of climate paladin that it acquired in the 2000s.[54] The aim of governments, that of the United States in particular, was to regain control over international climate experts, who were quick to brandish emission-reduction targets without weighing up their economic effects. In the mid-1980s, the United Nations Environment Programme (UNEP), under the aegis of the Egyptian biologist Mostafa Tolba, had played a major role in the Vienna Convention and the Montreal Protocol on the protection of the ozone layer. Tolba intended to repeat this success with greenhouse gases. In the small world of international climate expertise, Tolba's position stands out. For example, at the climate conference held in Villach, Austria, in October 1985, there was a striking contrast between his highly alarmist opening speech and the timid conclusions of the climatologists and economists. On the one hand, a common-sense reaction – to start reducing emissions without delay – on the other, a call for prudence based on a postponed transition.[55]

In 1986, UNEP, the World Meteorological Organization and the International Council for Science (ICSU) set up the Advisory Group on Greenhouse Gases (AGGG), a committee on global warming made up of a dozen carefully chosen scientists. For these experts, the time for scientific discussion was over; what was needed was a climate convention organizing an immediate reduction in emissions.[56] During the summer of 1988, this prospect seemed to be getting closer. In June, James Hansen made his famous statement to the US Senate that global warming had already begun in the stifling heat of a scorching summer. At the same time, an international climate conference was being held in Toronto, which was well attended by the press. Two heads of state, Brian Mulroney of Canada and

Gro Harlem Brundtland of Norway, were taking part, along with representatives of forty-eight governments. Brundtland compared the effects of climate change to those of a nuclear war, and a US senator called for a reduction by a quarter of global emissions by 2005. The final declaration of the conference took up this objective (a 20 per cent reduction) and added the creation of an atmospheric fund financed by a carbon tax levied on rich countries.[57]

For the US administration, it was out of the question to let the UN, a few international technocrats and a handful of scientists, sometimes linked to environmental NGOs, dictate the terms of future climate negotiations. A letter dated 27 January 1988 from the State Department's Bureau of Ocean, Environment and Science to the US representative to the World Meteorological Organization sheds a harsh light on the IPCC's initial function:

> I believe it important that we take an active role in shaping this panel to meet U.S. Government objectives . . . Governments, rather than individuals, should be invited to participate in the panel. The government representatives should reflect the full range of their governments' policy interests, including for instance, energy and agricultural policies as well as science and environmental policies.[58]

The end of the missive is just as clear: the AGGG must be disbanded. A subsequent document dated 15 August 1988 repeated the IPCC's objective: to define 'achievable and reasonable objectives'.[59]

In 1988, the IPCC was chaired by Bert Bolin, a Swedish climatologist who had been following these issues since the 1960s. More revealing was the distribution of the chairmanships of the three groups that make up the IPCC. The United States got the chairmanship of Group III, which was the group most likely to influence the content of the forthcoming climate convention. The USSR succeeded in placing the meteorologist Yuri Izrael at the head of Group II: so that the question of impacts was entrusted to one of the few openly climate-sceptical scientists in the field. In 2004, Izrael pleaded with Vladimir Putin *against* Russia's ratification of the Kyoto

Protocol, but this did not prevent him from remaining vice-chairman of the IPCC until 2008.[60]

To head Group III, the US government chose Frederick Bernthal, a nuclear energy specialist who had just been appointed by Ronald Reagan as Assistant Secretary of State for Oceans and International Environmental Affairs. Questioned by Senator Joe Biden at the time of his appointment, he was particularly evasive: 'there is no conflict between global warming and economic development . . . as demonstrated by the concept of "sustainable development".'[61] A memo from the White House in August 1989 sets out the guidelines for the work of Group III: 'Protecting the climate per se is not our objective – rather, our objective is to protect social, environmental, and economic well-being from the adverse effects likely to result from global climate change.'[62] The aim was not to stop global warming, but to slow it down. Adaptation was presented as the main response, which would have to be facilitated by transferring various technologies to poorer countries, in particular those that could protect coastlines from rising sea levels.[63] Bernthal was a supporter of laissez-faire. In August 1990, at a plenary meeting of the IPCC, Tolba summed up the work of Group I: stabilization of temperature required a 60 per cent reduction in CO_2 emissions, the 'facts are terrifying. They demand that we act now.'[64] The American retorted that one should not neglect the *positive* impacts of global warming.[65] In any case, Bernthal was sure the solution would come from technological progress, and he quoted the usual fable of the whales and the oil so dear to Exxon.[66]

In 1991, another American, Robert A. Reinstein, succeeded Bernthal as head of Group III. Rather problematically, he was at the same time chief negotiator for the United States for the UN Convention Framework on Climate Change (1992). In a fascinating interview he gave twenty years later to young American diplomats, he ticked off the list just about every argument of climate scepticism: correlation is not causation, CO_2 rise could be the result of global warming not its cause; water vapour is the main greenhouse gas; 'the vegetarians wouldn't have anything to eat if we eliminated

CO2'; scientists are ideologues attracted 'like moth to a flame' by the climate issue, etc.[67] After heading Group III of the IPCC (and briefly Group II), Reinstein became a lobbyist for the fossil-fuel industries. In 2004, he published an article containing all the classic arguments of the merchants of doubt.[68]

In the above-mentioned interview, Reinstein candidly outlined the American negotiating strategy that led to the 1992 United Nations Framework Convention, a text that sets no quantified objectives and which was a far cry from the ambitious goals of the 1988 Toronto conference. The United States was on the defensive:

> The whole world was against us and for various reasons. The developing countries wanted the money and technology for free, the Europeans wanted the binding targets because they had already decided that they were no longer competitive in energy intensive industries, and were going to be de-industrializing. Also they were jealous of us because we were energy rich and they were energy poor, and they wanted to hobble us in the same way.[69]

In Reinstein's view, the climate negotiations were just the continuation of trade negotiations. The Europeans were waving around purely aspirational climate objectives as a means of undermining American industrial competitiveness. 'Europe and the EU, old as it is, is kind of like a teenager. They know everything and understand nothing.'[70] In 1991, John Sununu, George H. W. Bush's chief of staff, gave Reinstein his road map for the climate negotiations: the United States would not provide any financial compensation and would refuse to accept any emission-reduction targets. In short: 'no money, no target'. Reinstein therefore proposed to focus the discussion on technology transfers and technical assistance. 'How you frame the issue determines how it gets negotiated' he summed up for future diplomats. To Sununu, who was concerned about intellectual property rights, he replied that there was nothing to worry about: these transfers would enable the United States to gain a foothold in the rapidly growing and liberalizing energy markets in poor countries.

President Bush's chief of staff gave him a blank cheque, with a phrase that sums up the essentially rhetorical status of the energy transition within the White House: 'Okay, play the technology card.'

This card suited many people: the oil-exporting countries, of course; the USSR, whose economy was particularly carbon-intensive; the majority of Asian countries with coal-based electricity mixes; and naturally the United States, the world's biggest emitter and leading technological power, which had every interest in dangling the prospect of salvation in innovation. Finally, the joker in the 'energy transition' pack belonged to the ideological atmosphere created by the business world at the turn of the 1980s and 1990s. For some years, multinationals had been turning their attention to the environment and promoting their ability to innovate and find solutions, provided they were allowed to operate without interference. It was at this time that voluntary commitments, codes of business conduct, green labels, and 'social and environmental responsibility' triumphed, and transition was just one aspect of the green logorrhoea that invaded entrepreneurial language.[71]

At the outset, the reports issued by Group III of the IPCC reflected American positions, showcasing a blend of a wait-and-see approach to climate change and faith in future technological solutions. Considering Reinstein's dual role, it is unsurprising that the proposed 'solutions' aligned well with those advocated by American climate diplomacy. Group III was also influenced by the 'smooth transition' proposed by IIASA, an institution whose influence on global energy modelling cannot be overstated. In the early 1990s, the Nordhaus line prevailed: he was the primary economist consulted by Reinstein[72] and at the Group III meetings held at IIASA he defended procrastination more than ever. He now had a new tool at his disposal, the model (DICE), which had the outrageous pretension of calculating the optimal temperature of the Earth.[73] According to the model, this temperature corresponded to a global warming of 3.5°C . . . This might seem like a lot but, Nordhaus argued, one should not forget that 'humanity is a technological and nomadic species . . . Doesn't *Homo adaptus* thrive in all climates from Hong Kong to Helsinki?'[74] His compatriot Jesse Ausubel, who had already played an important role in organizing the 1979 Geneva climate conference, made a similar point. He combined a confidence in humanity's capacity to adapt with a confidence in the inherent ability of the energy system to evolve towards less carbon and more hydrogen, and coined the term 'decarbonization' to encapsulate this 'historical law', discovered in 1975 by Cesare Marchetti. Ironically, 'decarbonization' provided an additional argument for procrastination.

In the 1990s, Group III of the IPCC followed this wait-and-see approach. At a meeting in Washington in February 1990, there was talk only of stabilizing rather than decreasing global emissions. The Greenpeace representative pointed out that it was necessary to stabilize the *concentration* of atmospheric CO_2 rather than emissions.[75] The first Group III reports bear witness to the influence of Nordhaus's delaying tactics. In 1991, the most ambitious scenario envisaged stabilizing emissions at just under 20 Gt of CO_2 per year by the end of the twenty-first century. The second report (1995) stated that 'slowing the transition away from fossil fuels provides valuable time to develop low-cost, carbon-free alternatives, to allow the capital stock to adapt, and to remove carbon from the atmosphere via the carbon cycle'.[76] No actual transition away from fossil fuels was yet envisaged.

The influence of Group III on the IPCC in general should not be underestimated. After the climatologists Bert Bolin and Robert Watson, the chairmen of the IPCC were two economists at the heart of the Asian fossil-fuel boom. Rajendra K. Pachauri came from the Tata Energy Research Institute, the forecasting centre of the famous Indian conglomerate. During his tenure as chairman of the IPCC, he sat on the boards of the Oil and Natural Gas Corporation and the National Thermal Power Corporation – an Indian electricity giant that ranked sixth among the world's emitters. His successor, the Korean economist Hoesung Lee, chairman of the IPCC from 2015 to 2023, began his career at the time of President Nixon's 'independence project' as an economist at Exxon. An advisor to the South

Korean government on energy matters – his brother was the country's prime minister – he was for a long time on the board of directors
of Hyundai, a conglomerate encompassing automotive factories as
well as thermal power stations, coal and steel.

Delusional scenarios

From the 2000s onwards, energy transition became a major issue.
By 2010 the expression had regained the lexical importance it had in
1979; by 2020 it was three times more frequently used than forty
years earlier.[77] Many companies, even the most polluting, that had
been the champions of 'sustainable development' declared themselves to be 'in transition' from the 2000s onwards.

This lexical success is also due to the profound changes in the
IPCC's expertise. The fact that the IPCC has become the 'voice of
the climate'[78] and Group III the apostle of transition was by no
means obvious, and reflects the strength of the climatological diagnosis. Under pressure from scientists, island states and the European
Union, climate targets became increasingly ambitious: 2°C in the
2000s and 1.5°C at the 2015 Climate Change Conference (COP)
meeting.[79] Within Group III of the IPCC, economists such as Minh
Ha-Duong, Michael Grubb and Jean-Charles Hourcade battled
against the Nordhaus line and developed models showing the
advantages of acting as soon as possible.[80] They insisted on the risk
of 'carbon lock-in' – the inertia of investment in fossil-fuel
infrastructures – and the importance of endogenizing technological
progress in emissions models. While it may appear to be a technical
detail, it holds fundamental significance: as progress does not
materialize out of thin air it was imperative that we commence
decarbonization efforts as early as possible in order to mitigate the
associated costs. Despite his Nobel Prize, Nordhaus had lost the scientific battle: the stabilization scenarios of the first two Group III
reports were thrown out and we saw the emergence of emissions
pathways corresponding to a rapid transition away from fossil fuels.

The problem is that the world had in the meantime followed Nordhaus's 'optimal' trajectory. The synchronized and paradoxical increase in climate ambition and CO2 emissions thus led to increasingly unrealistic emission-reduction scenarios, with steep declines projected after 2020. Modellers agreed to create 1.5°C scenarios in exchange for significant funding, often provided by the European Union.[81] The production of Integrated Assessment Models (IAMs) has become a scientific field in its own right, with its own journals, awards and careers, involving more than 1,500 researchers and dozens of teams around the world.[82] Models with a variety of acronyms (FAIR, FUND, PACE or even IMAGE, which dates back to Häfele's project) are becoming increasingly complex, requiring ever-greater computing power and money.[83] They are branching out into families and sub-families, forming an inextricable jungle that is difficult to understand for novices like me, but also, it would seem, even for insiders.

One thing is certain: in order to fit a growing global economy into carbon budgets that are melting like snow in the sun, *all* the scenarios are forced to resort to extraordinary means, namely huge quantities of 'negative emissions'. One of the perverse effects of modelling is that it has introduced into the climate debate some rather outlandish technological options. For example, the massive use of bioenergy combined with the capture and storage of CO2 (BECCS). In practical terms, the idea is to burn fast-growing trees in biomass-power stations, then capture the CO2 leaving the chimneys and bury it in the ground. In its latest report, Group III estimates that in order to avoid exceeding 2°C by 2100, this industry, which is still non-existent, would have to pump from the atmosphere and bury underground between 170 and 900 gigatonnes of CO2 by 2100 – absolutely gigantic quantities, equivalent to or even greater than the world's wood production.[84] To have an effect, this undertaking would have to be scaled up to staggering proportions, with some scenarios forecasting a forest plantation area dedicated to BECCS of 1.2 billion hectares, or more than three times the surface of India.[85]

The history of climate change expertise is riddled with weird technological proposals. Although geo-engineering is often presented as Plan B, it actually appeared *before* the idea of energy transition. In 1965, in *Restoring the Quality of our Environment*, a report submitted to President Johnson, the chapter on global warming, written by Roger Revelle and Charles Keeling, did not even mention a possible reduction in fossil fuels. Only one so-called 'compensatory' measure is envisaged: covering the oceans with reflective particles to increase their albedo.[86] Coming back to BECCS, this proposal dates back to 1977. It was put forward by the British scientist Freeman Dyson. Better known for his work in quantum physics and his far-fetched plans for interstellar travel than for his expertise in forestry, he nonetheless believed that it would be enough to plant 'a thousand billion fast-growing trees' to solve the climate problem.[87] This salvation in the trees was then pursued by the oil companies, which have discovered a sudden passion for protecting forests in poor countries.[88] Similarly, when it comes to carbon storage, the continuity of strange projects is impressive. In 2005, just as

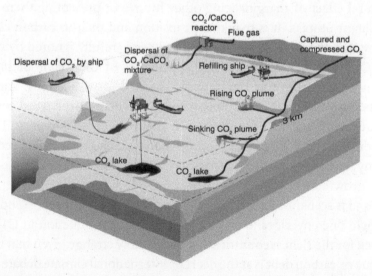

Permanent storage of CO2 in the form of underwater lakes. (IPCC, *Special Report on Carbon Dioxide Capture and Storage*, 2005, p. 280.)

George W. Bush's administration was launching a Carbon Seques-tration Leadership Forum with Australia – at the height of the coal boom – the IPCC's Group III published a special report on the sub-ject. It contained the same projects as those being pursued by American conservatives, such as artificial 'lakes' of carbon dioxide at the bottom of the oceans, where cold and pressure would keep the gas in a liquid state.

This report, which bears the IPCC stamp, borrowed a termin-ology ('CO_2 lake') that was actually coined thirty years earlier by Cesare Marchetti and William Nordhaus when they speculated about climate technofixes at Laxenburg Castle. Marchetti's famously imaginative ideas included controlling the Earth's albedo by spread-ing aerosols in the stratosphere, or balancing the carbon cycle by injecting CO_2 off the coast of Gibraltar using what he termed a 'giga-mixer'. It is also logical that the person who thought of the inertia of energy systems also coined the term 'geo-engineering', in 1975.[89]

These days, projects to capture and store hundreds of billions of tonnes of CO_2, ranging from the bizarre to the impossible, and 'net zero' 2050 scenarios that nobody believes in any more, have the col-lateral effect of marginalizing other futures or presenting them as militant utopias. It is thanks to transition and then to carbon cap-ture that the issue of sufficiency has been carefully ignored by the IPCC for thirty years: the first appearance of the theme of *suffi-ciency* dates from the 2022 report. As for 'degrowth', this is still a taboo for Group III economists: 20 occurrences of the word com-pared with 2,700 for 'transition' in their March 2022 report. The economists point out that they are merely analysing a global econ-omy that is in fact oriented towards growth – their models are based on growth forecasts drawn up by the OECD – but all the same: of the 3,131 scenarios examined by Group III in their last report, not a single one envisages, even as a hypothesis, any reduction in GDP, even for the richest countries. It's all the more strange given that the issue of carbon debt is at the heart of international climate debates.[90]

According to Frederic Jameson's oft-cited words, 'it is easier to imagine the world's end than the end of capitalism'. Some experts

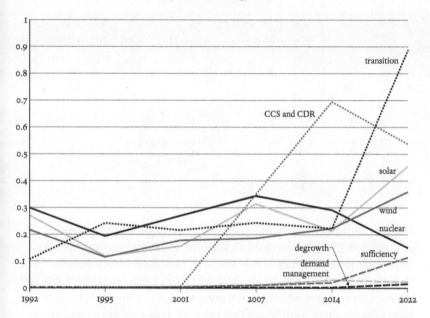

Frequency of a word per page, in the successive IPCC Group III reports. The scientific literature on 'solutions' summarized by Group III is clearly dominated by technological discussions. For example, 'demand management' is 20 times less frequent than 'carbon capture'. 'Sufficiency' makes a timid appearance in the last two reports. As for 'degrowth', the term is still almost impossible to find. In contrast, the 2007 report predicted the commercial availability of nuclear fusion reactors by 2050. The issue of carbon capture and storage took off in the 2014 and 2022 reports.

within Group III of the IPCC will have entertained visions of liquefied CO2 lakes resting on the ocean floor before considering the reduction of the size of any national economy.

In the 1980s other governments also recognized the inevitability of global warming. The main answer would reside in adaptation. In the UK, a government seminar on 26 April 1989 is particularly clear on this point. Margaret Thatcher had asked her ministers to present her with options for reducing British emissions. The responses were all along the same lines: there was no point in launching into a losing

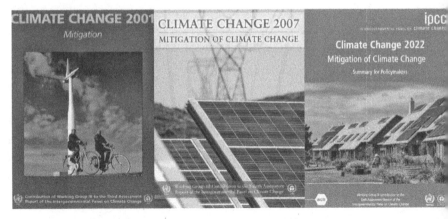

Despite the covers of its reports, Group III of the IPCC has more experts affiliated with fossil-fuel companies than from renewable energy, and, to my knowledge, none from bicycle manufacturers. Among the experts involved we find employees from Total, Exxon, ENI, Mobil Oil, Saudi Aramco, Elf, ESKOM, Du Pont, Japan Automobile Research Institute, Volvo, Aluminium Institute, World Coal Institute, Ford Motor Company, Air Transport Association of America, Mitsui Co. (commodity trading), IPIECA and the American Petroleum Institute (oil lobbies), as well as members from the Chinese Ministry of Electricity. At one point this presence of fossil-fuel companies became really embarrassing: Brian Flannery, a lead author of Group III for the 1998 and 2007 reports, was also the spokesperson for Exxon, which at that time was the main promoter of climate denialism. This infiltration should not be seen as manipulation: industry-affiliated experts are a minority, and researchers are not naive. However, it does reflect the IPCC's consensus-driven approach and its intention to include all 'stakeholders', even those contributing to the problem.

battle. According to the transport minister, we could certainly improve the efficiency of vehicles, but the gains would probably be cancelled out by rebound effects. As for improving public transport services, there was no guarantee that this would lead to a significant reduction in car use. 'Only a drastic increase in fuel prices . . . would have an appreciable effect.'[91] According to the minister for agriculture, 'to have an effect, the measures to be taken would have to be so severe that they would have catastrophic consequences for our competitiveness'.[92] The energy minister pointed out that the UK accounted for just 3 per cent of emissions, and that this share would fall rapidly with the emergence of China and India, so even heroic efforts would have no discernible effect on the climate:

> any attempt by the UK to make radical changes to our energy supply system would inevitably have very large costs. Whatever our aspirations . . . it would not be reasonable unilaterally to inflict such costs on ourselves, and to put ourselves as a consequence at a competitive disadvantage.[93]

The conclusion was clear: 'there is little we can do at national, or even international level to prevent global warming. We can only hope to mitigate its effects and adapt to them.'[94] It was at this time that Great Britain spoke out against the objectives of the 1988 Toronto conference, and then against the European eco-tax project. France, under the aegis of Michel Rocard, had initially promoted this scheme – which benefited its nuclear-powered industry – before doing an about-face just before the 1992 Rio conference.[95] Without saying so, without discussing it, in the 1980s and 1990s, the industrial countries chose – if that word has any meaning – growth and global warming and gave in to adaptation. This resignation was never made explicit. 'It would be wrong to give the impression that the United Kingdom's main response to the risk of climatic change was to be adaptation rather than prevention', stated a confidential note to Thatcher.[96] Populations were not consulted, especially those who will be and already are the victims.

Perception of an economic and climatic *fatum* presided over the coal revival, the oil counter-shock, suburbanization, consumerism in rich countries and the electrification of the poor world. This growth dynamic was more powerful than any climate warning, however clear and thunderous. 'Transition' is clearly not the cause of climate resignation, though it is merely its justification. Since the 1980s, it has accompanied general procrastination, and it continues to do so.

Conclusion:
The Weight of History

After so many false starts, has the transition finally begun? The fall in the cost of renewable energies and the fact that they are now competitive, including with coal, might have led some to believe that the material world was on the verge of a radical shift in its energy foundations. The aim of this book is not to criticize 'the transition', if by this term we mean the development of renewable energies, but this necessary condition is far from sufficient, and it is unreasonable to expect more from solar panels and wind turbines than they can deliver.

First, decarbonizing electricity remains difficult. The growth of renewable electricity is not incompatible with maintaining, and sometimes developing, fossil-fuel capacity. By 2022, despite the boom in renewables, emissions from the electricity sector were still rising globally.[1] Technical and economic constraints mean that renewable energies are not a 'like for like' substitute for fossil fuels. For example, in the Chinese region of Inner Mongolia, 'new energy bases', i.e. huge energy parks, have recently been inaugurated, combining solar panels, wind turbines and . . . new coal-fired power stations. These plants, which burn cheap local coal, make it possible to compensate for the variability of renewables and to recoup the particularly high connection costs, as the electricity is consumed 2,000 kilometres further east. It has been estimated that 35–40 per cent of the wind and solar power capacity built recently in China has been bundled with coal power.[2] At the 2023 COP, the Chinese envoy explained that it was 'unrealistic' to completely eliminate fossil fuels which are used to maintain grid stability.[3] This is partly why the somewhat vague term 'transition away from fossil fuels'

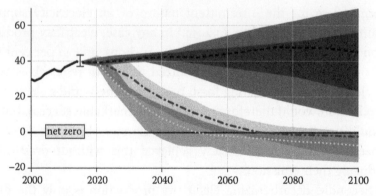

In 2023, CO2 emissions were around 50% higher than in 1990, but their rate of increase had fallen: from 2.1% for the period 2000–2010 to 1.3% for the period 2010–19. To avoid exceeding 1.5°C, emissions must be zero from 2050 and then become negative. The 2°C target allows two more decades. The upper curve corresponds to current policies and leads to a temperature rise of around 3.2°C. (IPCC, *Climate Change, Synthesis Report*, 2023, p. 22.)

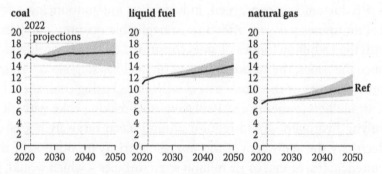

Global CO2 emissions in billions of tonnes. In its latest projections, which include the falling cost of renewables, the US Energy Agency predicts that coal will stabilize and oil and natural gas will rise until 2050. The EIA assumes economic growth of 2.6% per year and decarbonized electricity production of 54–67% in 2050. (Energy Information Administration, 'International Energy Outlook', 2023, p. 15.)

was preferred to 'phasing out'. The US Department of Energy, which does not play the net-zero scenario game, does forecast a reduction in the use of fossil fuels in electricity production, but this would be followed by a stabilization at a high level, in part to compensate for the intermittent nature of an electricity supply dominated by renewables in 2050.[4] In any case, electricity production accounts for only 40 per cent of emissions, and 40 per cent of this electricity is already decarbonized thanks to renewables and nuclear power. Eliminating fossil fuels from the world's electricity production would therefore represent a remarkable success, but it would not be enough to achieve the climate objectives. Several dozen countries have already achieved this without drastically reducing their emissions.[5]

Secondly, decarbonizing electricity production is only the first and easiest stage in the 'transition'. Without even mentioning aviation or maritime transport, the production of key materials such as steel, cement and, to a lesser extent, plastics and fertilizers, on which today's infrastructure, machinery, logistics and agriculture depend, remains very difficult to decarbonize.

As far as 'green steel' – that is steel produced by using hydrogen as a reductant – is concerned, industrialists are announcing a few million tonnes per year after 2030, a negligible quantity compared with the 1.7 billion tonnes of steel consumed each year worldwide.[6] Since the 2000s, the carbon intensity of steel has stagnated.[7] Today, three-quarters of the world's steel is produced using coal, and a lot of it: 1 billion tonnes in all.[8] Replacing steel-making coke with electrolytic hydrogen would require around 4,000 terawatt hours of electricity, the equivalent of the annual electricity production of the United States, or that of 1.2 million wind turbines – which would, in turn, require significant quantities of steel.[9] Moreover, growth in steel demand is to be expected in poorer countries, where steel stocks – mainly in the form of infrastructure and buildings – are 15 times lower than in rich countries (less than 1 tonne per capita compared with around 15 tonnes). And it is unlikely that this steel will be produced using hydrogen.[10]

As far as cement is concerned, its so-called 'greening' consists of replacing clinker with steel-making slag or fly ash from coal-power plants. These practices, which are sometimes presented as innovative, date from the 1920s and are entirely dependent on fossil fuels.[11]

Despite the rapid modernization of cement plants since the 2000s, the carbon intensity of cement has increased by 1.5 per cent per year over the last decade. Emissions from cement plants have tripled since 1990, accounting for 8 per cent of global emissions.[12]

Another example is plastic, which is responsible for 3–5 per cent of global emissions and whose growth seems unstoppable. Production has quadrupled since 1990 and vast markets remain to be conquered. On average, an American consumes 4 times more plastic than a Chinese person, and 15 times more than an Indian. As with cement, the carbon intensity of plastics has increased over the last few decades as more of them are produced in Asia from coal.[13] The problem is that substitute materials – paper and, especially, aluminium – have an even higher carbon footprint.[14] Whatever happens to the internal combustion engine, plastics will continue to ensure decades of profits for the oil industry.[15]

Finally, there are nitrogen fertilizers, which are responsible for 1.5 per cent of emissions at the production stage – which we might be able to reduce using 'green' hydrogen – but 5 per cent if we take into account their conversion into nitrous oxide by soil bacteria.[16]

Wind turbines and solar panels are remarkable technologies for producing electricity, but they are of little use in the production of these key materials.[17] To believe that innovation can decarbonize the steel industry, cement works, the plastics industry and fertilizer production and use in thirty or forty years, when recent trends have been the opposite, is a very risky technological and climatic gamble. Taken together, steel, cement, fertilizers and plastics account for more than a quarter of global emissions, enough to put the Paris Agreement target out of reach.[18] If 'green' electricity powers the same grey world of cars, cement, steel, plastic and industrial agriculture, global warming will only be slowed.

Thirdly, like all other energies, renewables are caught up in the infinite web of material symbioses. According to recent calculations, the construction of a renewable-energy-production infrastructure on a global scale would ultimately represent only a small amount of CO_2, on the order of 50 Gt, or a year of global emissions, to manufacture solar panels and wind turbines as well as the materials (silicon, steel, aluminium, etc.) that make them up – an undeniably worthwhile climate investment.[19] The problem is rather what we are going to do with this low-carbon electricity.

'Transition technologies' are not immune to rebound effects and ripple effects on other sectors. The climate benefits of renewables depend entirely on how this 'clean' electricity is used. In 2023, the world's largest floating wind farm was inaugurated in the Norwegian Sea: it belongs to Equinor – formerly Statoil – which uses it to power oil platforms. Similarly, in Qatar, Total is investing in a huge photovoltaic plant to 'green' gas extraction. In Texas windmills are now providing a large share of the electricity used by oil pumpjacks. Once again, this kind of symbiosis is nothing new: in the 1970s it was American oil companies that launched the solar-panel industry in an effort to diversify, and also because they were looking to power their installations in the Gulf of Mexico.[20] And if we go back further, at the beginning of the twentieth century, hydroelectricity was used to produce calcium carbide crystals, a half-fossil, half-renewable energy, which was extremely important because they powered acetylene welding sets. While solar panels and wind turbines reduce the carbon footprint of electricity production, the problem is that this electricity powers a world whose very materiality is, and will be for a long time to come, based on carbon.

A few historical analogies help us to understand the problem. The reduction in carbon intensity brought about by renewables is remarkable (a twelve-fold reduction compared with gas-fired power stations), but it is not unprecedented. Admittedly, industrialists in the twentieth century were not concerned about CO_2, but they did seek to reduce their production costs and therefore save fossil fuels. And, sometimes, they were very successful. For example, in the first quarter of that century, the switch from steam engines to steam turbines and electric motors reduced the carbon intensity of mechanical power by a factor of 10.[21] In the same way the switch from wood to coal as a fuel in the nineteenth century divided the 'wood intensity' of energy by 40 (a tonne of pit props made it possible to extract 20 tonnes of coal) but paradoxically led to an increase in wood consumption. Naturally, we have to be wary of these historical analogies, but the dynamics of the rebound effect and the symbiotic effect are empirically more accurate than simplistic stories of energy transitions.

With the falling cost of renewables, a second factor of hope is the reduction in the carbon intensity of the economy. Whereas 450 grams of CO_2 had to be emitted to produce one dollar of global GNP in 1980, this figure was 260 grams in 2020.[22] By extrapolation, it is easy to imagine a decarbonization of the world economy simply by accelerating this trend. But this ratio between two aggregates is obviously too crude to understand what is happening in the material world. The fall in carbon intensity since 1980 in fact conceals the unassailable and growing role of fossil fuels in the manufacture of just about everything, a role that they are fulfilling, it is true, more efficiently. Since the 1980s, global agriculture has become increasingly dependent on oil and methane as a result of advances in mechanization and the growing use of nitrogen fertilizers. Mining and metallurgy, faced with declining resource quality, are in some cases becoming more energy-intensive.[23] Building materials are becoming increasingly carbon-intensive: steel more so than wood, aluminium more so than steel, polyurethane more so than glass wool, wood panels more so than planks.[24] Although concrete is less energy-intensive than bricks, in many poor or formerly poor countries it has replaced low-carbon materials such as adobe and bamboo.[25] Finally, the extension of value chains, subcontracting and globalization are increasing the number of kilometres travelled by each commodity or component of a commodity, and therefore the role of oil in the smooth running of the economy. These phenomena have been masked by the growing efficiency of machines and the weight of services in global GNP, but they are nonetheless essential obstacles on the road to decarbonization.

What is more, the economy's growing energy efficiency is based in part on the use of ever-more sophisticated objects, blending ever-more finely a wider variety of materials. The imbroglio of wood, coal and oil that this book has studied obviously forms only the framework of an infinitely more vast and intertwined history of materials. For example, a tyre in 2020 contained as many different elements as a whole car a century earlier. A telephone in the 1920s contained twenty different materials; a century later, a smartphone uses sixty of the eighty-seven metals in the periodic table of elements.[26] By increasing the material complexity of objects, technological progress reinforces the symbiotic nature of the economy. It certainly increases energy efficiency, but it also makes recycling difficult if not impossible. Over time, the material world has become an increasingly vast and complex matrix, entangling a greater variety of materials, each consumed in greater quantities. These few historical observations do not derive from an irrefutable law of thermodynamics: they merely illustrate the enormity of the challenge ahead – or the scale of the disaster to come.

In the 2000s, scientists introduced the notion of the Anthropocene to describe the irreversibility of the processes set in motion by human action on the Earth system. In reality, the Anthropocene refers to a double irreversibility, a double accumulation, an accumulation of accumulations: not only are material flows piling up in the various compartments of the Earth system, but anthropogenic material flows are also following an additive logic.[27] Despite its symbiotic accumulation dynamic and the structural presence of carbon within it, we continue to attribute great malleability to the material world and to give history a weight it no longer has. For while the origins of global warming are easy to trace, what would stop it is beyond historical imagination. Ever since economic development spread across the globe, history has been slipping by, leaving only tiny traces on the curve of CO_2 emissions. The First World War, followed by the Spanish flu pandemic, led to a 17 per cent drop, while the Great Depression reduced emissions by a quarter. Conversely, the oil crisis of 1979 and the financial crisis of 2008 had modest effects (−6% and −1%).[28] Even the Covid confinements of

2020, which affected up to 4 billion people, only reduced global emissions by 5 per cent, and they picked up again in 2021. Despite these statistics, people still like to comment in the news about this or that specific event and set it up as a hypothetical 'tipping point' for the 'transition'. For example, it has been imagined that the invasion of Ukraine would push decarbonization, even though Russian gas exported to Europe accounts for only 1.5 per cent of global emissions.[29] Similarly, after the US Inflation Reduction Act was passed, the economist Paul Krugman wrote, without batting an eyelid, that it was 'a major step towards saving the planet', no doubt forgetting that the United States accounted for only 13 per cent of global emissions and that the Act subsidizes both renewables and fossil fuels – carrots without sticks.

Faced with the climate titan, economics and other social sciences have often promised much more than they could offer. Many studies propose 'solutions' without having assessed the depth of the problem. As the technical hurdles are left to the expertise of Group III of the IPCC, the transition becomes solvable in various economic or social reforms. Economists have long promoted 'creative destruction', guided by the universal carbon tax, a strategy that is certainly optimal in their models, but impracticable in a world riddled with inequalities and which also relies on extraordinary confidence in innovation. After the emphasis on the 'invisible hand' that characterized the climate policies of the 1990s and 2000s, it is now the financial arm of the State that is credited with great powers. A nebulous group of neo-Keynesian experts, NGOs and foundations thriving in the shadow of the COPs regularly put forward estimates of the 'cost of transition': 4 trillion dollars a year in a recent report, without any indication of how this fortune would change the chemistry of cement, steel or nitrogen oxides, or how it would convince producing countries to close their oil and gas wells. In the same way, contemporary political science is full of 'transition manuals' detailing 'post-carbon' coalitions, as if all this were within the reach of their enlightened advice. Every political project, no matter how just and necessary – from reducing inequality to ending patriarchy – has curiously discovered supposed climate virtues. It's all very well to mock the supposed 'techno-solutionism' of engineers, but the normative positions on climate that prevail in the social sciences are even more ridiculous.

This essay in materialist history offers no magic bullet, no 'real transition' programme, no emancipating green utopia. What it does show, however, is the danger of basing our visions of the future on bad history, and the need, if we are ever to hope to build a climate policy that is even remotely rigorous, for a new understanding of energy and material dynamics. Once again, the aim is not to criticize renewables or even to show that a transition is impossible – in the time allowed for the 2°C target, the answer would have been fairly predictable anyway. I simply wanted to understand where this strange and strangely consensual future came from. Born with the 'atomic age', envisaged as a distant response by rich countries to the depletion of fossil fuels, 'transition' has been taken up again, without any serious justification, as a way of thinking about the climate challenge.

Transition is the ideology of capital in the twenty-first century. It turns evil into cure, polluting industries into the green industries of the future, and innovation into our lifeline. Transition puts capital on the right side of the climate battle. Thanks to transition, we are talking about trajectories to 2100, electric cars and hydrogen-powered aircraft rather than material consumption levels and distribution. Very complex solutions in the future make it impossible to do simple things now. The seductive power of transition is immense: we all need future changes to justify present procrastination. The history of transition, though, and the unsettling sense of déjà vu it engenders should warn us. We must not let the technological promises of carbon-free material abundance repeat themselves again and again: after crossing the 2°C threshold in the second half of this century, they will just as surely lead us towards greater perils.

Notes

Introduction

1 It is because the historiography of technology is stagist that David Edgerton's key book, *The Shock of the Old: A Global History of Technology in the Twentieth Century* (London, 2006), was perceived as 'iconoclastic', even though it rightly highlighted a very widespread bias in the history of technology consisting of equating the techniques *used* in one era with the new techniques *appearing* in that era.

2 Food and Agriculture Organization (hereafter FAO), 'Forest Global Resources Assessment', 2020, graph p. 113 and FAO, 'Trends in Wood Products', 2005, p. 5; Dudley Stamp, 'The forest of Europe: present and future', *Empire Forestry Journal*, 7, 2, 1928, pp. 185–202.

3 In 2019, the IEA estimated that renewables, nuclear and biomass (including biofuels and waste) would provide 2.5%, 5% and 9.4% respectively of the world's primary energy. The 5% of nuclear power is primary energy, and given the heat losses, nuclear only provides 3% of the world's final energy. IEA, 'Key World Energy Statistics', 2019, p. 6. According to the FAO, wood provides 6% of the world's primary energy: FAO, 'State of the World's Forests', 2014.

4 See Chapter 5.

5 Calculations based on the database of the Carbon Dioxide Information Analysis Center of the US Department of Energy (https://cdiac.ess-dive.lbl.gov). It should be noted that this database and other works on the quantitative history of energy are based, for the period before 1985, on data collected by Bouda Etemad and Jean Luciani, *World Energy Production, 1800–1985* (Geneva, 1991), working under the direction of historians Paul Bairoch and Jean-Claude Toutain.

6 World Bank, 'Global Perspective on Coal Jobs and Managing Labor Transition out of Coal', 2021. Thanks to David Edgerton for this reference.

7 International Energy Agency (hereafter IEA), 'World Energy Outlook 2021', p. 59 and IEA, 'Nuclear Power in a Clean Energy System', 2019, p. 11.

8 EU, 'Raw Materials Scoreboard', 2021, pp. 81–2. In 2015, five of its members – Germany, the UK, France, Italy and the Netherlands – were among the top ten exporters of mining equipment. Cf. EU, 'Raw Materials Scoreboard', 2018.

9 https://climate-change.data.gov.uk/articles/emissions-embedded-in-trade-and-impacts-on-climate-change.

10 Calculations based on X. F. Wu and G. Q. Chen, 'Coal use embodied in globalized world economy: from source to sink through supply chain', *Renewable and Sustainable Energy Reviews*, 81, 2018, pp. 978–93. These figures are consistent with the recent findings of the French High Council for the Climate: 'the carbon footprint of the French', wrote the High Council, 'increased by 20% between 1995 and 2017. Since 1995, emissions linked to imports have doubled, while those linked to domestic production have fallen by a fifth ... In 2015, the French carbon footprint reached 11t of CO_2 e per capita, compared with national emissions estimated at 6.6t CO_2 e per capita'. See Haut Conseil pour le Climat, 'Annual Report 2019', p. 34.

11 On the issues involved in attributing emissions, see Antonin Pottier et al., 'Qui émet du CO_2? Panorama critique des inégalités écologiques en France', *Revue de l'OFCE*, 169, 2020, pp. 73–132.

12 *La Suisse sur sa montagne de charbon*, report by the NGO Public Eye, November 2022.

13 Bruce Podobnik, *Global Energy Shifts. Fostering Sustainability in a Turbulent Age* (Philadelphia, PA, 2005); Alfred W. Crosby, *Children of the Sun. A History of Humanity's Unappeasable Appetite for Energy* (New York, 2006); Manfred Weissenbacher, *Sources of Power: How Energy Forges Human History* (Santa Barbara, CA, 2009); Bent Sorensen, *A History of Energy: Northern Europe from the Stone Age to the Present Day* (London, 2012); Jean-Claude Debeir, Jean-Paul Deléage and Daniel Hémery, *A History of Energy. Les servitudes de la puissance* (Paris, 2013); Richard Rhodes, *Energy, A Human History* (New York, 2018); Anthony N. Penna, *A History of Energy Flows. From Human Labor to Renewable Power*

(London, 2021); Brian C. Black, *To Have and Have Not: Energy in World History* (London, 2022); Brian C. Black, *Energy Revolutions: A History* (Hoboken, NJ, 2023). Some authors, such as Podobnik, do note the cumulative nature of the history of energy on a global scale, but still propose 'transition' narratives. Note that pre-1970 works are less focused on the narrative of transitions, cf. Fred Cottrell, *Energy and Society. The Relation Between Energy, Social Change and Economic Development* (New York, 1955); Sam H. Schurr and Bruce Netschert, *Energy in The American Economy, 1850–1975* (Baltimore, MD, 1960).

14 John McNeill and Peter Engelke, *The Great Acceleration. An Environmental History of the Anthropocene since 1945* (Cambridge, MA, 2014), p. 9.

15 Astrid Kander, Paolo Malamina and Paul Warde, *Power to the People. Energy in Europe Over the Last Five Centuries* (Princeton, NJ, 2013), pp. 251–6.

16 Vaclav Smil, *Energy Transitions. History, Requirements, Prospects* (Santa Barbara, CA, 2010). In his latest book on the subject, *Energy and Civilization. A History* (Cambridge, MA, 2017), Smil briefly mentions the phenomenon that is central to this book: 'every transition to a new energy source has been powered by existing energies: the transition from wood to coal had to be powered by human muscles' (p. 230). But this symbiotic relationship that Smil mentions, in relation to child labour in the mines, is limited neither to the 'Victorian' phase of the transition to fossil fuels, nor indeed to human power.

17 For an extensive bibliography see: Daniel Yergin, *Prize: The Epic Quest for Oil, Money & Power* (New York, 2009); John Hatcher, Michael Flinn, Roy Church, Barry Supple, William Ashworth et al., *The History of the British Coal Industry*, 5 vols (Oxford, 1986–93); Joachim Radkau, *Wood: A History* (New York, 2012); Charles-François Mathis, *La civilisation du charbon* (Paris, 2021); Jean-Marie Martin-Amouroux, *Charbon, les métamorphoses d'une industrie. La nouvelle géopolitique du XXIe siècle* (Paris, 2008).

18 Andreas Malm, *Fossil Capital. The Rise of Steam Power and the Roots of Global Warming* (London, 2016).

19 Timothy Mitchell, *Carbon Democracy. Political Power in the Age of Oil* (London, 2011).

20 Thanks to Adam Lucas for sharing the results of his ongoing research.

21 Patrick Ruhemann, 'Vapeur motrice et industrie au XIXe siècle', University of Paris X Nanterre thesis, 2007, pp. 428 and 430.

22 Theodore Steinberg, *Nature Incorporated. Industrialization and the Waters of New England* (Cambridge, 1992).

23 Raphael Samuel, 'Workshop of the world: steam power and hand technology in mid-Victorian Britain', *History Workshop Journal*, 3, 1, 1977, pp. 6–72; Richard H. Schallenberg, 'Evolution, adaptation and survival: the very slow death of the American charcoal iron industry', *Annals of Science*, 32, 4, 1975, pp. 341–58; Louis C. Hunter, A *History of Industrial Power in the United States, 1750–1930*. Vol. 1, *Waterpower in the Century of the Steam Engine* (Charlottesville, VA, 1979); Serge Benoît, *D'eau et de feu: forges et énergie hydraulique, XVIIIe–XXe siècle. Une histoire singulière de l'industrialisation française* (Rennes, 2020); Chris Evans and Göran Rydén, *The Industrial Revolution in Iron: The Impact of British Coal Technology in Nineteenth-Century Europe* (London, 2005); Eric Baratay, *Bêtes de somme. Des animaux au service des hommes* (Paris, 2010); Joel Tarr, *The Horse in the City. Living Machines in the Nineteenth Century* (Baltimore, MD, 2007); Sabine Barle, *L'invention des déchets urbains, 1790–1970* (Seyssel, 2005); François Jarrige and Mohamed Kasdi, 'Moteurs animés des filatures', in François Jarrige and Alexis Vrignon (eds), *Face à la puissance. Une histoire des énergies alternatives à l'âge industriel* (Paris, 2020); François Jarrige, *La ronde des bêtes. Le moteur animal et la fabrique de la modernité* (Paris, 2023).

24 The title of Louis C. Hunter's classic book, *Waterpower in the Century of the Steam Engine*, is a good indication of this: the terms should have been swapped.

25 Terry G. Jordan, 'Windmills in Texas', *Agricultural History*, 37, 2, 1963, pp. 80–85; Lindsay Baker, 'Turbine-type windmills of the Great Plains and Midwest', *Agricultural History*, 54, 1, 1980, pp. 38–51; *idem*, 'Irrigating with windmills on the Great Plains', *Great Plains Quarterly*, 1989, 9, 4, pp. 216–30; Robert W. Righter, *Wind Energy in America. A History* (Norman, OK, 1996). Elisha Fales applies the lessons of aerodynamics from the First World War to wind turbines. Cf. Palmer Cosslett Putnam, *Power from the Wind* (New York, 1948), p. 2.

26 Charles Dupin estimates the work produced by the 66,000 mills in France in the 1820s as that of 1.5 million men. See Charles Dupin, *Forces productives et commerciales de la France*, vol. 1 (Paris, 1827). Industrial statistics for 1899 show 47,000 hydraulic motors producing 574,000 horsepower, or the power of 4.2 million men if we take the generally accepted equivalence of 7 men for 1 horsepower. Cf. *Répartition des forces motrices à vapeur et hydrauliques en 1899* (Paris, 1900), Table A, p. 1.

27 That the history of energy is one of accumulation is a truism that has been commented on by economists since the 1930s. The historian of technology David Nye mentions this phenomenon several times, while envisaging a history of six successive 'energy systems' and presenting his work as a reconceptualization of Lewis Mumford: David Nye, *Consuming Power. A Social History of American Energies* (Cambridge, MA, 1998), pp. 249–64. In 2013, I insisted on the fact that we should be talking about energy additions rather than transitions, see Christophe Bonneuil and Jean-Baptiste Fressoz, *The Shock of the Anthropocene. The Earth, History and Us* (London, 2016). This point was echoed by Richard York and Shannon Elizabeth Bell, 'Energy transitions or additions? Why a transition from fossil fuels requires more than the growth of renewable energy', *Energy Research & Social Science*, 51, 2019, pp. 40–43.

28 Bertrand Gille wrote that 'technical systems have succeeded one another over time'. Gille's encyclopaedic history of techniques is in fact a history of new techniques. This leads him to make certain chronological errors. 'Since the end of the eighteenth century, coal has become the main source of energy', he writes, or 'at the end of the nineteenth century, oil took first place in energy consumption' (pp. 871–2). This can also be seen in his depiction of the 'technical system of the industrial revolution' (which he traces back to the 18th century), with the steam engine at the centre (p. 706). Or the importance he attaches to nuclear reactors, rocket engines and tidal power plants when he talks about contemporary energy sources. More generally, the chapter entitled 'Towards a contemporary technical system' focuses on high tech and even the futurology of the 1970s. See Bertrand Gille, *Histoire des techniques* (Paris, 1978), pp. 859–1023.

29 Robert C. Allen, a specialist in the economic history of the English industrial revolution, saw in the 'transition from organic to fossil fuels some useful parallels for the future': see Robert C. Allen, 'Backward into the future: the shift to coal and implications for the next energy transition', *Energy Policy*, 50, 2012, pp. 17–23; *idem*, 'Energy transitions in history: the shift to coal', in Richard W. Unger (ed.), *Energy Transitions in History: Global Cases of Continuity and Change*, RCC Perspectives 2013, vol. 2, pp. 11–15. We shall see that using history to read the future of energy is an ancient gesture. Without going back to Jevons, we find the question of how long the transition might take posed in exactly these terms by the Italian nuclear physicist Cesare Marchetti, to whom we shall return in Chapter 8. His disciples at the IIASA continued this method with constancy and fidelity. Cf. Arnulf Grubler, 'Energy transitions research: insights and cautionary tales', *Energy Policy*, 50, 2012, pp. 8–16; Charlie Wilson and Arnulf Grubler, 'Lessons from the history of technological change for clean energy scenarios and policies', *Natural Resources Forum*, 35, 2011, pp. 165–84; Charlie Wilson and Arnulf Grubler, *Energy Technology Innovations. Learning from Historical Successes and Failures* (Cambridge, 2014).

30 Frank W. Geels, 'Technological transitions as evolutionary reconfiguration processes: a multi-level perspective and a case-study', *Research Policy*, 31, 2002, pp. 1257–74.

31 Benjamin Sovacool, 'How long will it take? Conceptualizing the temporal dynamics of energy transitions', *Energy Research & Social Science*, 13, 2016, pp. 202–15.

32 See for example Johan Schot and Laur Kanger, 'Deep transitions: emergence, acceleration, stabilization and directionality', *Research Policy*, 47, 6, 2018, pp. 1045–59. Benjamin Sovacool and David J. Hess, 'Ordering theories: typologies and conceptual frameworks for socio-technical change', *Social Studies of Science*, 47, 5, 2017, pp. 703–50.

33 IPCC, *Climate Change 2022. Mitigation of Climate Change*, ch. 2, pp. 256, 369. Benjamin Sovacool examines the transition to be made in the light of 'previous transitions such as that from wood to coal or coal to oil'.

34 We could also add that the transition has not yet taken place, so the one to come is bound to be quicker.

1. *A History of Energy by Candlelight*

1 William Nordhaus, 'Do real-output and real-wage measures capture reality? The history of lighting suggests not', in Timothy F. Bresnahan and Robert J. Gordon (eds), *The Economics of New Goods* (Chicago, 1996), pp. 27–70. Frédéric Bastiat would no doubt have objected that once the sun was taken into account, the average price of light actually remained remarkably stable.

2 Certain high-profile economists, promoters of green growth, have a fairly immaterial view of the economy, and can write without batting an eyelid that the electric car is a carbon-free technology. See Philippe Aghion, Céline Antonin and Simon Bunel, *The Power of Creative Destruction. Economic Upheaval and the Wealth of Nations* (Cambridge, MA, 2021), pp. 173–92. For a critique see Antonin Pottier, Jean-Charles Hourcade and Etienne Espagne, 'Modelling the redirection of technical change: the pitfalls of incorporeal visions of the economy', *Energy Economics*, 42, 2014, pp. 213–18; Frank Aggeri, *L'innovation, mais pour quoi faire* (Paris, 2023).

3 https://paulromer.net/conditional-optimism-technology-and-climate/.

4 On this point: David Edgerton, *The Shock of the Old: A Global History of Technology in the Twentieth Century* (London, 2006).

5 William Norwood Sparhawk, 'Why Grow Timber?', US Department of Agriculture, 1928, p. 2.

6 Vaclav Smil, *Making the Modern World: Materials and Dematerialization* (Chichester, 2013); Tessaleno C. Devezas, António M. Vaz and Christopher L. Magee, 'Global pattern in materials consumption: an empirical study', in Tessaleno C. Devezas, João Leitão and Askar Sarygulov, *Industry 4.0, Studies on Entrepreneurship, Structural Change and Industrial Dynamics*, Springer International Publishing (Berlin and New York, 2017), pp. 263–92.

7 Of the seventy main raw materials, Christopher Magee and Tessaleno Devezas list only six that have declined since 1960: asbestos, mercury, beryllium, tellurium, thallium and sheep's wool, to which we could add whale oil. Cf. Christopher L. Magee and Tessaleno C. Devezas, 'A simple extension of dematerialization theory: incorporation of

technical progress and the rebound effect', *Technological Forecasting & Social Change*, 117, 2017, pp. 196–205.

8 F. Krausman et al., 'From resource extraction to outflows of wastes and emissions: the socioeconomic metabolism of the global economy, 1900–2015', *Global Environmental Change*, 52, 2018, pp. 131–40.

9 The famous graph produced by Nordhaus showing the collapse of the price of light is misleading as data points are based on innovation dates, not dates of usage.

10 Nordhaus, 'Do real-output and real-wage measures capture reality?' Historians have shown little interest in the history of candles, oil lamps and paraffin lamps in the 19th and 20th centuries, with gas and electricity attracting all the attention. It has become customary to tell a story in three acts: the traditional candles and oil lamps, which have received little attention; gas lighting in the 19th century, produced from coal; and electricity in the 20th century. On the beginnings of gas in Paris: Jean-Pierre Williot, *Naissance d'un service public, le gaz à Paris* (Paris, 1999); Jean-Baptiste Fressoz, 'The gas lighting controversy: Technological risk, expertise and regulation in nineteenth-century Paris and London', *Journal of Urban History*, 33, 5, 2007, pp. 729–55. On London: Leslie Tomory, *Progressive Enlightenment: The Origins of the Gaslight Industry, 1780–1820* (Cambridge, MA, 2012). The bibliography on early electricity is immense. See Alain Beltran and Patrice Carré, *La Fée et la servante. La société française face à l'électricité au XIXe–XXe siècle* (Paris, 2000). For a history of light, admittedly disenchanted but still a history of modernity, see Wolfgang Schivelbuch, *Disenchanted Night. The Industrialization of Light in the Nineteenth Century* (Berkaley, CA, 1995). Historians have done more work on public lighting than on domestic lighting. Cf. David Nye, *American Illuminations. Urban Lighting 1800–1920* (Cambridge, MA, 2018). Candles and oil lamps have been studied but for earlier periods. Cf. Stéphane Castelluccio, *L'éclairage, le chauffage et l'eau aux XVIIe et XVIIIe siècles* (Paris, 2016); Benjamin Bothereau, 'Jeux de lumières et d'obscurités de la lanterne publique: entre renforments sécuritaires, extinctions par économie et limites des innovations techniques (Paris, Barcelone, XVIIIe siècle)', *Journal of Energy History (JEHRHE)*, 2, special issue 'Light(s) and darkness(es)' April 2019;

William O' Dea, *A Social History of Lighting* (London, 1958), pp. 213–32, focuses on luminous organic fuels. This chapter takes up the quantitative work on luminous fuels in France carried out in my 'Une histoire matérielle de la lumière', in François Jarrige and Alexis Vrignon (eds), *Face à la puissance. Une histoire des énergies alternatives à l'âge industriel* (Paris, 2020), pp. 84–99. The best sources on the technological progress of organic lighting are still the works of the 19th century. Cf. Louis Figuier, *L'Art de l'éclairage* (Paris, 1887); Jules Turgan, 'Usine de bougies de Clichy', *Les grandes usines de France* (Paris, 1860), vol. I, pp. 129–44.

11 In his 1845 lecture, Faraday was careful to distinguish stearic candles from tallow candles: 'a stearin candle is not that ugly greasy thing, but a very clean thing'. See Michael Faraday, *A Course of Six Lectures on the Chemical History of a Candle* (London, 1865), p. 13.

12 When it was taken over by Unilever in 1919, Price's Patent Candle Company had factories in Burma, India, Pakistan, Rhodesia, Chile, Morocco and Ceylon. For the history of this company, see Jon Newman, *Battersea's Global Reach: The Story of Price's Candles* (London, 2009).

13 *Notice historique sur le matériel des couleries de bougies stéariques presenté par P. Morane* (Paris, 1878).

14 5,000 to 20,000 tonnes a year between 1850 and 1900 in France, 20,000 to 80,000 tonnes at the same time in Great Britain.

15 These discoveries were made in the Paris laboratory of Théophile Pelouze, an industrial chemist working for Charles Milly, the owner of 'Bougies de l'Etoile', the first major candle factory in history. See Julian Turgan, *Les grandes usines de France* (Paris, 1860), p. 139; Kenne Fant, *Alfred Nobel: A Biography* (New York, 2006), pp. 96–100.

16 On Argand see John Wolfe, *Brandy, Balloons & Lamps. Ami Argand, 1750–1803* (Carbondale, IL, 1999).

17 Jules Janin, 'Exposition de l'industrie nationale', *Revue de Paris*, 1834, p. 127.

18 Calculation based on the 1852 agricultural survey: 3.5 million hectolitres of oilseeds (poppy and rapeseed) or 100,000 tonnes of oil. See Béatrice Marin and Mathieu Marraud, 'L'enquête agricole de 1852', *L'Atelier du Centre de recherches historiques*, published online on 14 April 2011: https://journals.openedition.org/acrh/3696.

19 This refutation was made by the historian and journalist Bill Kovarik in a blog in 2008. Go to: https://www.pbs.org/newshour/economy/ this-post-is-hopelessly-long-w. It was taken up by Richard York, 'Why petroleum did not save the whales', *Socius: Sociological Research for a Dynamic World*, 3, 2017, pp. 1–13.

20 Théophile Pelouze, 'The candle is an absolute substitute for wax and whiting [whale oil] candles'. In *Cours de chimie générale* (Paris, 1850), vol. 3, p. 623.

21 Roger Fouquet and Peter J. G. Pearson, 'Seven centuries of energy services: the price and use of light in the United Kingdom (1300–2000)', *The Energy Journal*, 27, 1, 2006, pp. 139–77.

22 *Tableaux décennaux du Commerce de la France avec ses colonies et les puissances étrangères* (Paris, 1847–1856), p. 267.

23 The figures for the 19th century are taken from E. Merril et al., 'The sperm whale, Physeter macrocephalus', *Marine Fisheries Review*, 46, 4, 1984, pp. 54–64. For the 20th century: Robert C. Rocha and Phillip J. Clapham, 'Emptying the oceans: a summary of industrial whaling catches in the 20th century', *Marine Fisheries Review*, 76, 4, 2015, pp. 37–48. Including all other whale species, the total for the 20th century is 2.9 million catches.

24 US Congress, *Whaling, Whale Oil, and Scrimshaw: Hearings Before the Subcommittee on Fisheries* (Washington DC, 1975).

25 On working days per tonne see Martin Lynn, *Commerce and Economic Change in West Africa: The Palm Oil Trade in the Nineteenth Century* (Cambridge, 1997), p. 49; Jonathan E. Robins, *Oil Palm, A Global History* (Chapel Hill, NC, 2021), p. 57.

26 Dominique Juhé-Beaulaton, 'Les paysages végétaux de la Côte des Esclaves du XVIIe siècle à la veille de la colonisation: essai d'analyse historique', dissertation, Paris-I, 1995, p. 239. Xavier Daumalin, *Marseille et l'Ouest Africain: l'outre mer des industriels, 1841–1956* (Marseilles, 1992); Lynn, *Commerce and Economic Change in West Africa*; Robins, *Oil Palm*, pp. 42–74.

27 Didier Terrier, 'Moulins à vent à huile', in Jarrige and Vrignon (eds), *Face à la puissance*, pp. 57–70.

28 In 1857, English mines began experimenting with gas lighting in certain galleries: cf. 'Sur le projet d'éclairage des mines par le gaz', *Annales des mines*, 12, 1857, p. 782. The daily lighting consumption indicated in the treatises varies from 90 grams for the best Davy lamps to 190 grams depending on the lamps used. Apart from Davy lamps, a delicate technical item used in coal mines, it was generally the miners who bought their oils and chose their means of lighting. A. T. Ponson, *Traité de l'exploitation des mines de houille* (Liège, 1854), vol. 4, pp. 31–6. On the costs of lighting and timbering, see M. Thélu, *Notice sur les étais de mines en France* (Paris, 1878, p. 69).

29 A mechanical cooperage in the 1910s consumed around 10 kg of coal and 3 hours of labour per barrel. See Archives départementales du Rhône, 272 J 178.

30 Nicholas Crafts, Jan de Vries and others have replaced the image of a sudden revolution based on coal and steam with that of an 'industrial revolution' dating back to the 17th century, based on increased work and productivity and operating across a wide range of sectors. Cf. Nicholas Crafts, *British Economic Growth During the Industrial Revolution* (Oxford, 1985); Jan de Vries, *The Industrious Revolution. Consumer Behavior and the Household Economy, 1650 to the Present* (Cambridge, 2008).

31 *Statistique sommaire des industries principales en 1873* (Paris, 1874), p. 71.

32 Helen C. Long, *The Edwardian House: The Middle-class Home in Britain, 1880–1914* (Manchester, 1993), p. 89. This puts into perspective the very impressive graphs by Roger Fouquet and Peter Pearson showing the overwhelming dominance of gas lighting in England in terms of light production from 1840 onwards. Cf. Fouquet and Pearson, 'Seven centuries of energy services'.

33 The yield of gas varies according to the coal and the plants, but industrial statistics for 1861–65 give an average of 220 cu. m per tonne of coal. In 1872, France produced 315 million cu. m of gas, requiring around 1.6 million tonnes of coal. From which must be subtracted the production of coke sold by the gas companies, 600,000 tonnes, i.e. 1 million tonnes of coal for the gas itself. The illuminating power of gas

is well known, as municipalities that pay for their gas in cubic metres want to ensure that they have a certain amount of light. In 1845, a commission charged with drawing up the specifications for the Compagnie parisienne du gaz d'éclairage concluded that 140 litres of gas burning in one hour produced the same luminous intensity as 45 grams of oil burning for the same amount of time. Other experts believed that the Company only supplied a gas that had half this luminous intensity. See Jean-Baptiste Dumas and Henri-Victor Régnault, *Etalon légal ou mesure type du pouvoir éclairant du gaz* (Paris, 1869), p. 9. With regard to oil consumption for lighting, three methods of calculation arrive at the same approximate estimate of 7 kilos of fat per person per year, or about 1½ hours of candlelight per day. For details and sources see Jean-Baptiste Fressoz, 'Une histoire matérielle de la lumière', in Jarrige and Vrignon (eds), *Face à la puissance*.

34 Paolo Malanima writes that 'it is impossible to gather information on oil for lamps and wax for candles' and that 'their contribution to the energy budget was negligible'. Cf. Paolo Malanima, *Energy Consumption in Italy in the XIXth and XXth Centuries*, Consiglio Nazionale delle Ricerche, 2006, p. 22. Paul Warde does not include lighting fuels either. See Paul Warde, *Energy Consumption in England and Wales*, Consiglio Nazionale delle Ricerche Istituto di Studi sulle Società del Mediterraneo, 2007, p. 17.

35 Hydraulic energy is calculated by multiplying the power of the mill by the time of use and by a coefficient designed to take into account not the energy actually supplied by the mill, but that of the water pressing on its wheel. Malanima assumed an efficiency of 70%, while Warde opted for an efficiency of 25% in the 18th century and 60% at the end of the 19th century. However, the efficiencies of steam engines are much lower: Watt's steam engine converted between 3% and 6% of the energy contained in coal, the best steam engines of the late 19th century only 20%. See Malanima, *Energy Consumption in Italy*, p. 40 and Warde, *Energy Consumption in England and Wales*, p. 57. The authors are well aware of this problem. Warde estimates that in the late 1840s steam power 'probably rivalled' animal and water power, while at the same time coal would account for at least 90% of Britain's energy. See

Astrid Kander, Paolo Malamina and Paul Warde, *Power to the People. Energy in Europe Over the Last Five Centuries* (Princeton, NJ, 2013), p. 196.

36 Smith, 'The coordination of fuel supply', *The Transactions of the First World Power Conference* (London, 1924), vol. 3, p. 249.

37 Wrigley makes the opposite hypothesis: according to him, primary energy statistics underestimate energy growth, given the progress in machine efficiency. This may be true from the end of the 19th century onwards, but it is not true for the earlier period. See E. A. Wrigley, *Energy and the English Industrial Revolution* (Cambridge, 2010), p. 98.

38 Gregory Clark and David Jacks, 'Coal and the Industrial Revolution, 1700–1869', *European Review of Economic History*, 11, 2007, pp. 39–72.

39 J. S. G. Thomas, 'Illumination by gas', *The Transactions of the First World Power Conference* (London, 1924), vol. 3, p. 266.

40 OECD, *Light's Labour's Lost. Policies for Energy-Efficient Lighting*, 2006, p. 32. On oil-based electricity, see Ricardo Pinto et al., 'The rise and stall of world electricity efficiency: 1900–2017, results and insights for the renewables transition', *Energy*, 269, 2023.

41 https://www.iea.org/reports/lighting. 875 Mt of CO_2 in 2021. Lighting-related CO_2 emissions are on a downward trend, but on a very gentle slope.

42 William Nordhaus and James Tobin, 'Is growth obsolete?', in Milton Moss (ed.), *The Measurement of Economic and Social Performance*, National Bureau of Economic Research, 1973, pp. 509–64.

2. 'The Age of . . . ': Material Stagism and Its Problems

1 Historians have coined the term 'chrononym' to describe this way of naming eras. See Paul Bacot, Laurent Douzou and Jean-Paul Honoré, 'Chrononymes. La politisation du temps', *Mots. Les langages du politique*, 87, 2008, pp. 5–12; 'Chrononymes. Dénommer le siècle', *Revue d'histoire du XIXe siècle*, 52, 2016; Dominique Kalifa (ed.) *Les noms d'époque. De 'Restauration' à 'Années de plomb'* (Paris, 2020). On the broader question of periodization see Arno J. Mayer, *The Persistence of the Old Regime. Europe to the Great War* (New York,

1981); Jacques Le Goff, *Faut-il vraiment découper l'histoire en tranches* (Paris, 2014).

2 In 1829 Carlyle proposed the 'mechanical age', a few years later we saw the appearance of an 'age of tin' and from 1845 an 'age of coal', but the meaning was still symbolic (moral decline, materialism). See Antonio Carlo Napoleone Gallenga, *The Age We Live In* (London, 1845). In the 1870s in the USA, Mark Twain spoke of a 'gilded age' (rapid economic growth after the American Civil War), but also of an age of make-believe.

3 On the omnipresence of coal in the landscape, intimacy and daily life of the English in the Victorian and Edwardian eras, see Charles-François Mathis, *La civilisation du charbon* (Paris, 2021).

4 For wood, see W. E. Hiley, *The Economics of Forestry* (Oxford, 1930), p. 38; for bricks, see Robert Lionel Sherlock, *Man as a Geological Agent* (London, 1922), pp. 218–20 (from 1 billion bricks a year in 1830 to 4.8 billion in 1907).

5 Edgard Hément, *Histoire d'un morceau de charbon* (Paris, 1868), p. 194.

6 Louis Simonin, *La vie souterraine* (Paris, 1867), p. 287.

7 Comité des houillères françaises, *Situation de l'industrie houillère en 1859* (Paris, 1860), p. 9.

8 Egon Glesinger, *Nazis in the Wood Pile. Hitler's Plot for Essential Raw Material* (New York, 1942), p. 260.

9 Ellsworth Huntington and Frank E. Williams, *Business Geography* (New York, 1922), pp. 15–17.

10 David Edgerton, *The Shock of the Old: A Global History of Technology in the Twentieth Century* (London, 2006).

11 This infatuation continues and, even today, public debate on technology often boils down to commentary on the speeches of tech gurus.

12 The theory of the three ages was popularized by Christian Thomsen, curator of the Royal Museum of Nordic Antiquities in Copenhagen, who used it to reorganize his collections. This material primacy was based on the observation that certain artefacts were never found in the same archaeological context: bronze swords were not found with iron swords, for example. See Bo Gräslund, *The Birth of Prehistoric Chronology. Dating Methods and Dating Systems in Nineteenth-century Scandinavian Archaeology* (Cambridge, 1987).

13 Hector Dufréné, 'Essai sur l'origine et les progrès de l'industrie', *Études sur l'Exposition de 1878* (Paris, 1878), vol. I, pp. 1–43; J. Riley, *The Age of Power* (London, 1921), pp. 1–6.

14 Simonin, *La vie souterraine*, p. 326 and William Tulloch Jeans, *The Creators of the Age of Steel* (London, 1884).

15 Karl Marx, *Capital*, vol. I, ch. 15, 'Machinery and large-scale industry'. See also Nick von Tunzelmann, *Steam Power and British Industrialization to 1860* (Oxford, 1978).

16 Christine MacLeod, *Heroes of Invention. Technology, Liberalism and British Identity 1750–1914* (Cambridge, 2007); François Jarrige, 'Le martyre de Jacquard ou le mythe de l'inventeur héroïque', *Tracés*, 16, 2009, pp. 99–117.

17 F. G. Tryon, 'An index of consumption of fuels and water power', *Journal of the American Statistical Association*, 22, 159, 1927, pp. 271–82. On this important article: Antoine Missemer and Franck Nadaud, 'Energy as a factor of production: historical roots in the American institutionalist context', *Energy Economics*, 86, 2020.

18 Thomas Read, *Our Mineral Civilization* (Baltimore, MD, 1932), p. 7.

19 Quoted in Allen Raymond, *What is Technocracy?* (New York, 1933), p. 82. The idea, if not the expression, of the 'energy slave' is obviously older. James Watt sometimes quantified the power of his machines in terms of the men they replaced. Charles Dupin in France also made an equivalence between installed steam power and the number of men. In the United States, during the American Civil War, the metaphor had an ideological function: the South was backward because of its slaves, who provided cheap energy that stifled the spirit of innovation.

20 Antoine Missemer, *Les Économistes et la fin des énergies fossiles (1865–1931)* (Paris, 2017); Nino Madureira, 'The anxiety of abundance: William Stanley Jevons and coal scarcity in the nineteenth century', *Environment and History*, 18, 2012, pp. 395–421.

21 Stanley Jevons, *The Coal Question* (London, 1867), p. 276. For a counterfactual showing the possibility of English economic growth without coal (until 1860) see Gregory Clark and David Jacks, 'Coal and the Industrial Revolution, 1700–1869', *European Review of Economic History*, 11, 1, 2007, pp. 39–72.

22 Jevons does not believe in the possibility of substitution, because water and wind provide energy that is too intermittent and not concentrated enough.

23 Pascal Grousset, 'De l'épuisement probable des mines de houille en Angleterre', *L'économiste belge*, 14, 22, 1868, p. 261.

24 Charles-François Mathis, 'Overthrowing the Coal King. Imagining the energy transition in Great Britain, 1865–1914', in Yves Bouvier and Léonard Laborie (eds), *L'Europe en transitions. Énergie, mobilité, communication, XVIIIe–XXIe siècles* (Paris, 2016), pp. 85–118.

25 Marcellin Berthellot, 'En l'an 2000', *Science et morale* (Paris, 1896), p. 510.

26 Howard P. Segal, *Recasting the Machine Age: Henry Ford's Village Industries* (Amherst, MA, 2005). Electricity is extolled precisely for its conservative political virtues. Cf. 'Linking up water, power and factory', *Industrial Power*, June 1920, pp. 17–50; Harper Leech, *The Paradox of Plenty* (New York, 1932), p. 22; Alain Beltran and Patrice Carré, *La vie électrique: Histoire et imaginaire (XVIIIe–XXIe siècles)* (Paris, 2016).

27 Eberhard Illner, 'Engels and electricity', in J. G. Backhaus et al. (eds), *200 Years of Friedrich Engels* (Berlin and Heidelberg, 2022), pp. 153–66.

28 Peter Kropotkin, *Champs, usines et ateliers* (Paris, 1910), pp. 210–330. This idea seems to have been fairly widespread within the anarchist movement. On Spanish anarchists and electricity: Daniel Pérez Zapico, 'Electricity in Gijón. Strategic control, social conflict and the rhetoric of violence (1880–1934)', *Écologie & politique*, 49, 2014, pp. 43–53.

29 August Bebel, *Women Under Socialism* (New York, 1904), p. 339.

30 G. Bernard Shaw, 'Transition', in G. Bernard Shaw (ed.), *Fabian Essays in Socialism* (New York, 1891). See in particular the essay by William Clarke in this volume.

31 This idea can be found in France with authors such as Panagiotis Argyriades, *Essai sur le socialisme scientifique. Critique économique de la production capitaliste* (Paris, 1891), and the former Communard Benoît Malon, *Le socialisme intégral: des réformes possibles et des moyens pratiques* (Paris, 1891).

32 Patrick Geddes, 'A national transition', *Sociological Review*, 18, 1, 1928, pp. 1–16. The other element of context is a feeling of slowness in the construction of the national electricity network. Cf. Hannah Leslie, *Electricity before Nationalisation* (London, 1979).

33 Chester Gilbert and Joseph Poge, *America's Power Resources* (New York, 1921); Erich Zimmerman, *World Resources and Industries* (New York, 1933).

34 C. K. Leith, *World Minerals and World Politics* (New York, 1931), p. 30.

35 Glesinger, *Nazis in the Wood Pile*, p. 260.

36 On coal estimates after Jevons, see Madureira, 'The anxiety of abundance'. On fears of timber depletion: Alphonse Mélard, *Insuffisance du bois d'oeuvre dans le monde* (Paris, 1900); Ian Tyrrell, *Crisis of the Wasteful Nation. Empire and Conservation in Theodore Roosevelt's America* (Chicago, 2015).

37 Gilbert and Poge, *America's Power Resources*, p. 83.

38 Zimmerman, *World Resources and Industries*, p. 448.

39 Edward Jeffrey, *Coal and Civilization* (New York, 1925).

40 *Royal Commission on Coal Supplies, Final Report*, 1905, p. 16.

41 Charles Van Hise, *The Conservation of Natural Resources in the United States* (New York, 1912).

42 Tyrrell, *Crisis of the Wasteful Nation*, p. 82.

43 Herbert S. Jevons, *The British Coal Trade* (London, 1915), p. 752.

44 David Cannadine, 'The present and the past in the English Industrial Revolution 1880–1980', *Past & Present*, 103, 1984, pp. 131–72.

45 'Emanzipation von den Schranken des Organischen', Werner Sombart, *Die deutsche Volkswirtschaft im neunzehnten Jahrhundert* (Berlin, 1903), p. 162.

46 Ibid., pp. 1–20. English translation in: 'Travel in Germany in 1800', *Economic Life in the Modern Age* (London, 2001), p. 196.

47 Werner Sombart, *The Jews and Modern Capitalism* (London, 1913), p. 340. On Sombart see Jeffrey Herf, *Reactionary Modernism: Technology, Culture, and Politics in Weimar and the Third Reich* (Cambridge, 1984), pp. 130–51.

48 Sombart, *Die deutsche Volkswirtschaft*, ch. 8.

49 As early as 1929, *Popular Science* referred to hydroelectricity as the 'second industrial revolution': see 'A new world run on dynamo', *Popular Science*, 115, 6, 1929, pp. 19–21. Leech, *The Paradox of Plenty*, p. 71.

50 Fred Henderson, *The Economic Consequences of Power Production* (London, 1931), p. 15.

51 Leech, *The Paradox of Plenty*, pp. 22–3, 40–42.

52 Ibid., p. 32.

53 Lewis Mumford, *Technics and Civilization* (London, 1934), p. 3. Mumford was one of the New York intellectuals associated with the New School of Social Research at Columbia University, where he studied under Veblen. We will return to this technocratic environment in Chapter 6. See Donald L. Miller, *Lewis Mumford, a Life* (New York, 1989), p. 110. On this work: Rosalind Williams, 'Technics and Civilization', Technology and Culture, 43, 1, 2002, pp. 139–49; Eric Schatzberg, *Technology: Critical History of a Concept* (Chicago, 2018), pp. 136–51.

54 Mumford, *Technics and Civilization*, pp. 83, 163. Many of Mumford's ideas can be found in later French historiography, in Bertrand Gille and Maurice Daumas, who equated industrialization with the conquest of fossil fuels and the rejection of wood. Cf. *Histoire générale des techniques*, vol. 3, *L'expansion du machinisme* (Paris, 1968), p. 6.

55 In the caption to a photo of a hydroelectric station in the USSR, Mumford notes: 'The calmness, cleanliness and order of the neotechnic environment. The same qualities prevail in the power station as in the kitchen or bathroom of the individual dwelling. In any of these spaces you could eat off the floor. Contrast that with the palaeotechnic environment.' Cf. *Technics and Civilization*, p. 372.

56 Ibid., p. 256.

57 Richard White, *The Organic Machine: The Remaking of the Columbia River* (New York, 1995), ch. 3.

58 *New York Times*, 12 August 1945. On the history of reactions to the atom bomb see: Paul Boyer, *By the Bomb's Early Light. American Thought and Culture at the Dawn of the Atomic Age* (New York, 1985).

59 *Le Monde*, 8 August 1945 and *L'aurore*, 7 August 1945. Other newspapers were not to be outdone: 'Atomic energy will revolutionise post-war industry' (*Sud Ouest*, 8 August 1945). *Paris Presse* announced an 'age of uranium'.

60 Dr A. Bonnet, *Comment prévenir la cellulite, fléau de l'âge atomique* (Paris, 1958).

61 Virgil Jordan, *Manifesto for the Atomic Age* (New Brunswick, NJ, 1946), p. 25.

62 Manuel Castells, *The Information Age: Economy, Society and Culture*, 3 vols (Oxford, 1996–98).

63 Jeremy Rifkin, *The Green New Deal. Why the Fossil Fuel Civilization Will Collapse by 2028, and the Bold Economic Plan to Save Life on Earth* (New York, 2019); Geoffrey B. Holland and James J. Provenzano, *The Hydrogen Age: Empowering a Clean-Energy Future*, (Santa Barbara, CA, 2007).

64 For example, 'Age of Steam' had 5 titles in the 1960s, then in the 1970s: 19, 1980s: 16, 1990s: 23, 2000s: 20, 2010s: 26.

3. Coal and Wood: A Tangled History

1 The trope of coal as a providential underground forest seems to have been invented by the German jurist Johann Philipp in his book *Sylva Subterranea* (1693). Cf. Rolf Peter Sieferle, *The Subterranean Forest: Energy Systems and the Industrial Revolution* ([1982] Winwick, Cambs., 2001), pp. 182–5. This idea of conserving wood through coal is found in the preamble to the French mining edicts of 1698, 1744 and 1783. See: Marcel Rouff, *Les mines de charbon en France au XVIIIe siècle, 1744–1791* (Paris, 1922), p. 68.

2 'The more men multiply, the more the forests will diminish: since wood can no longer suffice for their consumption, they will have recourse to these immense deposits of combustible matter, the use of which will become all the more necessary as the globe cools.' Cf. George Louis-Leclerc de Buffon, *Les Epoques de la nature, troisième époque* (Amsterdam, 1779), p. 50: 'The uses of coal have become an important object, not to save wood, but to make it less necessary, leaving more land for other productions.' Cf. Nicolas de Condorcet, 'Eloge de Morand', *Histoire de l'académie royale des sciences*, 1784, p. 50.

3 Reynald Abad, 'L'Ancien Régime à la recherche d'une transition énergétique? La France du XVIIIe siècle face au bois', in Yves Bouvier and Léonard Laborie (eds), *L' Europe en transitions: énergie, mobilité, communication: XVIIIe–XXIe siècles* (Paris, 2016).

4 The props are stacked up to ten metres high and extend for hundreds of metres. See M. Thélu, *Notice sur les étais de mines en France* (Paris, 1878), p. 43.

5 Louis Simonin, *La vie souterraine. Ou, la mine et les mineurs* (Paris, 1867), p. 108; Robert Boyle, 'Articles of inquiries concerning the mines . . .', *Philosophical Transactions*, 19, 19 November 1666; William Phillips, 'La luminosité des champignons', *Revue mycologique*, 33, 1887, pp. 120–26.

6 Lewis Mumford, *Technics and Civilization* (London, 1934), p. 69.

7 George Orwell, *The Road to Wigan Pier* ([1937] New York, 1958), p. 64. A 1911 film shot in Wigan shows the mass of props arriving in wagonloads, unloaded by female workers. Cf. https://www.youtube.com/watch?v=D581TDHFpmE.

8 Paul Warde, *Energy Consumption in England and Wales*, Consiglio Nazionale delle Ricerche Istituto di Studi sulle Società del Mediterraneo, 2007, p. 69 and appendix 2. E. A. Wrigley, *Energy and the English Industrial Revolution* (Cambridge, 2011), p. 37. The graph taken from this book has been very influential, as it is often found in the background to interpretations of the industrial revolution as an energy transition. Cf. Vaclav Smil, *Energy Transitions: History, Requirements, Prospects* (Santa Barbara, CA, 2010), p. 79; *idem, Energy and Civilization. A History* (Cambridge, MA, 2017), p. 233; Richard Rhodes, *Energy, A Human History* (New York, 2018), ch. 14. Paul Warde explains that 'organic energy' obviously persists after the industrial revolution, but he gives food as a significant example: 'humans still need to eat'. Cf. Astrid Kander, Paolo Malamina and Paul Warde, *Power to the People. Energy in Europe Over the Last Five Centuries* (Princeton, NJ, 2013), p. 144.

9 Richard Redmayne, *The British Coal Industry During the War* (Oxford, 1923), p. 44. FAO, *European Timber Statistics, 1913–1950* (Geneva, 1953), Table 15. According to Paul Warde, 3.6 million cu. m corresponds to the high end of the firewood peak in the middle of the 18th century in England and Wales. Cf. Warde, *Energy Consumption in England and Wales*, p. 38.

10 In 1876, French production was 2.22 cu. m/ha for firewood and 0.55 cu. m/ha for timber. See *Statistique forestière* (Paris, 1878), tables pp. 113, 115.

11 J. Beauverie, *Le Bois* (Paris, 1905), vol. 2, p. 1325.

12 Thélu, *Notice sur les étais de mines en France*, p. 6.

13 This is what a mining engineer explained in 1905. Roof collapse was 'the miner's real occupational accident', which hardly caused a ripple because they were so common. Cf. A. Leproux, 'Introduction', *Compte rendu des travaux de la Commission prussienne des éboulements* (Paris, 1905), pp. 1–3. It is thanks to comparisons of mortality rates between mines and between countries that this type of accident became recognized as a problem. For example, at the end of the 19th century, a Prussian Commission contrasted the relative safety of French mines with the dangers of German mines: the risk of death by landslide was 0.5/1000 per year in France, 0.6/1000 in England and 1 per 1000 in Germany. Deaths from all causes were 1/1000 in France, 1.6/1000 in England and 2.4/1000 in Germany. See also John E. Murray and Javier Silvestre, 'Small-scale technologies and European coal mine safety, 1850–1900', *Economic History Review*, 68, 3, 2015, pp. 887–910.

14 Thomas G. Andrews, *Killing for Coal, America's Deadliest Labor War* (Cambridge, MA, 2008).

15 G. Parlongue, 'Des bois tropicaux et subtropicaux en Belgique', *Congrès international du bois et de la sylviculture*, Paris, 1931, p. 336. Wood from Belgian mines came mainly from the Nordic countries, with the Congo playing a modest role in the timber trade in general. In the 1920s, total exports amounted to 15,000 cu. m.

16 Albert E. Boadle, *The British Lumber Market* (Washington DC, 1928), pp. 6, 26.

17 'L'accord franco-anglais poteaux-charbons', *Revue des eaux et forêts*, 72, 1934, pp. 650–51. The agreement provided for the exchange of 2 tonnes of Landes mine timber for 3 tonnes of English coal. This trade was famous enough to inspire Freeman Wills Crofts' crime thriller *The Pitprop Syndicate* (1922), set in the Landes.

18 *New York Times*, 15 December 1944, p. 3, and 12 December 1947, p. 11.

19 Karl Brandt, 'The fuel crisis in Europe', *Foreign Affairs*, 24, 2, 1946, pp. 337–40; William Diebold Jr, 'East–West trade and the Marshall Plan', *Foreign Affairs*, 26, 4, 1946, pp. 709–22; Nathaniel Samuels, 'The European Coal Organization', *Foreign Affairs*, 26, 4, 1948, pp. 728–36; US Department of State, 'The coal situation in Europe', *Foreign Affairs Background Summary*, October 1947.

20 'Power Economic Conference', *Current History*, 13, 75, 1947, pp. 297–302; Régine Perron, *Le marché du charbon, un enjeu entre l'Europe et les États-Unis de 1945 à 1958* (Paris, 1996), pp. 55–78.

21 Raphael Zon, 'Forestry and the mining industry', *Proceedings of the Lake Superior Mining Institute*, 21–24, 1916–1917, pp. 271–9.

22 'Statement of Conrad, Superintendent Timber Department Philadelphia Coal and Iron Company', *Reforestation: Hearings Before a Select Committee on Reforestation*, United States Senate, 7 and 8 March 1923, p. 1278.

23 K. Pochenkov, 'Coal basins of the USSR in the new five-year plan', *The Great Stalin Five-Year Plan*, 1946, pp. 39–41. The fourth five-year plan (1946–1950) emphasized the renovation, using Russian props, of thousands of kilometres of galleries in the mines of the Donbass.

24 V. Zvonkov, 'Volga–Don Canal opens new ship routes', *USSR Information Bulletin*, 12, 1952, pp. 387–91.

25 On the arrival of European capital and engineers in Chinese coal mines, see Tim Wright, 'Entrepreneurs, politicians and the Chinese coal industry, 1895–1937', *Modern Asian Studies*, 14, 4, 1980, pp. 579–602. On traditional roof support techniques, see: Peter J. Golas, *Joseph Needham's Science and Technology in China*, vol. 5, pt XIII, *Mining* (Cambridge, 1999), pp. 281–309. Lack of wood is a general trope in Western literature on Chinese mining. See for example: Bureau of Manufactures, *Monthly Consular and Trade Reports*, No. 325 (Washington DC, 1907), p. 190. The shortage of wood continued in the second half of the 20th century, see Everett D. Hawkins, 'China's fuel and power', *Current History*, 35, 208, 1958, pp. 336–41. Tim Wright, *Coal Mining in Chinese Economy and Society, 1895–1937* (Cambridge, 1984), p. 87.

26 On this case see Jessica Karlsson, 'Herbert Hoover's Apologia of His Chinese Mining Career 1899–1912. Untangling the Refutation Campaign', MSc thesis, Harvard University, 2018. Herbert Hoover, 'The Kaiping coal mines and coal-field, Chihle Province, North China', *Transactions of the Institution of Mining and Metallurgy*, 10, 1901–1902, p. 427.

27 *Decennial Reports on the Trade Navigation Industries 1912–1921*, vol. 1, 1924, p. 125; Rowland Gibson, *Forces Mining and Undermining China* (New York, 1914), p. 110. The author refers to a plantation of 10 million acacias.

28 Victor Seow, *Carbon Technocracy. Energy Regimes in Modern East Asia* (Chicago, 2021), pp. 70–80. On Japan's reforestation policy up to the end of the 1930s: Patrick J. Caffrey, 'Transforming the forests of a counterfeit nation: Japan's "Manchu Nation" in Northeast China', *Environmental History*, 18, 2, 2013, pp. 309–32.

29 William Shockley, 'Richesses minérales et procédés métallurgiques du Chan-Si (Chine Septentrionale)', *Le Génie Civil*, 45, 1904, pp. 309–12. Shockley reports prices half those charged by northern European mines. On Shanxi mines in the early 20th century, see Henrietta Harrison, 'Village industries and the making of rural–urban difference in early twentieth century Shanxi', in Jacob Eyferth (ed.), *How China Works: Perspectives on the Twentieth-Century Industrial Workplace* (London, 2006), pp. 25–40 and Wright, *Coal Mining*, pp. 15–31.

30 Redmayne, *The British Coal Industry During the War*, p. 141; The English press spoke of a war that Germany would wage against its props, cf. 'Germany's war on pit-props', *Manchester Guardian*, 26 June 1915.

31 George Samuel Rice and Irving Hartmann, *Coal Mining in Europe*, US Government Printing Office, 1939, p. 103.

32 Adrien Quièvre, 'Entendre le travail à la mine aux XIXe et XXe siècles', *Revue du Nord*, 435, 2020, pp. 311–25.

33 'Miners' objections to steel props', *Manchester Guardian*, 12 October 1929.

34 'Russian pit props arrive at Bo'Ness', *Scotsman*, 1 February 1938.

35 Albina Tretyakova and Meredith Heinemeier, *Cost Estimate for the Soviet Coal Industry, 1970 to 1980*, US Department of Commerce, 1986, p. 106.

36 https://www.cia.gov/readingroom/docs/CIA-RDP80-00809A000700 190197-2.pdf.

37 Central Intelligence Agency, *The Current Status of the Soviet Timber Industry*, CIA/RR ER 64–19, July 1964.

38 Lewis H. Siegelbaum and Daniel J. Walkowitz, *Workers of the Donbass Speak: Survival and Identity in the New Ukraine, 1989–1992* (Albany, NY, 1995), pp. 68, 138–43.

39 Alexander Ikonnikov, *The Coal Industry of China* (Canberra, 1977), p. 132.

40 Elspeth Thompson, *The Chinese Coal Industry: An Economic History* (London, 2003), p. 70, table 3.12.

41 Huaichuan Rui, *Globalization, Transition and Development in China, The Case of the Coal Industry* (London, 2005), p. 68.

42 The official statistics reported by Rui indicate between 10 and 18 deaths per million tonnes of coal (see table 3.8). Mortality in French and English mines in the 1900s was 5 per million tonnes. See US Geological Survey, *Coal Mines Accidents: Their Causes and Prevention*, 1907.

4. *The Timber Palace*

1 See Philip Landon, 'Great exhibitions: representations of the Crystal Palace in Mayhew, Dickens, and Dostoevsky', *Nineteenth-Century Contexts*, 20, 1, 1997, pp. 27–59. For a recent revival of the cliché, see Peter Sloterdijk, *In the World Interior of Capital* (Cambridge, 2006).

2 According to the contractor's report, the Crystal Palace required around 4,500 tonnes of cast iron, 500 tonnes of glass and at least 15,000 tonnes of wood. The budget also indicates that three times as much was spent on wood as on glass. Cf. *Report of the Commissioners for the Exhibition of 1851* (London, 1852), p. 69.

3 Dustin Valen, 'On the horticultural origins of Victorian glasshouse culture', *Journal of the Society of Architectural Historians*, 75, 4, 2016, pp. 403–23. In Worcester in the first half of the 19th century, there were farms with more than a hectare of fruit trees under glass, an area larger than that of the Crystal Palace. See Bill Gwilliam, *Old Worcester, People and Places* (Bromsgrove, 1993), p. 189.

4 Chris Evans and Göran Rydén, *The Industrial Revolution in Iron: The Impact of British Coal Technology in Nineteenth-Century Europe* (London, 2005); Serge Benoît, *D'eau et de feu: forges et énergie hydraulique, XVIIIe–XXe siècles. Une histoire singulière de l'industrialisation française* (Rennes, 2021).

5 In 1869, the forester E. P. Stebbing reported that Indian railways burned 5 to 10 times more wood than coal: *The Forests of India*

(London, 1923), vol. 2, table p. 103. Twenty years later, the situation had changed: in 1891, Indian railways burned 1 million tonnes of coal and 340,000 tonnes of wood. See Lieutenant-Colonel R. A. Sargeaunt, *Administration Report on the Railways in India* (London, 1892), p. 146. In 1913, Russian locomotives consumed 7.7 million cu. m of wood and 7.5 million tonnes of coal: *Socialist Construction in the U.S.S.R.: Statistical Abstract* (Moscow, 1956), table 11, p. 310.

6 Institute of Inter-American Affairs, 'Brazilian Technical Studies', p. 113. The case of the railways is not exceptional: wood remained the main source of energy in Brazil until the 1960s. Cf. Jean-Marie Martin, *Processus d'Industrialisation et développement énergétique du Brésil* (Paris, 1966), pp. 347–8.

7 Robin Doughty, *The Eucalyptus. A Natural and Commercial History of the Gum Tree* (Baltimore, MD, 2000), pp. 96–104.

8 US Department of Commerce, *Abstract of the Census of Manufactures*, 1914, table 216, pp. 495–502.

9 J. Beauverie, *Le Bois* (Paris, 1905), vol. 2, p. 707.

10 E. Tratman and B. Fernow, 'Consumption of ties by railways in the United States of America', *Revue générale des chemins de fer*, 14, 1891, pp. 44–9; Aishton, 'The railways and wood preservation', US Department of Agriculture, *Report of the National Conference on Utilization of Forest Products*, 1924, pp. 62–6.

11 Robert William Fogel, 'Railroads as an analogy to the space effort: some economic aspects', *The Economic Journal*, 76, 301, 1966, table 2, p. 28.

12 Edward Andrews, 'The Hayford process for preserving timber', *Journal of the Franklin Institute of the State of Pennsylvania*, 105, 1878, p. 182.

13 F. J. Angier, 'Timber preservation making big savings in cost of ties renewals', *Cross Tie Bulletin*, 15 June 1921, p. 161.

14 Herman Haupt, *Military Bridges* (New York, 1864).

15 'L'exploitation des forêts et les chemins de fer à rail en bois en Amérique', *La Nature*, 1883, pp. 404–06.

16 Nicholas A. Bill, 'Timber bridge construction on British and Irish railways, 1840–1870: the scale of construction and factors influencing material selection', *Construction History*, 31, 1, 2016, pp. 75–98.

17 Göran Rydén, 'Responses to coal technology without coal. Swedish iron making in the nineteenth century', in Evans and Rydén, *The Industrial Revolution in Iron.*

18 E. F. Söderlund, 'The Swedish iron industry during the First World War and the post-war depression', *Scandinavian Economic History Review*, 6, 1, 1958, pp. 53–94.

19 Ian Blanchard, 'Russian railway construction and the Urals charcoal iron and steel industry, 1851–1914', *Economic History Review*, 53, 1, 2000, pp. 107–26.

20 The consumption of charcoal per tonne of cast iron fell from 8 tonnes to 1.5 tonnes between 1800 and 1900. Cf. Ian Blanchard, 'Nineteenth-century Russian and Western ferrous metallurgy: complementary or competitive technologies', in Evans and Rydén, *The Industrial Revolution in Iron*, table 8.1, p. 138.

21 US Department of Agriculture, *Charcoal Production in the United States*, 1957, p. 2. Richard H. Schallenberg, 'Evolution, adaptation and survival: the very slow death of the American charcoal iron industry', *Annals of Science*, 32, 4, 1975, pp. 341–58; Kris E. Inwood, 'The decline and rise of charcoal iron: the case of Canada', *Business and Economic History*, 14, 1985, pp. 237–43.

22 Joachim Radkau, *Technik in Deutschland: Vom 18. Jahrhundert bis heute* (Frankfurt, 2008), p. 134. Thanks to Jawad Daheur for this reference.

23 Jeffrey L. Meikle, *American Plastics: A Cultural History* (New Brunswick, NJ, 1997), pp. 40–45.

24 Egon Glesinger, *Demain l'âge du bois* (Paris, 1951), p. 147.

25 So as to produce 10 million tonnes of cast iron and 5 million tonnes of steel. See Frank Rosillo-Calle and Guilherme Bezzon, 'Production and use of industrial charcoal', in Frank Rosillo-Calle, Sergio Bajay and Harry Rothnam (eds), *Industrial Uses of Biomass Energy. The Example of Brazil* (London, 2000), pp. 183–99. By way of comparison, in 1860 the French iron and steel industry consumed only 315,000 tonnes of charcoal: Serge Benoît and Gérard Emptoz, 'L'actualité du combustible végétal: l'évolution des procédés de carbonisation du bois', in Benoît, *D'eau et de feu.*

26 Gerrit Ralf Surup et al., 'Charcoal as an alternative reductant in ferroalloy production: a review', *Processes*, 8, 11, 2020. In Yunnan, a major

silicon refining centre, these hundreds of thousands of tonnes of charcoal are illegally imported from Myanmar every year: https://dialogue.earth/en/business/10228-burning-down-the-house-myanmar-s-destructive-charcoal-trade/.

27 W. E. Hiley, *The Economics of Forestry* (Oxford, 1930), p. 38.

28 Alphonse Mélard, *Insuffisance du bois d'oeuvre dans le monde* (Paris, 1900). On Germany, Jawad Daheur, 'La sylviculture allemande et ses "hectares fantômes" au tournant des XIXe et XXe siècles', *Revue Forestière Française*, 69, 2017, pp. 227–39.

29 Alfred J. Van Tassel, *Mechanization in the Lumber Industry*, National Research Project, March 1940, p. 1.

30 In 1901, Paris had 1.6 million sq. m of wooden roadways out of a total surface area of 9 million sq. m. See Beauverie, *Le Bois*, vol. 2, p. 1327. André Guillerme, *Bâtir la ville: révolutions industrielles dans les matériaux de construction* (Paris, 1995), pp. 220–22. *Bartholomew's Road Surface Map of London & Neighbourhood* of 1910 shows the very large numbers of streets paved with wooden blocks. Cf. https://vu.contentdm.oclc.org/digital/collection/krt/id/1618/rec/1 (accessed 21 October 2020).

31 W. B. Greely et al., 'Timber: mine or crop?', *Yearbook of Agriculture*, 1922, pp. 83–180.

32 Robert Lionel Sherlock, *Man as a Geological Agent* (London, 1922), pp. 218–20. Faversham in Kent, rich in clay banks deposited during the last ice age, specialized in the production of bricks for the construction of London.

33 Henri Le Chatelier, *Le Chauffage industriel* (Paris, 1925), p. 454; 'How much coal is burned in clay products plants', *Black Diamond*, 63, 1, 1919, p. 321; Jefferson Middleton, *Statistics of the Clay-Working Industries in the United States* (Washington DC, 1897); Bureau of the Census, *The Clay Products Industries*, 1922, 1924, 1928, 1932.

34 Ian Tyrrell, *Crisis of the Wasteful Nation. Empire and Conservation in Theodore Roosevelt's America* (Chicago, 2015); Nino Madureira, 'The anxiety of abundance: William Stanley Jevons and coal scarcity in the nineteenth century', *Environment and History*, 18, 2012, pp. 395–421.

35 Roy R. Hornor and Harry Earle Tufft, *Mine Timber: Its Selection, Storage, Treatment, and Use* (Washington DC, 1925), p. 7.

36 Michael Williams, *Americans and Their Forests: A Historical Geography* (Cambridge, 1989), p. 441.

37 On this point, see the key book by Sherry Olson, *The Depletion Myth* (Cambridge, MA, 1971).

38 William D. Middleton, 'Logging railways', *Encyclopedia of North American Railroads* (Bloomington, IN, 2007), p. 628.

39 Judith Koll Healey, *Frederick Weyerhaeuser and the American West* (St Paul, MN, 2013).

40 Michael Koch, *The Shay Locomotive: Titan of the Timber* (Denver, CO, 1971).

41 *Statistical Abstract of the United States* (Washington DC, 1912), p. 320.

42 *Socialist Construction in the U.S.S.R. Statistical Abstract*, p. 304.

43 For example, it took four sailors to transport 100 tonnes of wood in 1870, but only two in 1900. See Lewis R. Fischer and Helge W. Nordvik, 'Myth and reality in Baltic shipping: the wood trade to Britain, 1863–1908', *Scandinavian Journal of History*, 12, 1987, pp. 99–116; Saif I. Shah Mohammed and Jeffrey G. Williamson, 'Freight rates and productivity gains in British tramp shipping, 1869–1950', NBER Working Paper 9531, 2003; C. K. Harley, 'Ocean freight rates and productivity, 1740–1913: the primacy of mechanical invention reaffirmed', *Journal of Economic History*, 48, 4, 1988, pp. 851–76.

44 Paul Warde, 'Firewood consumption and energy transition: a survey of sources, methods and explanations in Europe and North America', *Historia Agraria*, 77, April 2019, pp. 7–32. Zon and Sparhawk, two American foresters, estimated that in 1920, in North America as in Europe, half the wood was felled for burning, and the proportion was four-fifths on other continents. Dudley Stamp, 'The forest of Europe: present and future', *Empire Forestry Journal*, 7, 2, 1928, pp. 185–202. Egon Glesinger, a specialist in forestry statistics, also emphasized the relative stability of firewood in Europe between 1910 and the 1930s. See Egon Glesinger, *Le Bois en Europe. Origines et étude de la crise actuelle* (Paris, 1932), p. 71.

45 Gary Bryan Magee, *Productivity and Performance in the Paper Industry, 1860–1914* (Cambridge, 1997), p. 70.

46 Ibid., p. 158.

47 E. Arnould, *Traité classique d'enseignement de la fabrication du papier* (Fontainebleau, 1927), p. 237.

48 Glesinger, *Le Bois en Europe*, p. 315.

49 Paul Josephson, *Industrialized Nature. Brute Force Technology and the Transformation of the Natural World* (Washington DC, 2002), ch. 2.

50 Martin Meiske and Christian Zumbragel, 'Holz im Zeitalter von Kohle und Stahl zur Persistenz und Wandelbarkeit eines Werkstoffes in der Hochindustrialisierung', *Technikgeschichte*, 88, 2021, pp. 251–85.

51 Samuel Bagster Boulton, *On the Antiseptic Treatment of Timber* (London, 1884), p. 66.

52 Mark Aldrich, 'From forest conservation to market preservation: invention and diffusion of wood-preserving technology, 1880–1939', *Technology and Culture*, 47, 2, 2006, pp. 311–40.

53 Frederick Marshall, 'Creosoting timber', *The New Monthly Magazine*, 97, 385, January 1853, pp. 69–71.

54 Lionel B. Moses, 'A review of the Pinchot–Capper Bill', *Cross Tie Bulletin*, 2, 1921, p. 11.

55 Mélard, *Insuffisance du bois d'oeuvre*, p. 3.

5. Liaisons carbone

1 George Orwell, *The Road to Wigan Pier* ([1937] New York, 1958), p. 34.

2 Astrid Kander, Paolo Malamina and Paul Warde, *Power to the People. Energy in Europe Over the Last Five Centuries* (Princeton, NJ, 2013), p. 258.

3 John McNeill, *Something New Under the Sun. An Environmental History of the Twentieth-century World* (New York, 2000); John McNeill and Peter Engelke, *The Great Acceleration. An Environmental History of the Anthropocene since 1945* (Cambridge, MA, 2014); Kander, Malamina and Warde, *Power to the People*.

4 On Barak, *Powering Empire. How Coal Made the Middle East and Sparked Global Carbonization* (Oakland, CA, 2020).

5 National Automobile Chamber of Commerce, *Automobile Facts and Figures*, a publication that changed its title several times. This source has been little used by historians, apart from Chris Wells in his remarkable book *Car Country. An Environmental History* (Seattle, WA, 2012).

6 'Effects of coal and railway strikes on highway construction', *Highway Engineer and Contractor*, 7, 4, 1922, pp. 25–6.

7 'A permanent coal supply', Ford Industries, *Facts about the Ford Motor Company and Subsidiaries* (Detroit, MI, 1924), p. 73; James M. Rubenstein, *Making and Selling Cars. Innovation and Change in the U.S. Automotive Industry* (Baltimore, MD, 2001), p. 56.

8 Louis Pineau, 'Le Pétrole', *Le Génie civil*, 106, 14, 1935, pp. 338–40. Ford achieved a similar result: 6 tonnes of coal per car in 1941. See Wells, *Car Country*, p. 205.

9 Robert Brunschwig, 'Charbon et pétrole dans l'économie moderne', *Annales de l'Office national des combustibles liquides*, 8, 2, 1933, p. 266. The author singles out maritime transport, where there is effectively a substitution thanks to the superior efficiency of diesel engines compared with steam engines.

10 Dalley, 'Oil as an ally of coal', in John R. Bradley, *Fuel and Power in the British Empire*, US Department of Commerce, 1935, p. 17.

11 H. C. George, *Surface Machinery and Methods for Oil-well Pumping* (Washington DC, 1925).

12 G. R. Hopkins, *Survey of Fuel Consumption at Refineries in 1934*, US Bureau of Mines, 1934.

13 *Iron and Coal Trades Review*, January 1923, p. 42; *Steel Needs for the Oil and Gas Industry*, 1947, p. 219.

14 Robert William Fogel, 'Railroads as an analogy to the space effort: some economic aspects', *The Economic Journal*, 76, 301, 1966, table 2, p. 28.

15 Nebojsa Nakicenovic, 'Diffusion of pervasive systems: a case of transport infrastructures', in Nebojsa Nakicenovic and Arnulf Grübler, *Diffusion of Technologies and Social Behavior* (Berlin, 1991), p. 495.

16 Alessio Miatto et al., Modeling material flows and stocks of the road network in the United States 1905–2015, *Resources, Conservation and Recycling*, 127, 2017, pp. 168–78.

17 Nelo Magalhães, 'Matières à produire l'espace. Une histoire environnementale des grandes infrastructures depuis 1945', dissertation, Université Paris-Cité, 2022.

18 Graham West, *The Technical Development of Roads in Britain* (London, 2000), pp. 211–14; T. W. Delahanty, 'The contribution of chemical products to highway progress', Commerce reports, 5 January 1931, p. 11.

19 Paul Lesieur, 'Batailles pour la route. Une histoire de la genèse de la route moderne en France (1895–1914)', EHESS Master's thesis, 2018; Patrick Harismendy, 'Du caillou au bitume, le passage à la "route moderne"' (1900–1936)', *Annales de Bretagne et des pays de l'Ouest*, 106, 3, 1999, pp. 105–28.

20 'The Great War', wrote a truck promoter in 1918, 'demonstrated the merits of the truck far better than thousands of advertisements.' Cf. S. V. Morton, *The Motor Truck as an Aid to Business Profits* (Chicago, 1918), p. 14.

21 Jean-Michel Boniface and Gabriel Jeudy, *Les camions de la victoire 1914–1918* (Paris, 1996).

22 Quoted in B. E. Seely, 'The scientific mystique in engineering: highway research at the Bureau of Public Roads, 1918–1940', *Technology and Culture*, 25, 4, 1984, pp. 798–831.

23 *Automobile Facts and Figures*, 1929, p. 3.

24 Earl Swift, *The Big Roads: The Untold Story of the Engineers, Visionaries, and Trailblazers Who Created the American Superhighways* (Boston, MA, 2011); US Department of Transportation, *America's Highways, 1776–1976. A History of the Federal Aid Program*, US Government Printing Office, 1976.

25 70 million of the 127 million barrels in 1937, or 11 out of 19 million tonnes of cement produced. *Hearings to Amend the Federal Aid Highway Act before the Committee on Post Offices and Roads*, United States Senate, 26 January 1938, p. 34.

26 Swift, *The Big Roads*, p. 86.

27 *Concrete Highway Magazine*, 8, 1924, p. 231.

28 Nicolas Yaworski et al., *Fuel Efficiency in Cement Manufacture 1909–1935*, Work Progress Administration, 1937, table p. 39.

29 W. Geiger, 'Combined motor truck and cement mixer', *The Motor Truck*, 18, 5, 1927, p. 6.

30 *Concrete Highway Magazine*, 9, 1, 1925, p. 3. Between 1924 and 1928, the United States produced 84% of the world's cars. In 1928, of the 32 million trucks and cars in use worldwide, more than three-quarters (77%) were driven in the United States. See *Automobile Facts and Figures*, 1929, p. 21.

31 Yaworski et al., *Fuel Efficiency in Cement Manufacture 1909–1935*, pp. 17, 52: 84% of cement was produced with coal in 1919, 65% in 1935. The same work indicates an average consumption of 130 pounds per barrel of cement. A 1938 statistic gives a consumption of 3,800 barrels of cement per mile of concrete road, i.e. 670 tonnes of cement per 1.6 km.

32 Gabriel Dupuy, *La dépendance automobile: symptômes, analyses, diagnostic, traitements* (Paris, 1999).

33 Charles-François Mathis, 'Du pétrole *made in UK*? La liquéfaction du charbon dans l'Angleterre de l'entre-deux-guerres', in Charles-François Mathis, Christophe Bouneau, Renan Viguié and Jean-Pierre Williot (eds), *L'énergie à tous les étages. Autour d'Alain Beltran* (Paris, 2022).

34 William Telfair Daugherty, *German Chemical Developments in 1926*, US Bureau of Commerce, Trade Information Bulletin, no. 451, 1927, p. 18.

35 *Bulletin municipal officiel de la ville de Paris*, 5 December 1911, p. 4299. By the 1900s, all Paris buses were running on this mixture. On the national fuel, see Camille Molles, 'Faire carburer la France à l'alcool', in François Jarrige and Alexis Vrignon (eds), *France à la puissance. Une histoire des énergies alternatives à l'âge industriel* (Paris, 2020), pp. 83–195.

36 Emile Guarini, 'Foreign automobile trucks', *Scientific American*, no. 1525, 24 March 1905, pp. 24436–8; dump trucks were used from 1912 according to the *Coal and Coal Trade Journal*, 43, 1912, p. 162; 'Horses and trucks', *Black Diamond*, no. 26, 1914, p. 534. During the war, the United States exported 1.1 million horses, three-quarters of them to England and France. To this must be added 340,000 mules. This represented around one-twentieth of the American horse population. Cf. Jonathan Levin, *Where Have All the Horses Gone? How Advancing Technology Swept American Horses from the Road, the Farm, the Range and the Battlefield* (Jefferson, NC, 2017), p. 15. On dump trucks see Donald F. Wood, *Dump Trucks* (Osceola, WI, 2001).

37 'Quick-discharging coal trucks', *The Motor Truck*, March 1918, p. 138.

38 Louis S. Weber, 'Motor trucks revolutionize coal delivery system in New York City', *Good Roads*, 5 January 1921, p. 8; 'How trucks extended a selling zone', *Black Diamond*, 53, 12, September 1914, pp. 224–5.

39 'The economics application of the motor truck to coal transportation', *Commercial Vehicle*, 7, 4, April 1912, p. 6; George W. Grupp, *Economics of Motor Transportation* (New York, 1924), p. 52. On the difficulties of delivering coal to London before the lorry, see Charles François Mathis, *La civilisation du charbon* (Paris, 2021), pp. 55–67.

40 Jovan Milenkovic, *La question du pétrole et des carburants de remplacement en France* (Paris, 1936), p. 174; Charles Bihoreau, 'Le benzol et son emploi comme carburant', *Annales de l'office nationale des carburants liquides*, 1927, pp. 281–308.

41 Thomas Parke Hughes, 'Technological momentum in history: hydrogenation in Germany 1898–1933', *Past & Present*, 44, 1969, pp. 106–32; Anthony N. Stranges, 'Friedrich Bergius and the rise of the German synthetic fuel industry', *Isis*, 75, 4, 1984, pp. 642–67; David Edgerton, The *Shock of the Old: A Global History of Technology in the Twentieth Century* (London, 2006).

42 Shawn P. Keller, 'Turning Point: A History of German Petroleum in World War II', Air Command and Staff College thesis, 2011.

43 Albert Speer confided after the war that the Allied raids on these facilities in the summer of 1944 had dealt a fatal blow to the German war machine. The Germans also tried to bury these factories. See *United States Strategic Bombing Survey, Oil Division, Final Report*, January 1947, pp. 28–9. These difficulties had been wholly anticipated. See Luc Fauvel, *Problèmes économiques de la guerre totale*, dissertation, Paris Faculty of Law, 1939.

44 David Edgerton, *Britain's War Machine: Weapons, Resources and Experts in the Second World War* (London, 2011), p. 187; Anthony N. Stranges, 'From Birmingham to Billingham: high-pressure coal hydrogenation in Great Britain', *Technology and Culture*, 26, 4, 1985, pp. 726–57.

45 Jean Chardonnet, 'Une industrie nouvelle: les carburants de remplacement', *Annales de géographie*, 283, 1941, pp. 168–79. Jean-Louis Crussard, a mining engineer, was in charge of the French programme. See https://www.annales.org/archives/x/crussard.html.

46 'L'hydrogénation du charbon et du lignite', *Revue industrielle*, no. 2230, June 1937, pp. 201–4.

47 As Stephen Sparks has shown, SASOL, a symbol of the autarky and techno-nationalism of the Apartheid period, was also an international project, founded in 1950 with the help of the World Bank and German, British and American experts. Under the combined impact of the oil crisis and the Apartheid blockade, SASOL built a huge synthetic fuel plant in Secunda that would become a model for the industry. After the oil shocks, engineers from all over the world visited the plant, before the oil counter-shock led to the abandonment of the 'coal to fuels' projects. See Stephen John Sparks, 'Apartheid Modern: South Africa's Oil from Coal Project and the History of a South African Company Town', PhD thesis, University of Michigan, 2012.

48 The CTL figure is taken from official Chinese statistics, cf. http://www.stats.gov.cn/sj/ndsj/2022/indexeh.htm. On fuel methanol, see https://www.methanol.org/wp-content/uploads/2020/04/China-Methanol-Fuel-Report-2020_final-1.pdf.

49 IEA, *Global EV Outlook 2021. Accelerating Ambitions Despite the Pandemic*, p. 7.

50 Alain Maire, *Le transport par pipeline* (Paris, 2011), pp. 3–4; https://www.offshore-technology.com/analyst-comment/north-america-has-the-highest-oil-and-gas-pipeline-length-globally/.

51 John Frey, *History of Petroleum Administration for War, 1941–1945* (Washington DC, 1946); Maury Klein, *A Call to Arms: Mobilizing America for World War II* (New York, 2013).

52 Incomplete because there is also a lot of sheet metal for tanks. A comprehensive 1967 report on the material consumption of the US oil industry indicates that OCTG accounted for 69% of the mass of steel used in US oil production. Steel accounted for most of the metal requirements (2.55 million tonnes out of 2.6 million in 1967), the rest being copper, aluminium and nickel. See National Petroleum Council, *Material Requirements for Petroleum Exploration and Production* (Washington DC, 1967).

53 *Stockpile and Accessibility of Strategic and Critical Materials in a Time of War*, part 6, Petroleum, gas, and coal (Washington DC, 1954), p. 1044.

54 The fortunes of US Steel are partly linked to those of the American oil industry. Cf. Ronald G. Garay, *U.S. Steel and Gary, West Virginia: Corporate Paternalism in Appalachia* (Knoxville, TN, 2011), pp. 85–7.

55 S. A. Martanus and D. V. Khmelnitskii, 'Key aspects of steel consumption in Russia', *Metallurgist*, 56, 2013, pp. 637–46.

56 Tao Wang, Daniel B. Müller and Seiji Hashimoto, 'The ferrous find: counting iron and steel stocks in China's economy', *Journal of Industrial Ecology*, 19, 5, 2015, pp. 877–89.

57 Maureen Heraty Wood, Ana Lisa Vetere Arellano and Lorenzo Van Wijk, 'Corrosion-related accidents in petroleum refineries', EU Joint Research Centre report, 2013, p. 13.

58 For the figure of 7%, see National Petroleum Council, *Material Requirements*; the sulphur content of American crude has risen by half since the 1980s, see https://www.eia.gov/dnav/pet/hist/LeafHandler.ashx?n=PET&s=MCRSiUS2&f=M. The American Association of Corrosion Engineers estimates the cost of maintenance in US refineries alone at $3.7 billion for the cost of corrosion. See Aisha H. Al-Moubarakia and Ime Bassey Obot, 'Corrosion challenges in petroleum refinery operations: sources, mechanisms, mitigation, and future outlook', *Journal of Saudi Chemical Society*, 25, 12, 2021. Refineries in both the United States and Europe are ageing, with none having been built since 1977.

59 See IEA, *Iron and Steel Technology Roadmap Towards More Sustainable Steelmaking*, 2020. In the United States, the automotive industry consumes almost 30% of steel. Cf. Yongxian Zhu, Kyle Syndergaard and Daniel R. Cooper, 'Mapping the annual flow of steel in the United States', *Environmental Science & Technology*, 53, 19, 2019, pp. 11260–68.

60 K. P. Jain, J. F. J. Pruyn and J. J. Hopman, 'Quantitative assessment of material composition of end-of-life ships using onboard documentation', *Resources, Conservation and Recycling*, 107, 2016, pp. 1–9.

61 Car manufacturers prefer to use primary steel from blast furnaces rather than recycled steel containing impurities. Nabila Iken, 'Transition soutenable à l'échelle de l'entreprise: approche de la performance par les outils de gestion', Mines Paris-Tech thesis, 2021, p. 129.

62 Xiaoyu Yan, 'Energy demand and greenhouse gas emissions during the production of a passenger car in China', *Energy Conversion and Management*, 50, 12, 2009, pp. 2964–6.

63 IEA, *Technology Roadmap. Low-Carbon Transition in the Cement Industry*, 2015, p. 28 and https://www.globalcement.com/magazine/articles/974-coal-for-cement-present-and-future-trends.

64 Zijan Ren et al., 'Stocks and flows of sand, gravel, and crushed stone in China 1978–2018', *Resources, Conservation and Recycling*, 180, 2022.

65 https://www.usgs.gov/centers/national-minerals-information-center/cement-statistics-and-information.

66 Armelle Choplin, *Matière grise de l'urbain. La vie du ciment en Afrique* (Geneva, 2020).

67 For uses of cement in France, see ADEME, *Plan de transition sectoriel de l'industrie cimentière en France*, February 2021. For the importance of infrastructure in Europe: Dominik Wiedenhofer, Julia K. Steinberger, Nina Eisenmenger and Willi Haas, 'Maintenance and expansion modeling material stocks and flows for residential buildings and transportation networks in the EU25', *Industrial Ecology*, 19, 4, 2015, pp. 538–51.

68 For a study of opencast coal mines, see Victor Seow, *Carbon Technocracy. Energy Regimes in Modern East Asia* (Chicago, 2021); on opencast copper mines in the United States: Timothy J. Le Cain, *Mass Destruction. The Men and Giant Mines that Wired America and Scarred the Planet* (New Brunswick, NJ, 2009).

69 It should be noted that surface mining is obviously older than underground mining – coal outcrops were first mined.

70 C. L. Christenson, *Economic Redevelopment in Bituminous Coal. The Special Case of Technological Advance in United States Coal Mines, 1930–1960* (Cambridge, MA, 1962), p. 128.

71 Steam shovels were used in opencast mines as early as 1877. The figures from the US in 1930: 13 tonnes per miner per day in opencast mines, compared with 4.6 tonnes from underground mines. The Rosebud mine in Montana reached the record of 45 tonnes of coal per man per day. See O. E. Kiessling and F. G. Tryon, *The Economics of Strip Coal Mining* (Washington DC, 1931), table 1.

72 Philip G. LeBel, *Energy Economics and Technology* (Baltimore, MD, 1982), p. 121.

73 'USSR: Coal Industry Problems and Prospects: A Research Paper', CIA, National Foreign Assessment Center, 1980; Pyotr Moskatov, *Along the Road of Technical Progress*, 1960. English translation by the CIA: https://www.cia.gov/readingroom/document/cia-rdp81–01043r00450 0020002–4.

74 Albert Chiraz, 'Le lignite ou houille brune, en France et à l'étranger', *La science et la vie*, 13, 37, 1918, pp. 321–8; 'Une mine à ciel ouvert. La "découverte" de Decazeville', *Bibliothèque de travail*, no. 506, 20 November 1961, https://www.icem-freinet.fr/archives/bt/bt506/bt506.pdf.

75 'Opencast coal production in UK', *Foreign Commerce Weekly*, 26 August 1944, p. 22; *International Coal Trade*, 25, 9, 1956, p. 18; *International Coal Trade*, 47, 2, 1978, p. 22.

76 One billion tonnes of lignite for world production, 250 Mt for the GDR and 130 Mt for the FRG. 'World lignite production', *International Coal Trade*, 47, 5, 1978, p. 36; George Rabchevsky, 'The mineral industry of the German Democratic Republic', *Minerals Yearbook*, 1977, vol. 3, Area Reports: International, pp. 347–63. German lignite production has fallen sharply since then. It will reach 150 Mt in 2020.

77 *The United States Strategic Bombing Survey: Summary Report*, 30 September 1945, p. 93, table 56.

78 Julia Krümmelbein, Oliver Bens, Thomas Raab and Anne Naeth, 'A history of lignite coal mining and reclamation practices in Lusatia, eastern Germany', *Canadian Journal of Soil Science*, 92, 1, 2012; Michel Deshaies, 'Metamorphosis of mining landscapes in the Lower Lusatian lignite basin (Germany): new uses and new image of a mining region', *Les Cahiers de la recherche architecturale urbaine et paysagère*, 7, 2020.

79 Petrus J. Terblanche, Michael P. Kearney, Clay S. Hearn and Peter F. Knights, 'Technology selection and sizing of on-board energy recovery systems to reduce fuel consumption of diesel-electric mine haul trucks', in Kwame Awuah-Offei (ed.), *Energy Efficiency in the Mineral Industry. Best Practices and Research Directions* (Berlin and New York, 2018), p. 302.

80 Australian Renewable Energy Agency, 'Renewable Energy in the Australian Mining Sector', 2017; In South Africa 10% of oil and 15% of electricity are used by the minerals industry (https://www.sbpr.co.za/energy-in-mining/). In the United States, the figure is only 2%.

81 https://www.pwc.com.au/consulting/assets/publications/productivity-scorecard-mar12.pdf, p. 7, figure 4.

82 https://www.sciencedirect.com/science/article/pii/S2667111521000025.

83 Bruce Netschert, 'The energy company: a monopoly trend in the energy markets', *Bulletin of Atomic Scientists*, October 1971, pp. 13–18.

84 Energy Information Administration, 'Privatization and the Globalization of Energy Markets', October 1996; Jean-Martin Amouroux, *Charbon, les métamorphoses d'une industrie. La nouvelle géopolitique du XXIe siècle* (Paris, 2008), p. 220.

85 https://www.youtube.com/watch?v=9GOlPpr9-oY.

86 Lee Grieveson, 'The work of film in the age of Fordist mechanization', *Cinema Journal*, 51, 3, 2012, pp. 25–51. See for example the film about the Dagenham factory in England: https://www.youtube.com/watch?v=W2wpBnwxvzk.

87 In 1933, at the Chicago World's Fair, the company was already displaying samples of raw materials.

88 https://www.youtube.com/watch?v=3ntmZqrDZnA.

6. The Carbon Fallacy

1 Philip G. LeBel, *Energy Economics and Technology* (Baltimore, MD, 1982), table 5.7, p. 121.

2 Marie-France Conus and Jean-Louis Escudier, 'Cycle de vie et relation capital/travail. Application à l'industrie houillère française 1720–2004', in Xavier Daumalin, Sylvie Daviet and Philippe Mioche (eds), *Territoires européens du charbon. Des origines aux reconversions* (Aix en Provence, 2006), pp. 53–73; idem, 'Analyse économique du cycle de vie de l'industrie houillère française: la phase ultime: 1970–2004', in Alain Beltran, Christophe Bouneau, Yves Bouvier, Denis Varaschin and

Jean-Pierre Williot (eds), *Etat et Energie, XIXe–XXe siècles* (Vincennes, 2009), pp. 153–82.

3 In 1960, 98% of coal in the United States was mined by cutting machine and 86% was loaded mechanically. See LeBel, *Energy Economics*, p. 121.

4 Pyotr Moskatov, *Along the Road of Technical Progress*, 1960, p. 203, https://www.cia.gov/readingroom/document/cia-rdp81-01043r004500020002-4.

5 *US Census of Mineral Industries 1958, Summary and Industrial Statistics*, vol. 1, pp. 3 and 14; United States Congress Economic Joint Committee, *Automation and Technological Change: Report of the Joint Committee* (Washington DC, 1956), p. 489, table 2.

6 William Ashworth, *The History of the British Coal Industry. Vol. 5, 1946–1982: The Nationalised Industry* (Oxford, 1986), pp. 75–82.

7 John Temple, *Mining: An International History* (London, 1972), p. 86.

8 Bernard Pache, 'La politique de charbonnages de France', *Annales des mines, réalités industrielles*, January 1992, pp. 8–13; Conus and Escudier, 'Cycle de vie et relation capital/travail'.

9 Several American reports from the 1970s stressed the modernity of European mines: James Olson and Sathit Tandanand, 'Mechanized Longwall Mining. A Review Emphasizing Foreign Technology', Information circular 8740, US Bureau of Mines, 1977; Raja V. Ramani, *Longwall–Shortwall Mining. State of the Art* (New York, 1981).

10 After the war, the National Coal Board employed the considerable number of 300 researchers. Cf. David Edgerton, *The Rise and Fall of the British Nation: A Twentieth Century History* (London, 2020), p. 189. In 1947, Charbonnages de France created its Centre d'Études et de Recherche (CHERCHAR), which employed 150 people in the 1960s.

11 The Chinese government has been encouraging this method since 1949. See Alexander Ikonnikov, *The Coal Industry of China* (Canberra, 1977), p. 110.

12 John Phipps, 'Coal Mine Equipment. A Market Assessment for the People's Republic of China', US Department of Commerce, Bureau of East–West Trade, 1977.

13 *China Economic News*, 2, 1981, p. 7; *Mine and Quarry Mechanisation*, 1983, p. 127.

14 In particular, Chinese mining companies have developed new vertical coal-cutting machines that are better suited to thick veins. Cf. Zhenyu Fu, *Industrial Innovation in China: The Factors Determining Success or Failure* (New York, 2022), ch. 2.

15 US Bureau of Mines, 'The popularity of long wall electra continues to grow', *Mineral Yearbook*, 1991, p. 59.

16 Hans K. Schneider, 'International energy trade: recent history and prospects', *Annual Review of Energy*, 2, 1977, pp. 31–65.

17 Per Högselius, Eric van der Vleuten and Arne Kaijser, *Europe's Infrastructure Transition, Economy, War, Nature* (London, 2015), p. 86. In 1965, the Ruhrgas network reached 3,400 kilometres, distributing more than 3 billion cu. m of which only 10% was natural gas, see: http://www.fundinguniverse.com/company-histories/ruhrgas-ag-history/. In Great Britain in the 1960s, 12% of coal was transformed into gas, mixed with gas from oil refineries with a higher calorific value. See C. Chaline, 'Tendances actuelles de la production de charbon en Grande-Bretagne', *L'information géographique*, 26, 4, 1962, pp. 169–71.

18 M. Bulle, 'Quelques considérations sur l'emploi du charbon pulvérisé', *Chaleur et Industrie*, 12, 1921, pp. 184–8.

19 Edwin Austin, *Developments in Power Station Design* (New York, 1924), p. 7.

20 Fred Henderson, *The Economic Consequences of Power Production* (London, 1931), p. 24; Cecil Frederic Herington, *Powdered Coal as a Fuel* (New York, 1920), pp. 2, 160–65; François Giraumont, 'L'utilisation comme combustible du charbon pulvérisé', *La Science et la vie*, 15, 43, 1919, pp. 309–18; 'Standard locomotive stockers', in Roy V. Wright (ed.), *Locomotive Cyclopedia of American Practice* (New York, 1938), pp. 419–49.

21 Dipak K. Sarkar, *Thermal Power Plant, Design and Operation* (Amsterdam and London, 2015), pp. 139–49.

22 B. E. A. Jacobs, *Design of Slurry Transport Systems* (London, 1991); Jinfeng Wang, Kang Li and Lijie Feng, 'Tracing the technological trajectory of coal slurry pipeline transportation technology: an HMM-based topic modeling approach', *Sustainable Energy Systems and Policies*, 23 August 2022.

23 Interstate Commerce Commission, *Railroad Petroleum Traffic*, 1948, 1950, 1953, p. 54.

24 André Lévy, 'Le Commerce et l'industrie du pétrole en France', doctoral thesis, Université de Paris, 1923, p. 77.

25 In France in the 1970s, pipelines carried far less oil than trucks. Adam Soussana, 'L'or noir des "Trente Glorieuses". Une approche historique et matérielle de la pétrolisation de la France entre 1946 et 1973', EHESS Master's thesis, 2022, p. 105. The first pipeline linking the refineries in Normandy to the oil depots in the Paris suburbs was inaugurated in 1953.

26 Myrna Santiago, *The Ecology of Oil. Environment, Labor, and the Mexican Revolution, 1900–1938* (Cambridge, 2006).

27 Peyman Jafari, 'Fluid history: oil workers and the Iranian Revolution', in Touraj Atabaki, Elisabetta Bini and Kaveh Ehsani (eds), *Working for Oil: Comparative Social Histories of Labor in the Global Oil Industry* (New York, 2018), pp. 69–98.

28 Philippe Pétriat, *Aux pays de l'or noir. Une histoire arabe du pétrole* (Paris, 2021), pp. 121–9.

29 Marion Fontaine and Xavier Vigna, 'La grève des mineurs de l'automne 1948 en France', *Vingtième siècle*, 121, 2014, pp. 21–34; Darryl Holter, *The Battle for Coal. Miners and the Politics of Nationalization in France, 1940–1950* (DeKalb, IL, 1992).

30 David Montgomery, *Workers' Control in America: Studies in the History of Work, Technology, and Labor Struggles* (Cambridge, 1979). Among their feats of arms was the great Minneapolis strike of 1934, which began with that of the coal-delivery drivers.

31 'Aggravation de la situation dans les raffineries', *Le Monde*, 4 May 1952.

32 See Timothy Mitchell, *Carbon Democracy. Political Power in the Age of Oil* (London, 2011), pp. 28–32. Mitchell follows David Painter, 'The Marshall Plan and oil', *Cold War History*, 9, 2, 2009, pp. 159–75.

33 On coal and the Marshall Plan: John Gillingham, *Coal, Steel, and the Rebirth of Europe, 1945–1955* (Cambridge, 1991); Régine Perron, *Le marché du charbon, un enjeu entre l'Europe et les États-Unis de 1945 à 1958* (Paris, 1996); Jean-Paul Thuillier, 'Les Charbonnages de France et le plan Marshall', in *Le Plan Marshall et le relèvement économique de l'Europe* (Paris, 1993), pp. 331–3; Keisuke Mamehara, 'Du plan Monnet au plan

Béthancourt. Comment ont évolué la politique charbonnière et la politique énergétique pendant les trente glorieuses', dissertation, University of Paris IV, 2016.

34 Letter from Leo T. Crowley (Administrator of the Foreign Economic Administration) to Harold Ickes (Director of the Solid Fuels Administration for War). Quoted in Perron, *Le marché du charbon*, p. 60.

35 Gillingham, *Coal, Steel, and the Rebirth of Europe*, p. 118.

36 Darryl Holter, 'Politique charbonnière et guerre froide 1945–1950', *Le mouvement social*, 130, 1985, pp. 33–53; Jean-William Dereymez, 'La CGT et le plan Schuman (1950)', in Elyane Bressol, Michel Dreyfus, Joël Hedde and Michel Pigenet (eds), *La CGT dans les années 1950* (Rennes, 2015).

37 Jean Chardonnet, 'Le problème du charbon', *La revue économique*, 3, 1951, pp. 315–25; aid which represented three-quarters of the Charbonnages de France investments. Cf. *Rapport sur les aspects économiques du plan de modernisation des houillères* (Paris, 1949), pp. 7–9.

38 *Foreign Aid by the United States Government, 1940–1951* (Washington DC, 1952). On this point, see Alain Milward, *The Reconstruction of Western Europe 1945–1951* (London, 1984).

39 James Barr, *Lords of the Desert: Britain's Struggle with America to Dominate the Middle East* (London, 2023).

40 Irwin M. Wall, *France, the United States and the Algerian War* (Berkeley, CA, 2001); Marta Musso, ' "Oil will set us free": the hydrocarbon industry and the Algerian decolonization process', in Andrew W. M. Smith and Chris Jeppesen (eds), *Britain, France and the Decolonization of Africa: Future Imperfect?* (London, 2017), pp. 62–84.

41 Elisabetta Bini, 'A transatlantic shock: Italy's energy policies between the Mediterranean and the EEC, 1967–1974', *Historical Social Research*, 39, 4, pp. 145–64.

42 Bruce Jentleson, *Pipeline Politics: The Complex Political Economy of East–West Energy Trade* (Ithaca, NY, 1986), p. 119. On the other hand, De Gaulle complied with the American embargo policy and guaranteed that the equipment from the USA that had been used to modernize the Dunkirk steelworks would not be exported to the USSR. The reason for this was that, at the time, he saw France as an oil-producing

nation thanks to Algeria, and feared that Soviet production would adversely affect oil prices.

43 Hubert Bonin, 'Business interests versus geopolitics: the case of the Siberian pipeline in the 1980s', *Business History*, 49, 2, 2007, pp. 235–54; J. Perović and D. Krempin, '"The key is in our hands": Soviet energy strategy during Détente and the global oil crises of the 1970s', *Historical Social Research*, 39, 4, 2014, pp. 113–44; Per Högselius, *Red Gas. Russia and the Origins of European Energy Dependence* (New York, 2015), p. 217.

44 Roger Brunet, 'Le pétrole en Grande-Bretagne', *L'Information géographique*, 25, 2, 1961, pp. 69–77; Fernand Scheurer, 'Histoire des centrales thermiques de 1946 à 1980', *Bulletin d'histoire de l'électricité*, 10, 1987, pp. 121–42.

45 Louis Puiseux, 'Les bifurcations de la politique énergétique française depuis la guerre', *Annales*, 37, 4, 1982, pp. 609–20; Giuliano Garavini, *The Rise and Fall of OPEC in the Twentieth Century* (Oxford, 2019), pp. 88–133.

46 Ricardo Pinto et al., 'The rise and stall of world electricity efficiency: 1900–2017, results and insights for the renewables transition', *Energy*, 269, 2023.

47 A tax equivalent to 30% of the price of fuel oil was imposed in the United Kingdom in April 1961. Martin Chick, *Electricity and Energy Policy in Britain, France and the United States Since 1945* (Cheltenham, 2007), p. 10. For Germany: Alain Clément, 'Le gouvernement de Bonn prépare une taxe spéciale sur le fuel pour aider les charbonnages à résister à la concurrence du pétrole', *Le Monde*, 15 August 1959.

48 Eric Kocher-Marboeuf, *Le patricien et le général. Jean-Marcel Jeanneney et Charles de Gaulle 1958–1969* (Paris, 2003), vol. 1, pp. 99–138; Robert J. Lieber, 'Energy policies of the Fifth Republic: autonomy versus constraint', in William G. Andrews and Stanley Hoffmann (eds), *The Impact of the Fifth Republic on France* (Albany, NY, 1978), pp. 179–96.

49 'Rapport général sur l'évolution de l'énergie', 16 December 1958, AN 80 AJ 123. Gilbert Mathieu, 'La production de charbon, au lieu de croître, diminuera. Le pétrole et le gaz vont se tailler la part du lion. Incertitude sur l'avenir des centrales hydrauliques et nucléaires', *Le Monde*, 7 July 1959.

50 Jean-Pierre Anglier, 'Le charbon, industrie nouvelle', *Revue d'économie industrielle*, 16, 1981, pp. 1–15; Jeff Goodell, *Big Coal: The Dirty Secret Behind America's Energy Future* (New York, 2006).

7. The Roots of Growth

1 S. J. M. Eaton, *Petroleum. A History of the Oil Region of Venango County, Pennsylvania* (Philadelphia, PA, 1866), pp. 104–10, 280; J. H. Newton, *History of Venango County, Pennsylvania: And Incidentally of Petroleum* (Columbus, OH, 1879), p. 278; John James McLaurin, *Sketches in Crude Oil: Some Accidents and Incidents of the Petroleum Development in all Parts of the Globe* (Harrisburg, PA, 1896), pp. 260–70; Charles Whiteshot, *The Oil-well Driller: A History of the World's Greatest Enterprise, The Oil Industry* (1905), p. 380; Franklin F. Coyne, *The Development of the Cooperage Industry in the United States, 1620–1940* (Chicago, 1940), p. 18; Harold F. Williamson and Arnold R. Daum, *The American Petroleum Industry. The Age of Illumination, 1859–1899* (Evanston, IL, 1955), pp. 178–83.

2 Christopher F. Jones, *Routes of Power. Energy and Modern America* (Cambridge, MA, 2014), pp. 108–9.

3 Walter Henry Jeffery, *Deep Well Drilling: The Principles and Practices of Deep Well Drilling, and a Hand Book of Useful Information for the Well Driller* (Toledo, OH, 1921), p. 44. On the quantity of wood per derrick: Victor Ziegler, *Oil Well Drilling Methods* (New York, 1923). On the number of wells drilled: US Department of Commerce, *Mineral Resources of the United States*, 1930, part II, p. 801. The figure of 810,000 is a minimum, as 'dry wells' are poorly counted. See Diana Davids Hinton and Roger M. Olien, *Oil in Texas: The Gusher Age, 1895–1945* (Austin, TX, 2002), p. 58; Bobby D. Weaver, *Oilfield Trash: Life and Labor in the Oil Patch* (Austin, TX, 2010), p. 20.

4 'Good missionary work', *Packages*, 21, November 1918, p. 34.

5 William Ganson Rose, *Cleveland: The Making of a City* (Kent, OH, 1990), p. 449. Bob Gilding, *The Journeymen Coopers of East London: Workers' Control in an Old London Trade* (Oxford, 1971). The author lists 1,000 coopers in the mid-19th century and 2,400 fifty years later.

6 M. Gascheau, *La question des pétroles en France* (Paris, 1903), p. 112.

7 'Machine à cercler les tonneaux', *La Nature*, 1884, p. 381.

8 *British Parliamentary Papers*, Select committee on petroleum report, evidence 2 April 1897. In the years 1910–1920, there were many advertisements and articles in petroleum literature extolling the merits of wooden barrels compared with metal barrels, which were 2 to 4 times more expensive. See 'Why the wooden barrel is cheapest to use', *National Petroleum News*, 7, 11, January 1916, p. 21.

9 Christian Rouxel, *D'Azur à Total. Desmarais Frères, le premier grand pétrolier français* (Toulouse, 2007), p. 10; Timothée Dhotel, 'Naissance d'un torrent noir. Enquête sur les premiers dépôts de pétrole en Côte-d'Or (1877–1939)', Master's thesis, University of Burgundy, 2021.

10 Bureau of the Census, *Tight Cooperage Stock, 1911* (Washington DC, 1913).

11 'Machine à cercler les tonneaux', *La Nature*, 1884, p. 381.

12 *Rapport sur la législation douanière appliquée aux futailles étrangères présenté par le syndicat général français du commerce des merrains et de la tonnellerie* (Bordeaux, 1903).

13 *National Coopers Journal*, 38–39, 1922, p. 14. It seems that the Atlantic Refining Company, near Philadelphia, could even reach a million barrels a year. 'Coopers' union', *American Federationist. The Official Magazine of the American Federation of Labor*, 9, 1902, p. 712.

14 M. W. Kovalesvsky, *La Russie à la fin du 19e siècle* (Paris, 1900), p. 430. In 1885, the English company Ransomes sold its barrel-making machines to Baku. See *Timber and Wood-working Machinery*, 1, 6 June 1885, p. 171. In 1877, American machines were installed in Chistopol to make 1,000 barrels a day. See Waitzenbreier, 'Le pétrole dans les gouvernements de Samara, Simbirsk et Kazan', *Revue universelle des mines, de la métallurgie, des travaux public*, 2, 1877, p. 293.

15 A. M. Sowder, 'Timber Requirements of the Cooperage Industry', US Forest Service, 1942. Industrial cooperages complained in particular about the departure of black workers, who found work for better wages.

16 Philippe Pétriat, 'Le baril', in Pierre Singaravelou and Sylvain Venayre, *Le Magasin du monde* (Paris, 2020), pp. 269–72.

17 Frank Rosillo-Calle, Sergio V. Bajay and Harry Rothman (eds), *Industrial Uses of Biomass Energy: The Example of Brazil* (London, 2000), pp. 187–90; Frank J. Nellissen, *Das Mannesmann-Engagement in Brasilien von 1892 bis 1995* (Munich, 1997), pp. 355–9.

18 This quantity is difficult to estimate, but all the American derricks built between 1860 and 1930 weighed around 30 million tonnes of wood, representing an average consumption of less than 1 million cu. m per year over the period.

19 Egon Glesinger, *Nazis in the Woodpile: Hitler's Plot for Essential Raw Materials* (New York, 1942), pp. 79–93. On Glesinger's career, see Martin Bemmann, 'Cartels, Grossraumwirtschaft and statistical knowledge. International organizations and their efforts to govern Europe's forest resources in the 1930s and 1940s', in Liesbeth van de Grift and Amalia Ribi Forclaz (eds), *Governing the Rural in Interwar Europe* (London, 2018), pp. 234–58.

20 'Summary of investigators' reports on technical industrial forest products development in Germany', *Journal of Forestry*, 44, 6, June 1946, pp. 401–10; British Intelligence Objectives Subcommittee, *The Timber Industry in Germany During the Period 1939–1945* (London, 1948). Nevertheless, there was an increase in pit wood and a transfer of pulpwood from the paper industry to the production of wood alcohol (a fuel), nitrocellulose (an explosive) and rayon (a textile fibre). Germany increased its consumption because it could tap the forests of conquered countries. Cf. 'German forest resources and forest products industries', *Reports of the Technical Industrial Disarmament Committees*, vol. 2, July 1945, table I, p. 10, table II, p. 34.

21 W. N. Sparhaw, 'Forests and employment in Germany', US Department of Agriculture, 1938.

22 Pulpwood consumption stagnated between 1939 and 1945 but doubled over the following decade. See US Department of Agriculture, *Agricultural Statistics 1956* (Washington DC, 1957), p. 553. As for construction, with an index of 100 for the period 1947–49, it was 40 in 1944 and 134 in 1953. Cf. US Department of Commerce, *Construction and Building Materials*, 9, 7, 1953, p. 14.

23 Forest harvesting fell from 27 million cu. m before the war to 24 million cu. m in 1942 and 1943. See *Annuaire statistique*, vol. 56 (Paris, 1946), p. 124, table 2. Egon Glesinger, *Le Bois en Europe. Origines et étude de la crise actuelle* (Paris, 1932), p. 305.

24 Throughout the war, Great Britain consumed 27 million tonnes of timber, 16 million of which was produced on its own territory. See Frank H. House, *Timber at War* (London, 1965), p. 328. Consumption between the wars was around 30 million cu. m/year. See W. E. Hiley, *The Economics of Forestry* (Oxford, 1930) and Iñaki Iriarte-Goñi and Maria-Isabel Ayuda, 'Not only subterranean forests: wood consumption and economic development in Britain (1850–1938)', *Ecological Economics*, 77, 2012, pp. 176–84. In Canada, timber production increased during the war but only returned to its 1929 level. See US Tariff Commission, 'Softwood Lumber', *Changes in Industry Series*, report no. 25, 1947, p. 84.

25 'Forest resources, lumber industry and trade of Sweden', *World Trade in Commodities*, 5, 3, March 1947, p. 3; Timo Myllyntaus and Timo Mattila, 'Decline or increase? The standing timber stock in Finland, 1800–1997', *Ecological Economics*, 41, 2002, pp. 271–88.

26 Chris Pearson, 'Environments, states and societies at war', in Michael Geyer and Adam Tooze (eds), *The Cambridge History of the Second World War* (Cambridge, 2015), vol. 3, pp. 220–29. For example, German removals from French forests during the occupation (18 million cu. m) are put into perspective when we know that one storm in 1999 felled 140 million cu. m of wood in a few hours, or that felling in French forests currently stands at around 40 million cu. m per year. Commission Consultative, *Dommages subis par la France*, vol. 6, 1948, pp. 48–9. Similarly, John McNeill describes 5 million cu. m of wood removed by the Germans in Lithuania as an enormous mass of timber. Cf. J. R. McNeill, 'Woods and warfare in world history', *Environmental History*, 9, 3, 2004, pp. 388–410.

27 In the United States and Europe, the share of buildings in final energy consumption figures has risen from one-third in 1950 to 40% today. Worldwide, buildings account for 30% of energy and 27% of

emissions; 43% of energy and 36% of emissions in Europe. In China, they account for 43% of emissions (including construction). See: IEA, Buildings, 2022, https://www.iea.org/reports/buildings; Marie Rousselot and Frédéric Pinto Da Rocha, 'Energy efficiency trends in buildings in the EU', EU Enerdata, June 2021; US Energy Information Administration, *Monthly Energy Review*, November 2022, p. 36; Yan Zhang et al., 'China's energy consumption in the building sector: a life cycle approach', *Energy and Buildings*, 94, 2015, pp. 240–51. https://www.energy.gov/sites/prod/files/2017/03/f34/qtr-2015–chapter5.pdf.

28 Thomas Piketty, *Le Capital au XXIe siècle* (Paris, 2013).

29 There are significant differences between the UK (63%), France (71%) and Spain (89%). See https://ec.europa.eu/energy/eu-buildings-data base_en; Justine Piddington et al., 'The Housing Stock of the United Kingdom', BRE Report, 2020. For China, see Kenneth S. Rogoff and Yuanchen Yang, 'Peak China Housing', NBER Working Paper, No. 27697, 2020, fig. 19.

30 *Timber Resources for America's Future*, US Department of Agriculture, Forest Service, 1958, pp. 380–81. In 2020, 92% of new American homes were timber-framed.

31 In the United States in the 1990s, the value of construction timber was $17 billion, compared with $4 billion for cement. See US Department of Commerce, *U.S. Industrial Outlook*, 1994, tables 7.2 and 6.4.

32 Thierry Paradis et al., 'Le bois dans la construction', *Revue Forestière Française*, 56, special issue, 2004, pp. 81–94.

33 Vincent Farion, *Placoplatre et autres histoires industrielles* (Paris, 2019). https://www.flickr.com/photos/reconstruction1945–1979/195410450 29/in/album-72157655519712208/.

34 It was patented at the end of the 19th century in the United States by Augustine Sackett, a rather obscure paper manufacturer specializing in disposable shirt collars. The patent was bought by US Gypsum. In the United States, gypsum plasterboards were introduced earlier, in the 1920s. Thomas Leslie, 'Dry and Ready in Half the Time: Gypsum Wallboard's Uneasy History', 7th International Congress on Construction History, 2021. The history of building materials other than concrete in the 20th century remains relatively unexplored. Thomas

Jester, *Twentieth Century Building Materials. History and Conservation* (Los Angeles, 2014). From the 1970s onwards, plasterboard was made using synthetic gypsum, based on the desulphurization of flue gases from thermal power stations using milk of lime. In Germany, for example, the closure of coal-fired power stations led to the opening of new gypsum quarries.

35 *Minerals Yearbook: Metals and Minerals (Except Fuels) Year 1954*, vol. 1, 1958, p. 542, table 6 and *Minerals Yearbook: Metals and Minerals (Except Fuels) Year 1965*, vol. 1, 1966, p. 466, table 5. *Historical Statistics of the United States, Colonial Times to 1970: Labor*, p. 142.

36 In 1929, IG Farben patented a new formaldehyde resin for plywood. In 1934 Norman Adrian de Bruyne, a Cambridge student, founded Aero Research Ltd, backed by the manufacturer de Haviland. See Christopher Wilk, *Plywood. A Material History* (London, 2017), pp. 73–147 and Janet Ore, 'Mobile home syndrome: engineered woods and the making of a new domestic ecology in the post-World War II era', *Technology and Culture*, 52, 2, 2011, pp. 260–86.

37 F. J. Champion, *Products of American Forests*, US Department of Agriculture, Forest Service, 1961, pp. 4–10.

38 FAO, *Forest Products Statistics*, Part II, Apparent Consumption, 1975, table page 9. Although formaldehyde was recognized as a carcinogen in the 1980s, US production rose from 1 to 3 million tonnes between 1960 and 1980 and has remained at this level ever since. https://www.atsdr.cdc.gov/toxprofiles/tp111–c4.pdf (Table 4.2).

39 Jeffrey L. Meikle, *American Plastics: A Cultural History* (New Brunswick, NJ, 1997), p. 192.

40 The Marcel Breuer archives have been digitized by Syracuse University in the United States. See: https://breuer.syr.edu.

41 FAO, *Global Forest Products, Facts and Figures*, 2018.

42 Rolf Thelen, 'The Substitution of Other Materials for Wood', US Department of Agriculture, 1917; 'Le Cintrage des murs en béton', *Le Ciment*, 10, 1908, p. 151; Alan Graham, 'Forms for concrete work', *The Canadian Engineer*, 26, 1914, p. 546. In 1917, in the United States, a wooden warehouse floor required 0.2 cu. m of wood per sq. m, while a cement floor required 0.1 cu. m of wooden formwork per

sq. m. The construction of major infrastructure required gigantic preparatory works in wood. Books describing the construction of dams often devote a chapter to the wooden structures (cofferdams) used to divert the river. See, for example, US Bureau of Reclamation, *The Grand Coulee Dam and the Columbia Basin Reclamation Project*, 1938.

43 Robert G. Knutson, 'Trends in the Highway Market for Wood Products', USDA Forest Research Service, 1975.

44 Wei-yi Li and David Evison, 'Consumption of plywood and sawn timber for concrete formwork in the Chinese construction industry', *New Zealand Journal of Forestry*, 62, 4, 2018, pp. 30–37.

45 https://www.mckinsey.com/industries/paper-forest-products-and-packaging/our-insights/2022-and-beyond-for-the-packaging-industrys-ceos-the-priorities-for-resilience.

46 David McKeever, *Domestic Market Activity in Solid Wood Products in the United States, 1950–1998*, US Department of Agriculture, 2002; https://www.epa.gov/facts-and-figures-about-materials-waste-and-recycling/containers-and-packaging-product-specific; *Containers and Packaging, Industry Report*, 3, 1950, p. 63. Conversion: 1 board foot = 2.3 kilos of wood. The figures from the two sources are not entirely consistent. McKeever was preferred because it allows a distinction to be made between crates and pallets.

47 Roland Geyer et al., 'Production, use, and fate of all plastics ever made', *Science Advances*, 3, 7, 2017, pp. 1–5.

48 In 2020, Europeans threw away an average of 72 kilos of cardboard and paper packaging and 27 kilos of wooden packaging, compared with 34 kilos of plastic and the same amount of glass: https://ec.europa.eu/eurostat/statistics-explained/index.php?title=Packaging_waste_statistics#Waste_generation_by_packaging_material. For the United States see https://www.epa.gov/facts-and-figures-about-materials-waste-and-recycling/containers-and-packaging-product-specific#C&POverview.

49 Susan Strasser, *Satisfaction Guaranteed. The Making of the American Mass Market* (New York, 1989).

50 Sowder, 'Timber Requirements of the Cooperage Industry', p. 51.

51 Thomas Heinrich and Bob Batchelor, *Kotex, Kleenex, Huggies: Kimberly-Clark and the Consumer Revolution in American Business* (Columbus, OH, 2004).

52 Hannes Toivanen, 'Learning and Corporate Strategy: The Dynamic Evolution of the North American Pulp and Paper Industry, 1860–1960', Georgia Institute of Technology thesis, 2004; Diana Twede, 'The birth of modern packaging', *Journal of Historical Research in Marketing*, 4, 2, 2012, pp. 245–72. For France, see Denis Woronoff, *Histoire de l'emballage en France du XVIIIe siècle à nos jours* (Valenciennes, 2014).

53 Daniel Horowitz, *Putting Meat on the Table. Taste, Technology, Transformation* (Baltimore, MD, 2005), pp. 130–35.

54 R. M. Frost, *World Paper Consumption, 1927–1938*, US Department of Commerce, 1941, pp. 11–15.

55 Albert B. Cluman, 'The cellophane industry', *Containers and Packaging, Industry Report*, 13, 1, 1960, pp. 31–7.

56 Toivanen, 'Learning and Corporate Strategy', pp. 82–90; Diana Twede, 'The history of corrugated fiberboard shipping containers', *Proceedings of the Biennial Conference on Historical Analysis and Research in Marketing*, 13, 2017, pp. 241–6.

57 Sowder, 'Timber Requirements of the Cooperage Industry', p. 24.

58 Baudry de Saunier, 'Le chariot électrique', *Le véhicule électrique*, 30, 1936, p. 31. The device was part of a line of manual devices, perfected hand trucks, using a crank to lift a load and move it. In Le Havre, the Transatlantique company had four forklift trucks in 1921 and fifty in 1928. The first forklift trucks, those of the pioneers Clark, Yale, Ransomes and Fenwick, were powered by electricity. More powerful petrol-powered models appeared in the 1940s.

59 Alvin P. Stauffer, *Quartermaster Depot Storage and Distribution Operations*, Q. M. C. Historical Studies, vol. 18, 1948, p. 2. This work, which shows its key role in palletizing loads, is strangely not mentioned in books on US army logistics. See *Logistics in World War II. Final Report of the Army Service Forces* (Washington DC, 1993); Alan Gropman (ed.), *The Big 'L': American Logistics in World War II* (Washington DC, 1997).

60 Stauffer, *Quartermaster Depot Storage*, pp. 107–20; John T. Lucas, *The Department of Defense Market for Wooden Pallets*, US Department of Agriculture, Forest Service, 1965, p. 2.

61 *Building the Navy's Bases in World War II. History of the Bureau of Yards and Docks and the Civil Engineer Corps, 1940–1946*, vol. 1 (Washington DC, 1947), p. 293.

62 Ibid., p. 313.

63 And that figure would be a quarter without recycling. Peter Berg and Oskar Lingqvist, 'Pulp, Paper and Packaging in the Next Decade: Transformational Change', 7 August 2019: https://www.mckinsey.com/industries/paper-forest-products-and-packaging/our-insights/pulp-paper-and-packaging-in-the-next-decade-transformational-change.

64 A. Camia et al., *The Use of Woody Biomass for Energy Production in the EU*, JRC Science for Policy Report, 2021, pp. 42, 50. In the United States, in 2018 more than 3 million tonnes of paper and pallets were burned in incinerators where the energy is recovered: https://www.epa.gov/facts-and-figures-about-materials-waste-and-recycling/containers-and-packaging-product-specific.

65 US Energy Information Administration, 'Monthly Energy Review', October 2022, p. 185.

66 IIASA, *Global Energy Assessment*, 2008, ch. 8: https://previous.iiasa.ac.at/web/home/research/Flagship-Projects/Global-Energy-Assessment/GEA_Chapter8_industry_lowres.pdf; https://www.iea.org/reports/pulp-and-paper.

67 Camia et al., *The Use of Woody Biomass for Energy Production in the EU*.

68 Ibid., p. 43.

69 Ibid., p. 49.

8. The Pétrolization of Wood

1 Alexander S. Mather, 'The forest transition', *Area*, 24, 4, 1992, pp. 367–79. Mather also cited Sherry Olson's important book, *The Depletion Myth* (Cambridge, MA, 1971). Along the same lines: Lloyd C. Irland, 'Is

timber scarce?' The economics of a renewable resource', *Yale University School of Forestry Bulletin*, 83, 1974.

2 Florence Pendrill et al., 'Deforestation displaced: trade in forest-risk commodities and the prospects for a global forest transition', *Environmental Research Letter*, 14, 2019, pp. 1–14.

3 Paul Josephson, *Industrialized Nature: Brute Force Technology and the Transformation of the Natural World* (Washington DC, 2002), pp. 69–130; Nancy Farm Mannikko, 'Technological Innovation in Forest Harvesting', PhD thesis, Virginia Polytechnic Institute, 1990.

4 A. Debauve, *Procédés et matériaux de construction*, vol. 3 (Paris, 1894), pp. 481–2.

5 *Bulletin des Séances de la société centrale d'agriculture*, 37, 1877, p. 130.

6 In 1921, 600 logging trucks were at work in the forests of Washington State, which seems to be where they were first used. See Frederick Malcolm Knapp, *Motor Truck Logging Method* (Seattle, WA, 1921).

7 R. Villiers, 'L'abattage mécanique des arbres', *La Nature*, 1919, pp. 15–18.

8 It was nevertheless used by the Wehrmacht. It should be pointed out that its inventor was an important member of the SS.

9 *Historical Statistics of the United States, Colonial Times to 1970*, part 1, p. 145. There were 117,000 loggers in 1900, 196,000 in 1950 and 89,000 in 1970. The number of loggers halved between 1950 and 1970, while timber production increased by 40%. Productivity increased thanks to the chainsaw, but much less than 'by 100 or 1000', as John McNeill wrote. See John McNeill, *Something New Under the Sun. An Environmental History of the Twentieth-century World* (New York, 2000), ch. 10. In Sweden, the productivity of loggers increased fivefold between 1950 and 1970. See Jonny Hjelm, 'The chainsaw in Swedish forestry', in Nebojsa Nakicenovic and Arnulf Grübler (eds) *Diffusion of Technologies and Social Behavior* (Berlin, 1991), pp. 549–64.

10 Ellis Lucia, *The Big Woods: Logging and Lumbering, from Bull Teams to Helicopters, in the Pacific Northwest* (Garden City, NY, 1975); C. R. Silversides, 'Mechanized forestry, World War II to the present', *The Forestry Chronicle*, August 1984, pp. 231–6. In Finland in 1962, half the trees were

still felled by hand, but the transition to the chainsaw was completed in 1970. The chronology is similar in Sweden. See Pentti Hakkila, 'Logging in Finland', *Acta Forestelia Fennica*, 207, 1989, p. 11; Hjelm, 'The chainsaw in Swedish forestry'.

11 H. Duteil, 'La mécanisation dans l'abattage et le façonnage', *Revue forestière française*, 1956, pp. 400–424.

12 William Boyd, *The Slain Wood: Papermaking and Its Environmental Consequences in the American South* (Baltimore, MD, 2015), pp. 83–95. In France, production and productivity in the timber industry increased in the 2000s. See Dominique Dangue des Deserts, 'Adéquation emploi formation dans la filière forêt', CGAAER report, 2010.

13 'U.S. Timber Production, Trade, Consumption, and Price Statistics' 1965–1997, fig. 9.

14 One calorie of diesel would recover 10 calories of wood. Piotr Lijewski et al., 'Fuel consumption and exhaust emissions in the process of mechanized timber extraction and transport', *European Journal of Forest Research*, 136, 2017, pp. 153–60.

15 Hearle Clapp, *Report to Committee on Roads*, US Forest Service, 1939, fig. 19; Billy Goodman, 'US Forest Service proposes ban on road construction', *BioScience*, 50, 9, 2000, p. 744.

16 The pace of construction peaked in the 1980s, with 5,000 kilometres of new forest roads built every year. See Hakkila, 'Logging in Finland', fig. 6.

17 Statistics from the Finnish Ministry of Transport: https://vayla.fi/en/transport-network/road-network (accessed 9 November 2022).

18 Jean Messines, 'L'équipement routier de la forêt et le Fonds Forestier National', *Revue forestière française*, 1952, pp. 636–53.

19 Michel Bartoli, 'Lombardi à Arudy! Images de l'exploitation forestière dans les Pyrénées françaises de 1916 à 1975', *Revue forestière française*, 59, 1, 2007, pp. 85–92.

20 'Progrès général en matière d'équipement des forêts', *Revue forestière française*, 24, 1972, p. 653; for France: Julien Bouillie, 'État du réseau routier en forêt domaniale', *ONF RDV techniques*, 13, 2006, pp. 53–6; CRPF Rhône-Alpes, 'Les pistes et routes forestières', 2013.

21 Yuri Gerasimov, 'Prospects of forest road infrastructure development in northwest Russia with proven Nordic solutions', *Scandinavian Journal of Forest Research*, 8, 8, 2013.

22 Jonas Botelho et al., 'Mapping roads in the Brazilian Amazon with Artificial Intelligence and Sentinel-2', *Remote Sensing*, 14, 2022, p. 3625.

23 In particular in Sweden, Finland, the United States, Germany and Japan. See William A. Groman, 'Forest Fertilization: A State-of-the-art Review and Description of Environmental Effects', EPA R2 72–016, August 1972; Anna Saarsalmi and Eino Mälkönen, 'Forest fertilization research in Finland: a literature review', *Scandinavian Journal of Forest Research*, 16, 6, 2001, pp. 514–35; Anna Lindkvist, Örjan Kardell and Christer Nordlund, 'Intensive forestry as progress or decay? An analysis of the debate about forest fertilization in Sweden, 1960–2010', *Forests*, 2, 2011, pp. 112–46.

24 USDA Forest Service, *Forest Fertilization Symposium Proceedings*, 1973, p. 21; Andrew H. Malcolm, 'Supertrees: more wood for an energy-hungry world', *Popular Mechanics*, 145, 5, May 1976, pp. 235–46.

25 Robin Doughty, *The Eucalyptus. A Natural and Commercial History of the Gum Tree* (Baltimore, MD, 2000); Patricia Marchak, *Logging the Globe* (Montreal, 1995), pp. 55–6. Eucalyptus accounts for 11% of Portugal's forest area. In Spain, it is associated with the industrialization of forestry during the Franco era.

26 Robert Sedjo, 'The Forest Sector: Important Innovations', *Resources for the Future*, Discussion Paper 97–42, 1996.

27 Philip J. Smethurst, 'Forest fertilization: trends in knowledge and practice compared to agriculture', *Plant Soil*, 335, 2010, pp. 83–100.

28 Doughty, *The Eucalyptus*, p. 108.

29 Laércio Couto, Ian Nicholas and Lynn Wright, 'Short Rotation Eucalypt Plantations for Energy in Brazil', IEA, 2011; Lais Silva, 'Fertilization of eucalyptus stands at advanced ages in Minas Gerais, Brazil', *Floresta Ambiental*, 26, 3, 2019.

30 Pine plantations in the Landes reached 5 cu. m per hectare in the 1950s and 10 cu. m today. See Olivier Mora et al., *Le massif des Landes de Gascogne à l'horizon 2050. Rapport de l'étude prospective*, Aquitaine Regional Council-INRA, 2012.

31 James Carle, 'The future of planted forests', *International Forestry Review*, 22, 2, 2020, pp. 1–16.

32 The problem with extraordinary yields is that they are temporary. In the case of eucalyptus plantations in China, it would appear that three-quarters of the plots have been abandoned after 20 years of intensive exploitation. See YuXing Zhang and XueJun Wang, 'Geographical spatial distribution and productivity dynamic change of eucalyptus plantations in China', *Nature Scientific Reports*, 11, 2021.

33 'This policy would make the wood industries even more dependent on the petrochemical industry': Donald Arganbright, 'Les usages du bois dans l'avenir', *Revue forestière française*, 28, 3, 1976, pp. 239–40. 'It's not sustainable, despite what the timber industry claims. It's not even agriculture, it's mining' wrote the biologist Eliot Norse. See Eliot Norse, *Ancient Forests of the Pacific Northwest* (Washington DC, 1990,) p. 219.

34 FAO, *Global Forest Resources Assessment 2020 Main Report*, p. 32. To be distinguished from less intensively cultivated 'planted forests', whose surface area has increased from 170 million hectares in 1990 to 294 million hectares in 2020.

35 Mainly in Brazil, Argentina, Chile, Portugal, China and South Africa. See Zhang and Wang, 'Geographical spatial distribution'.

36 A. P. Brodell, 'Tractors don't eat oats', US Department of Agriculture, *Land Policy Review*, 4, 6, August 1941, pp. 25–9.

37 In the United States, the number of sheep fell from 56 million in 1942 to 6 million in the early 2000s. See National Research Council, *Changes in the Sheep Industry in the United States: Making the Transition* (Washington DC, 2008).

38 Aapo Rautiainen et al., 'A national and international analysis of changing forest density', *PLoS One*, 6, 2011; Anaïs Denardou-Tisserand, 'Changements du stock de bois sur pied des forêts françaises: description, analyse et simulation sur des horizons temporeaux pluri-décennal (1975–2015) et séculaire à partir des données de l'inventaire forestier national et de statistiques anciennes', PhD thesis, University of Lorraine, 2019; Simone Gingrich, Andreas Magerl, Sarah Matej and Julia Le Noë, 'Forest transitions in the United States, France and Austria: dynamics of forest change and their socio-metabolic drivers', *Journal*

of Land Use Science, 17, 1, 2022, pp. 113–33; Juan Infante-Amate et al., 'From woodfuel to industrial wood: a socio-metabolic reading of the forest transition in Spain (1860–2010)', *Ecological Economics*, 201, 2022; Jawad Daheur, 'Estimer le volume de bois dans les forêts du passé: enjeux, sources et méthodes', *Histoire et mesure*, 38, 2, 2023, pp. 163–88.

39 Roberto Pilli, 'The European forest carbon budget under future climate conditions and current management practices', *Biogeosciences*, 19, 3, 2022, pp. 3263–82.

40 FAO, *Yearbook of Forest Products*; F. I. Cermak and A. H. Lloyd, 'Supplement – Timber transportation in the tropics', *Unasylva*, 16, 2, 1962; Joanne C. Burgess, 'Timber production, timber trade and tropical deforestation', *Ambio*, 22, 2, 1993, pp. 136–43.

41 Virgilio De La Cruz, *Small-scale Harvesting of Timber and Other Forest Products*, FAO, 1989, pp. 31–47.

42 Emilien Dubiez, Adrien Peroches, Claude Akalakou Mayimba and Laurent Gazull, 'Rapport d'étude de la filière bois-énergie de la ville de Kinshasa', CIRAD-CAFI, 2022; Jean-Noël Marien et al. (eds), *Quand la ville mange la forêt: les défis du bois-énergie en Afrique centrale* (Versailles, 2013).

43 Eunhye Kim, 'Les transitions énergétiques urbaines du XIXe au XXIe siècle: de la biomasse aux combustibles fossiles et fissiles à Paris (France)', PhD thesis, University of Paris I, 2013, table p. 203. The only historical precedent is probably the Tokyo–Yokohama conurbation, which in the 1940s consumed around one million tonnes per year. Tokyo–Yokohama had a population of 12 million at the time, and American experts estimated charcoal consumption at 100 kilos per person per year. See United States Strategic Bombing Survey, *The Japanese Wartime Standard of Living and Utilization of Manpower*, 1947, p. 43. Charcoal exports, which began in the 1990s, pale into insignificance compared to local consumption: Indonesia, the world leader, exports 500,000 tonnes, Nigeria less than 300,000 tonnes. The scandal is that most of this charcoal ends up in the barbecues of rich countries. France, for example, consumes 130,000 tonnes of charcoal a year, of which 100,000 tonnes is imported. FAO data (data.un.org).

44 A. Bertrand, 'Les problèmes du bois de chauffage et du charbon de bois en Afrique tropicale', *Bois et forêts des tropiques*, 173, 1977, pp. 39–48.

45 From 5 to 35 million tonnes, while it remained stable on other continents. FAO data consulted on data.un.org.

46 Derek Earl has shown that charcoal is generally cheaper than wood from a distance of 80 kilometres, as the losses due to carbonization are offset by the gains from transport. See Derek Earl, *Forest Energy and Economic Development* (Oxford, 1975), p. 74.

47 In Senegal in the 1990s, loggers and charcoal-makers earned three times less per tonne of charcoal than merchants in Dakar. See Jesse Ribot, 'Theorizing access: forest profits along Senegal's charcoal commodity chain', *Development and Change*, 29, 2, 1998, pp. 307–41. In Uganda in the 2000s, the Kampala bourgeoisie, supported by the military, appropriated vast areas of the north of the country, sending teams of loggers to produce charcoal on the land of rural communities. See Adam Branch and Giuliano Martiniello, 'Charcoal power: the political violence of non-fossil fuel in Uganda', *Geoforum*, 97, 2018, pp. 242–52. In Brazil in the 2000s, 45,000 tonnes of charcoal were being transported every day on 3,000 lorries. See José Brito et al., 'Le charbon de bois au Brésil', *Bois et forêts des tropiques*, 288, 2006, pp. 59–68.

48 According to satellite readings, the forest gained 100,000 km of roads during the 2010s. See Fritz Kleinschroth et al., 'Road expansion and persistence in forests of the Congo Basin', *Nature Sustainability*, 2, 2019, pp. 628–34.

49 Leo Zulu and Robert Richardson, 'Charcoal, livelihoods, and poverty reduction: evidence from sub-Saharan Africa', *Energy for Sustainable Development*, 17, 2, 2012, pp. 127–37; Rémi de Bercegol, 'Transition urbaine et électrification domestique en Afrique de l'Est: La diversification énergétique des périphéries de Dar Es Salaam', *Territoire en mouvement*, 55, 2022.

50 There is a great deal of literature on the sustainable production of charcoal in Africa, Asia and Latin America. CIRAD has been particularly active in this field. See Michel Matly, 'La mort annoncée du bois énergie à usage domestique', *Bois et forêts des tropiques*, 266, 2000, pp.

43–54; Yves Nouvellet, Malick Ladji Sylla and Amadou Kassambara, 'La production de bois d'énergie dans les jachères au Mali', *Bois et forêts des tropiques*, 276, 2003, pp. 5–15; Franck Bisiaux, Régis Peltier and Jean-Claude Muliele, 'Plantations industrielles et agroforesterie au service des populations des plateaux Batéké, Mampu, en République démocratique du Congo', *Bois et forêts des tropiques*, 301, 2009, pp. 21–32. See also the FAO reports: *Eucalyptus in East Africa. The Socio-economic and Environmental Issues*, 2009; S. Rose, E. Remedio and M. A. Trossero (eds), *Criteria and Indicators for Sustainable Woodfuels: Case Studies from Brazil, Guyana, Nepal, Philippines and Tanzania*, FAO, 2009. The area planted with eucalyptus has increased significantly, particularly in forest-poor East Africa. In 1956, at the time of the first international conference on eucalyptus, Ethiopia had barely 4,000 hectares of plantations, compared with over 500,000 today. Cf. Dominique Loupp and Denis Depommier, 'Expansion, Research and Development of the Eucalyptus in Africa. Wood Production, Livelihoods and Environmental Issues: An Unlikely Reconciliation?', paper given at the FAO/MEEATU 'Eucalyptus in East Africa' conference, 2010.

51 J. Van Dam, *The Charcoal Transition: Greening the Charcoal Value Chain to Mitigate Climate Change and Improve Local Livelihoods*, FAO, 2017.

52 https://www.drax.com/wp-content/uploads/2022/03/Drax_AR2021_ 2022–03–07.final_.pdf p. 46.

9. Technocracy Inc.

1 On technological unemployment see John Maynard Keynes, 'Economic possibilities for our grandchildren', *Essays in Persuasion* ([1930] New York, 1963), pp. 358–73; Ester Fano, 'The problem of "technological unemployment" in the industrial research of the 1930's in the United States', *History and Technology*, 1, 3–4, 1984, pp. 277–306.

2 Walter Polakov, *The Power Age: Its Quest and Challenge* (New York, 1933), p. 17.

3 Stuart Chase, *Waste and the Machine Age* (New York, 1931), p. 38.

4 From 1.8 million to 38 million CV. See Polakov, The *Power Age*, pp. 74–5, which reproduces the American industrial censuses.

5 The less radical idea of 'cultural lag' was theorized in 1922 by the sociologist William Ogburn. See Harper Leech, *The Paradox of Plenty* (New York, 1932); Polakov, The *Power Age*; *Technocracy Study Course*, 1934. On the history of Futurism, see Richard B. Halley and Harold G. Vatter, 'Technology and the future as history: a critical review of Futurism', *Technology and Culture*, 19, 1, 1978, pp. 53–82.

6 On social credit: John L. Finlay, 'John Hargrave, the Green Shirts, and social credit', *Contemporary History*, 5, 1, 1971, pp. 53–71. The most in-depth study of the American technocrat movement is William E. Akin, *Technocracy and the American Dream: The Technocrat Movement, 1900–1941* (Berkeley, CA, 1977); John Elsner, 'Messianic Scientism: Technocracy, 1910–1960', University of Michigan thesis, 1960; Eric Schatzberg, *Technology. Critical History of a Concept* (Chicago, 2018), pp. 141–5; Sean F. Johnston, *Techno-Fixers: Origins and Implications of Technological Faith* (Montreal, 2020), pp. 22–45. And more generally: Charles S. Maier, 'Between Taylorism and Technocracy: European ideologies and the vision of industrial productivity in the 1920s', *Journal of Contemporary History*, 5, 1970, pp. 27–61; John Jordan, *Machine Age Ideology. Social Engineering and American Liberalism, 1911–1939* (Chapel Hill, NC, 1994); Richard H. Pells, *Radical Visions and American Dreams: Culture and Social Thought in the Depression Years* (Champaign, IL, 1998).

7 These are in two lectures given at Birkbeck College by Frederick Soddy in 1921 and published in *Cartesian Economics. The Bearing of Physical Science upon State Stewardship* (London, 1922). On Soddy's economic thinking, see Juan Martinez-Alier, *Ecological Economics. Energy, Environment and Society* (Cambridge, MA, 1987), pp. 127–48.

8 Clifford Hugh Douglas, *Economic Democracy* (London, 1922), p. 112.

9 Finlay, 'John Hargrave, the Green Shirts, and Social Credit', pp. 53–71.

10 Quoted ibid., p. 56.

11 Chase, *Waste and the Machine Age*, pp. 9–13.

12 William Henry Smyth, 'Technocracy: industrial national management. Practical suggestions for national reconstruction', *Industrial*

Management, 57, March 1919, pp. 208–12; *idem, Technocracy, First, Second and Third Series. Social Universals* (Berkeley, CA, 1921).

13 Leroy Allen, 'Technocracy – a popular summary', *Social Science*, 8, 2, 1933, pp. 175–88. The University of Alberta has made available online a large archive of the technocracy movement, in particular the various periodicals it produced. See https://archive.org/details/ualberta_technocracy.

14 Thorstein Veblen, *The Engineers and The Price System* (New York, 1919), pp. 42–82. Even Veblen's disciples were taken aback by the book's schematism. Samuel Haber called it a 'technological hallucination'. Daniel Bell explains that it was partly a satire that was taken seriously. Cf. Jordan, *Machine Age Ideology*, p. 107. Nevertheless, this book is considered to be the 'bible' of the technocratic movement. Cf. Allen Raymond, *What is Technocracy?* (New York, 1933), p. 120.

15 Ronald R. Kline, *Steinmetz. Engineer and Socialist* (Baltimore, MD, 1992), pp. 242–4; John Jordan, ' "Society improved the way you can improve a dynamo": Charles P. Steinmetz and the politics of efficiency', *Technology and Culture*, 30, 1, 1989, pp. 57–82.

16 Charles P. Steinmetz, *America and the New Epoch* (New York, 1916).

17 Quoted in Jordan, *Machine Age Ideology*, pp. 54–5.

18 Veblen, *Engineers and the Price System*, pp. 99–106.

19 James MacKaye, *Americanized Socialism: A Yankee View of Capitalism* (New York, 1918), p. 177.

20 Akin, *Technocracy and the American Dream*, p. 101.

21 Over ten thousand people in Los Angeles in 1932. Elsner, 'Messianic Scienticism', p. 122; Akin, *Technocracy and the American Dream*, p. 98; Henry Mayers, *The What, Why, Who, When, and How of Technocracy; Amazing Revelations of Foremost U.S. Engineers and Economists Concerning Our Past Prosperity, Present Depression and Future*, 1932.

22 Raymond, *What is Technocracy?* pp. 18–23.

23 'Industrial growth of nation is traced', *New York Times*, 6 August 1934. Allen Raymond rightly points out that it is impossible to find 3,000 or even 50 similar goods over a century, which casts doubt on the very existence of this survey. Cf. Raymond, *What is Technocracy?* p. 161.

24 This was the analysis of Wesley Mitchell, a leading specialist in the business cycle. This debate between cycle and change of state has been the subject of a number of popular publications (see Paul H. Douglas, *Collapse or Cycle?* (Chicago, 1933)).

25 Raymond Pearl, *The Biology of Population Growth* (New York, 1925), p. 63. On the importance of the logistic curve in population ecology, see Sharon Kingsland, *Modeling Nature* (Chicago, 1986). Predictions spread rapidly outside demography. Garrett Hardin, famous for his theorizing on the 'tragedy of the commons', also uses this curve as a starting point. Cf. Fabien Locher, 'Les pâturages de la Guerre froide: Garrett Hardin et la "Tragédie des communs"', *Revue d'histoire moderne & contemporaine*, 60–61, 2013, pp. 7–36. See also Michelle Murphy, *The Economization of Life* (Durham, NC, 2017).

26 Cf. Raymond Pearl, 'The population problem' *Geographical Review*, 12, 4, 1922, pp. 636–45.

27 Ibid.

28 In 1927, for example, he opened the first 'International Population Congress' in Geneva. Cf. Alison Bashford, *Global Population. History, Geopolitics and Life on Earth* (New York, 2014), p. 81.

29 This is a commonplace among neo-Malthusians, defended in particular by Albert Thomas, John Maynard Keynes, Alexander Carr-Saunders and others, Cf. Bashford, *Global Population*, pp. 60–65. Harold Cox, *The Problem of Population*, quoted in Pearl, *Biology of Population Growth*, p. 2. In an article in *Harper's Magazine*, Pearl presents population growth as a global environmental problem and a tragedy of the commons: 'Birth control is great when it's your neighbour who does it.' The target: prolific Germany threatening its Malthusian French neighbour. See Raymond Pearl and Fred C. Kelly, 'Forecasting the growth of nations', *Harper's Magazine*, 1921, pp. 704–13.

30 Charles P. Steinmetz, 'America's energy supply: the available sources of energy', *General Electric Review*, 21, 7, 1918, pp. 454–66.

31 Steinmetz regularly gave interviews on the future of energy and politics in the USA, as reported in the *New York Times*. Cf. 'Dr. Steinmetz says coal will end within our time. Electricity will then prove the world's salvation', *New York Times*, 18 May 1908, and 'Electricity will

keep the world from freezing up', *New York Times,* 12 November 1911.

32 Raymond B. Prescott, 'Law of growth in forecasting demand', *Journal of the American Statistical Association,* 18, 140, 1922, pp. 471–9.

33 *American Petroleum Supply and Demand* (New York, 1925).

34 On Hubbert, see the interviews conducted by the historian Ron Doel, https://www.aip.org/history-programs/niels-bohr-library/oral-histo ries/5031-5 (accessed March 2020), and Mason Inman's biography, *The Oracle of Oil, A Maverick Geologist's Quest for a Sustainable Future* (New York, 2016).

35 *Technocracy Study Course,* 1934, p. 98.

36 Ibid., p. 77.

37 Raymond, *What is Technocracy?,* p. 96

38 'A continental hydrology', in *Pamphlets and Leaflets on Technocracy,* 1938, pp. 33–6.

39 'Technocracy has no objection to Europeans killing other Europeans; it doesn't care if Asians kill their fellow Asians.' Howard Scott, 'Pax Americana', *Technocracy,* 17, 1939, p. 4.

40 'Would freeze Europe to death. Technocrats aims to divert the Gulf Stream', *Winnipeg Tribune,* 6 October 1939. See Technocracy Archives, Box 2012–19–1, Folder 7, University of Alberta: https://archive.org/ details/technocracy201219if7/page/n85/mode/2up (accessed 4 March 2019).

41 Philip Scranton, *Endless Novelty. Specialty Production and American Industrialization, 1865–1925* (Princeton, NJ, 2000), pp. 340–43.

10. *Atomic Malthusians*

1 Glen T. Seaborg, 'Our nuclear future, 1995', *Bulletin of Atomic Scientists,* 26–6, 1970, pp. 7–14.

2 Ian Tyrrel, *Crisis of the Wasteful Nation. Empire and Conservation in Theodore Roosevelt's America* (Chicago, 2015), pp. 79–97.

3 Paul Boyer, *By the Bomb's Early Light. American Thought and Culture at the Dawn of the Atomic Age* (New York, 1985), pp. 20–24. On the history

of the assessment of the risks of radioactivity, see Soraya Boudia, 'Global regulation: controlling and accepting radioactivity risks', *History and Technology*, 23, 4, 2007, pp. 389–406.

4 'Il y a un an, Hiroshima', *Le Franc Tireur*, 6 August 1946.

5 Sam Schurr and Jacob Marshak, *Economic Aspect of Nuclear Energy* (Princeton, NJ, 1950), p. 247. See also Warren Young, *Atomic Energy Costing* (New York, 1998), pp. 9–19.

6 Quoted in Boyer, *By the Bomb's Early Light*, p. 114.

7 In a secret briefing to Eisenhower in January 1959. See Brian Balogh, *Chain Reaction. Expert Debate and Public Participation in American Commercial Nuclear Power, 1945–1975* (Cambridge, 1991), p. 178.

8 Farrington Daniels, *Factors Involved in the Production of Atomic Power*, Oak Ridge Operations, 1947.

9 President's Material Policy Commission, *Resources for Freedom*, 1952, vol. I, p. 122. The Commission was even concerned that the nuclear industry would become a major consumer of electricity: *Resources for Freedom*, vol. III, p. 39.

10 *Resources for Freedom*, vol. I, p. 127.

11 John Krige, 'Atoms for Peace, scientific internationalism, and scientific intelligence', *Osiris*, 21,1, 2006, pp. 161–81.

12 Peaceful uses of atomic energy, report of the Panel on the Impact of the Peaceful Uses of Atomic Energy to the Joint Committee on Atomic Energy, Background material for the report, 'Summary of Power Seminar', vol. 2, January 1956, p. 3

13 Farrington Daniels, *Direct Use of the Sun's Energy* (New Haven, CT, 1964), p. 9.

14 D. S. Halacy, *The Coming Age of Solar Energy* (New York, 1963).

15 United Nations, *New Sources of Energy, Rome 21–31 August* (New York, 1961), pp. 5, 9.

16 The same applies to coal consumption, which remains close to the (local) peak of 1946. See Sam H. Schurr and Bruce Netschert, *Energy in The American Economy, 1850–1975* (Baltimore, MD, 1960), pp. 37–41. This book, which was the first to offer a modern quantitative history of energy, is geared towards short-term forecasting. Its historical data was taken up by all the futurologists of the 1970s.

17 See for example H. C. Hottel and J. B. Howard, *New Energy Technology: Some Facts and Assessments* (Cambridge, MA, 1971).

18 Alvin Weinberg, *The First Nuclear Era. The Life and Times of a Technological Fixer* (New York, 1994), p. 40; Gabrielle Hecht, *Being Nuclear. Africans and the Global Uranium Trade* (Cambridge, MA, 2012), pp. 61–8; Richard Rhodes, *Energy. A Human History* (New York, 2018), pp. 272–92.

19 Alvin Weinberg, 'Burning the rocks, forty years later', in Kirk Smith (ed.), *Earth and The Human Future. Essays In Honor of Harrison Brown* (Boulder, CO, 1986), p. 110.

20 Weinberg, *The First Nuclear Era*, p. 129. Sean F. Johnston, 'Alvin Weinberg and the promotion of the technological fix', *Technology and Culture*, 59, 3, 2018, pp. 620–51. On disarmament: Lawrence S. Wittner, *The Struggle Against the Bomb*. Vol. 1, *One World or None: A History of the World Nuclear Disarmament Movement through 1953* (Redwood, CA, 1993).

21 Historians generally give a start to the history of futurology during the Cold War. See Kaya Tolon, 'The American futures studies movement (1965–1975)', PhD dissertation, Iowa State University, 2011; the special issue of the *American Historical Review*, 117, 5, 2012; Jenny Andersson, *The Future of the World. Futurology, Futurists, and the Struggle for the Post-Cold War Imagination* (Oxford, 2018). As the previous chapter suggests, other chronologies are possible.

22 See AEC, *Ninth Semi-Annual Report of the Atomic Energy Commission* (Washington DC, 1951). See also the interview with Hans Bethe, 8 May 1972, American Institute of Physics (www.aip.org/history-programs/niels-bohr-library/oral-histories/4504-3). Richard Hewlett and Oscar Anderson, *A History of the United States Atomic Energy Commission* (Washington DC, 1972), 621–55.

23 Palmer Cosslett Putnam, *Energy in the Future* (New York, 1953), p. 2. Weinberg, *The First Nuclear Era*, p. 215, confirms that it was Carroll Wilson who took this initiative. Note that the AEC will continue to publish global energy forecasts, but on a smaller scale than Putnam's: see Milton Searl, *Fossil Fuels in the Future*, AEC, 1960. My warmest thanks to Michel Lepetit for this key and little-known reference. See https://www.lajauneetlarouge.com/histoire-climatique/.

24 Vannevar Bush, *Pieces of the Action* (New York, 1970). Putnam developed the DUKW amphibious vehicles that would be used at D-Day.

25 Putnam, *Energy in the Future*, pp. 254 and 214–15. In his view, the most promising market for solar energy is passive home heating. See *Resources for Freedom*, vol. 4, p. 220; Putnam believed that wind could supply 4% of American electricity: See P. C. Putnam, *Power from the Wind* (New York, 1982), p. xiii.

26 Weinberg, *The First Nuclear Era*, p. 215.

27 Putnam, *Energy in the Future*, p. 452.

28 Ibid., p. 254. Putnam introduced a new unit, the 'Q' (equivalent to 10^{18} BTU or 38 billion tonnes of coal). According to Putnam, in 1947, the world consumed 0.1 Q/year and it would consume 1 Q/year in 2000 and therefore at least 100 Q during the 21st century. Geologists estimate global coal reserves at 60 Q. These estimates are criticized by Schurr and Netschert, *Energy in the American Economy*, p. 344.

29 Charles Galton Darwin, *The Next Million Years* (Garden City, NY, 1953), p. 66.

30 Matthew Connelly, *Fatal Misconception. The Struggle to Control World Population* (Cambridge, MA, 2008), p. 188. On the importance of the neo-Malthusian movement in Anglo-Saxon countries, see Bjorn-Ola Linner, *The Return of Malthus: Environmentalism and Post-War Population–Resource Crises* (Winwick, Cambs., 2003); Thomas Robertson, *The Malthusian Moment. Global Population Growth and the Birth of Environmentalism* (New Brunswick, NJ, 2012); Alison Bashford, *Global Population. History, Geopolitics and Life on Earth* (New York, 2014). For more on Brown, see Roger Revelle, *Harrison Brown 1917–1986* (Washington DC, 1994), and Caltech's oral history archives (https://oralhistories.library.caltech.edu/), in particular interviews with Rud Brown, James Bonner, Alan Sweezy and Samuel Epstein.

31 Harrison Brown, *The Challenge of Man's Future* (New York, 1954). Brown envisages an energy future that is essentially nuclear, with solar energy providing a small supplement. Coal would be used as a raw material for synthetic fuels. See H. Brown et al., *The Next Hundred Years* (New York, 1957), p. 113.

32 H. Brown and L. T. Silver, 'The possibilities of securing long range supplies of uranium, thorium and other substances from igneous rocks', *Proceedings of the International Conference on the Peaceful Uses of Atomic Energy*, 8, 1955, pp. 129–32.

33 Brown, *The Challenge of Man's Future*, p. 221.

34 John Surrey and William Walker, 'Energy R&D: a UK perspective', *Energy Policy*, 3, 2, 1975, pp. 90–115.

35 Alvin Weinberg, 'Energy as an ultimate raw material, or – problems of burning the sea and burning the rocks', *Physics Today*, 12, 1959, pp. 18–25; H. E. Geoller and A. Weinberg, 'The age of substitutability', *American Economic Review*, 68, 6, 1978, pp. 1–11.

36 H. Brown, 'Population, food and the energy transition', in S. J. Sherman (ed.), *Fertility and Family Planning. A World View* (Ann Arbor, MI, 1967), pp. 180–88. Participants included John D. Rockfeller III, Frank Notestein and Simon Kuznets.

37 Jacob Darwin Hamblin, 'An American miracle in the desert: environmental crisis and nuclear-powered desalination in the Middle East', in Astrid Mignon Kirchhoff and John McNeill (eds), *Nature and the Iron Curtain. Environmental Policy and Social Movements in Communist and Capitalist Countries, 1945–1990* (Pittsburgh, PA, 2019), pp. 205–18.

38 On Hubbert, see the interviews conducted by the historian Ron Doel (https://www.aip.org/history-programs/niels-bohr-library/oral-histo ries/5031-5) and Mason Inman, *The Oracle of Oil, A Maverick Geologist's Quest for a Sustainable Future* (New York, 2016). Tyler Priest, 'Hubbert's Peak', *Historical Studies in the Natural Sciences*, 44, 1, 2014, pp. 37–79.

39 Joint Committee on Atomic Energy, *Industrial Radioactive Waste Disposal*, 1959, 3, pp. 2036–86.

40 Other options are being explored: oceans, salt domes, ice caps, space. William Alley and Rosemarie Alley, *Too Hot to Touch. The Problem of High-Level Nuclear Waste* (Cambridge, 2012). On the sometimes conflicting links between the AEC and Hubbert, see interview 5 with Ron Doel (https://www.aip.org/history-programs/niels-bohr-library/oral-histories/5031-5).

41 Putnam had already shown that oil deposits were becoming smaller despite deeper wells. Peak oil would occur as early as 1960, peak coal around 1990. Putnam, *Energy in the Future*, pp. 169–252.

42 M. K. Hubbert, 'Nuclear Energy and the Fossil Fuels', Shell Development Company, 95, 1956. Hubbert explains that before Brown's conference in Geneva he saw no interest in nuclear energy because of limited uranium resources (https://www.aip.org/history-programs/niels-bohr-library/oral-histories/5031–5).

43 M. K. Hubbert, *Energy Resources* (Washington DC, 1962).

44 Atomic Energy Commission, *Civilian Nuclear Power. A Report to the President*, 1962, p. 19.

45 Joint Committee on Atomic Energy, *Hearings*, 9, 10 April and 2 May 1963 (Washington DC, 1963), pp. 168–88. On the limited supervision provided by this committee, see Balogh, *Chain Reaction*, pp. 66–83.

46 National Academy of Science, National Research Council, *Resources and Man. A Study and Recommendations* (San Francisco, 1969), p. 228.

47 Spencer Weart, *The Discovery of Global Warming* (Cambridge, MA, 2003); Paul Edwards, *A Vast Machine* (Cambridge, MA, 2010); Ron Doel, 'Quelle place pour les sciences de l'environnement physique dans l'histoire environnementale?', *Revue d'histoire moderne & contemporaine*, 56, 4, 2009, pp. 137–64; Joshua Howe, *Behind the Curve. Science and the Politics of Global Warming* (Seattle, WA, 2014); Jacob Hamblin, *Arming Mother Nature. The Birth of Catastrophic Environmentalism* (Oxford, 2014); Allan Bentley, 'Second only to nuclear war: science and the making of existential threat in global climate governance', *International Studies Quarterly*, 61, 2017, pp. 809–20.

48 Putnam, *Energy in the Future*, p. 459.

49 Gladwin Hill, 'Warming Arctic climate melting glaciers faster, raising ocean level, scientist says', *New York Times*, 30 May 1947, p. 23.

50 Doel, 'Quelle place pour les sciences de l'environnement physique dans l'histoire environnementale'.

51 'Industrial gases warming up the Earth', *Washington Post*, 5 May 1953; 'How industry may change climate', *New York Times*, 24 May 1953; Leonard Engel, 'The weather is *really* changing', *New York Times Magazine*, 12 July 1953.

52 Putnam, *Energy in the Future*, p. 459.

53 Interview with Samuel Epstein, 1986, Caltech Oral History Archives (https://oralhistories.library.caltech.edu/). He also approached the American Petroleum Institute to finance his work. Ben Franta, 'Early oil industry knowledge of CO2 and global warming', *Nature Climate Change*, 8, 2018, pp. 1024–5.

54 Charles D. Keeling, 'Rewards and penalties of monitoring the earth', *Annual Review of Energy and the Environment*, 23, 1998, p. 32.

55 Hans Suess, 'Natural radiocarbon and the rate of exchange of carbon dioxide between the atmosphere and the sea', in National Research Council Committee on Nuclear Science, *Nuclear Processes in Geologic Settings* (Washington DC, 1953), pp. 52–6.

56 Roger Revelle and Hans Suess, 'Carbon dioxide exchange between atmosphere and ocean and the question of an increase of atmospheric CO2 during the past decades', *Tellus*, 9, 1, 1957, pp. 18–27; Weart, *The Discovery of Global Warming*, p. 28; Jacob Darwin Hamblin, *Poison in the Well. Radioactive Waste in the Oceans at the Dawn of the Nuclear Age* (New Brunswick, NJ, 2008), p. 73–98.

57 Samuel Epstein emphasizes the role of this character. See https://oralhistories.library.caltech.edu/197/. On Urey: Matthew Shindell, 'From the end of the world to the age of the Earth: the Cold War development of isotope geochemistry at the University of Chicago and Caltech', in Naomi Oreskes and John Krige (eds), *Science and Technology in the Global Cold War* (Cambridge, MA, 2014) and *idem*, *The Life and Science of Harold Urey* (Chicago, 2019), ch. 6. On the accuracy of spectrometers see Harold Urey et al., 'Measurement of paleotemperature of the Upper Cretaceous', *Bulletin of the Geological Society of America*, 62, 1951, pp. 399–416.

58 Willi Dansgaard, *Frozen Annals, Greenland Ice Sheet Research* (Copenhagen, 2005); Sarah Dry, *Waters of the World. The Story of the Scientists Who Unravelled the Mysteries of Our Seas, Glaciers and Atmosphere and Made the Planet Whole* (London, 2019), ch. 7.

59 Morgan Jouvenet, *Des glaces polaires au climat de la terre* (Paris, 2022), pp. 207–30.

60 See Edward Teller, 'Energy patterns of the future', in Allan Nevis and Robert G. Dunlop (eds), *Energy and Man. A Symposium* (New York, 1960), pp. 55–72.

61 Hans E. Suess, 'Fuel residuals and climate', *Bulletin of Atomic Scientists*, 17, 9, 1961, pp. 374–5.

62 See for example the testimony of James T. Ramey: *Environmental Effects of Producing Electric Power Hearings Before the Joint Committee on Atomic Energy* (Washington DC, 1969), p. 141. Or the testimony of a Los Alamos physicist: *Frontiers in Atomic Energy Research. Hearings Before the United States Joint Committee on Atomic Energy* (Washington DC, 1960), p. 167.

63 *Construction of Nuclear Desalting Plants in the Middle East. Hearings, Ninetieth Congress, First Session. October 19, 20, and November 17* (Washington DC, 1967), p. 66. In 1971, Weinberg and Hammond took up this argument at the fourth Atom for Peace conference. See Alvin Weinberg and Philip Hammond, 'Global Effects of Increased Use of Energy', Proceedings of the Fourth United Nation Conference on the Peaceful Use of Atomic Energy, 1971.

64 *Inadvertent Climate Modification: Report of the Study of Man's Impact on Climate (SMIC)* (Cambridge, MA, 1971); Milton Lomask, 'One of a Kind: Carroll L. Wilson', unpublished manuscript, MIT Library, 1986, pp. 145–50; Bert Bolin, *A History of the Science and Politics of Climate Change. The Role of the Intergovernmental Panel on Climate Change* (Cambridge, 2007) p. 27; Howe, *Behind the Curve*, pp. 72–5.

65 'Economic and environmental implications of US nuclear moratorium, 1985–2019', Institute for Energy Analysis, IEA-76-4, 1976.

66 Alvin Weinberg and Gregg Marland, 'Some long range speculations about coal', Institute for Energy Analysis, IEA-77, 22 August 1977.

67 *Coal as an Energy Resource. Conflict and Consensus* (Washington DC, 1977), pp. 289.

68 Joseph Barnea, 'Is nuclear energy necessary?', *Bulletin of Atomic Scientists*, 36, 7, 1980, p. 62.

69 Alvin Weinberg strongly criticized a reassuring 1983 report by the National Academy of Sciences led by William Nierenberg. See Naomi Oreskes, Erik Conway and Matthew Shindell, 'From Chicken Little to Dr. Pangloss: William Nierenberg, global warming, and the social

deconstruction of scientific knowledge', *Historical Studies in the Natural Sciences*, 38, 1, 2008, pp. 109–52.

70 http://www.climatefiles.com/exxonmobil/1977-exxon-memo-about-doe-environmental-advisory-committee-subgroup-studying-co2-effects/.

11. The Invention of the Energy Crisis

1 David Nye, *Consuming Power. A Social History of American Energies* (Cambridge, MA, 1998), pp. 217–48; Meg Jacobs, *Panic at the Pump. The Energy Crisis and the Transformation of American Politics in the 1970s* (New York, 2016). The prevailing view at the time was that the crisis was artificially provoked by the major oil companies. See James Ridgeway, *The Last Play. The Struggle to Monopolize the World's Energy Resources* (New York, 1973); Robert Sherrill, *The Oil Follies of 1970–1980. How the Petroleum Industry Stole the Show* (Garden City, NY, 1983); Bruce Netschert, 'The energy company: a monopoly trend in the energy markets', *Bulletin of Atomic Scientists*, 1971, pp. 13–18; J. Stork, *Middle East Oil and the Energy Crisis* (New York, 1975); Timothy Mitchell, *Carbon Democracy: Political Power in the Age of Oil* (London, 2011), pp. 173–99.

2 David Nye, *When Light Goes Out. A History of Blackouts in America* (Boston, MA, 2010).

3 On anti-nuclear mobilizations, see Brian Balogh, *Chain Reaction. Expert Debate and Public Participation in American Commercial Nuclear Power, 1945–1975* (Cambridge, 1991), pp. 221–301.

4 Joint Committee on Atomic Energy, *Selected Materials on Environmental Effects of Producing Electric Power* (Washington DC, 1969), p. 26.

5 Joint Committee on Atomic Energy, *Hearings, Environmental Effects of Producing Electric Power*, 27 January–26 February 1970, vol. 2 (Washington DC, 1970), pp. 2318–39.

6 Philip M. Boffey, 'Energy crisis: environmental issue exacerbates power supply problem', *Science*, 168, 3939, 26 June 1970, pp. 1554–9.

7 'Editorial: Ecological backlash', *New York Times*, 25 April 1970; 'The coming power crisis', *Journal of Commerce*, 7 May 1970; *Oil and Gas Journal*, 3 May 1970.

8 Glenn T. Seaborg and Benjamin S. Loeb, *The Atomic Energy Commission Under Nixon. Adjusting to Troubled Times* (New York, 1993), pp. 155–68. On 4 June 1971, Nixon asked Congress to finance the fast-breeder reactor programme.

9 'A crisis in fossil fuels', *Nuclear Industry*, 17, 6, 1970.

10 'Federal Power Commission chairman Nassikas on the fuel crisis', *Selected Readings on the Fuels and Energy Crisis* (Washington DC, 1972), p. 131; *New York Times*, 11 August 1970.

11 'Energy crisis predicted', *New York Times*, 23 October 1971.

12 John Noble Wilford, 'Energy crisis: it won't go away soon', *New York Times*, 6 July 1971; 'Energy crisis: a nuclear future looms', *New York Times*, 7 July 1971; 'Nation's energy crisis: is unbridled growth indispensable to the good life?', *New York Times*, 8 July 1971. See also 'Heading off an energy crisis', *Nation's Business*, 1971, p. 26.

13 Joint Committee on Atomic Energy, *Hearings*, 4 March 1971 (Washington DC, 1971), p. 509.

14 See Gerard Gambs, *The Twentieth Century Fossil Fuel Crisis. Current and Projected Requirements* (New York, 1971); Reed Millard, *How Will We Meet the Energy Crisis?* (New York, 1971); Lawrence Rocks and Richard P. Runyon, *The Energy Crisis* (New York, 1971). In autumn 1971, the *Bulletin of Atomic Scientists* devoted three issues to this theme. See also David Inglis, 'Nuclear energy and the Malthusian dilemma', *Bulletin of Atomic Scientists*, 1971, pp. 14–18.

15 This section overlaps in part with Duccio Basosi, 'A small window: the opportunities for renewable energies from shock to counter-shock', in Duccio Basosi, Giuliano Garavini and Massimiliano Trentin, *Counter Shock. The Oil Counter Revolution of the 1980s* (London, 2018), pp. 336–56.

16 Jay Forrester, *World Dynamics* (Cambridge, 1971), p. 130; Donella Meadows et al. (eds), *The Limits to Growth* (New York, 1972), p. 180; Kenneth E. Boulding, 'The economics of the coming Spaceship Earth', in H. Jarrett (ed.), *Environmental Quality in a Growing Economy* (Baltimore, MD, 1966), pp. 3–14; Herman E. Daly, 'The economics of the steady state', *American Economic Review*, 64, 2, 1974, pp. 15–21.

17 Reference to the 'zero population growth' of the neo-Malthusians. David Freeman (ed.), *A Time to Choose. America's Energy Future* (Cambridge, MA, 1974), p. 85.

18 Ibid., p. 107. The Ford Foundation is a highly influential institution headed then by McGeorge Bundy, former National Security Advisor to presidents Kennedy and Johnson. The author of the report on energy, David Freeman, played an important role under President Carter. Speaking of the report, the Westinghouse chairman called it a 'misleading' document that risked plunging the nation 'into energy chaos'. The ZEG scenario is a figment of the imagination, given the correlation between growth and energy in the past. On the other hand, as the history of energy in the United States proves, a transition to nuclear power is possible, and it must begin as soon as possible.

19 Denis Hayes, *Energy: The Solar Prospect*, World Watch Paper 11, 1976; Amory Lovins, 'Scale, Centralization and Electrification in Energy Systems', 21 October 1976; *Joint Hearings Before the Select Committee on Small Businesses. Alternative Long-range Energy Strategies*, 9 December 1976 (Washington DC, 1977), pp. 218–82; Amory Lovins, 'Energy strategy: the road not taken', *Foreign Affairs*, 1976, pp. 65–96; Robert H. Murray and Paul A. LaViolette, 'Assessing the solar transition', in Ervin Laszlo and Judah Bierman, *Goals in a Global Community. The Original Background Papers for Goals for Mankind, a Report to the Club of Rome* (New York, 1977), pp. 221–78; D. Hayes, *Rays of Hope. Transition to a Post-Petroleum World* (New York, 1977).

20 John P. Holdren and Philip Herrera, *Energy. A Crisis in Power* (San Francisco, 1971); Michael McCloskey, 'Energy crisis: issues and a proposed response', *Environmental Affairs Law Review*, 1, 3, 1971, pp. 587–605.

21 Jennifer Thomson, 'Surviving the 1970s: the case of Friends of the Earth', *Environmental History*, 22, 2, 2017, pp. 235–56. The author describes a 'normalization' of the association, which under the Reagan presidency shifted from criticism of capitalism to reformism. Considering the case of Lovins, one might think that capitalism had never been the issue.

22 Lovins talks about innovations that enable 'clean use of coal at all scales', see 'Scale, Centralization and Electrification'.

23 Roger F. Naill, *Managing the Energy Transition. A System Dynamic Search for Alternatives to Oil and Gas* (Cambridge, MA, 1977).

24 For Wilson Clark of Friends of the Earth, the solar transition is a matter of survival. See Wilson Clark, *Energy for Survival. The Alternative to Extinction* (New York, 1974).

25 Preface to Hayes, *Rays of Hope*, p. 9.

26 Committee on Nuclear and Alternative Energy Systems, *Energy in Transition, 1985–2010* (Washington DC, 1980).

27 James Everett Katz, 'Impact of the Reagan Administration', *Energy Policy*, 12, 2, 1984, pp. 135–45.

28 On the history of American energy policies: Craufurd D. Goodwin (ed.), *Energy Policy in Perspective. Today's Problems, Yesterday's Solutions* (Washington DC, 1981).

29 'President's National Energy Plan', *New York Times*, 30 April 1977.

30 https://millercenter.org/the-presidency/presidential-speeches/april-18–1977–address-nation-energy. The aim of Carter's speeches was to justify higher energy prices. Hence the importance of talking about transition: the sacrifice is only temporary.

31 'An interview with Jacques Lesourne', *OECD Observer*, no. 100, 1979, pp. 4–8. Thanks to Michel Lepetit for this reference.

32 Duccio Basosi, 'Lost in transition. The world's energy past, present and future at the 1981 United Nations Conference on New and Renewable Sources of Energy', *Revue d'histoire de l'énergie*, 4, 2020; Frank N. Laird, 'Avoiding transitions, layering change: the evolution of American energy policy', in Carol Hager and Christoph H. Stefes (eds), *Germany's Energy Transition. A Comparative Perspective* (New York, 2016), pp. 111–22.

33 The disappearance of wood is, moreover, a contrivance due to the source of the graph – the book by Sam H. Schurr and Bruce Netschert, *Energy in the American Economy, 1850–1975* (Baltimore, MD, 1960), whose data on wood stops in 1955. In reality, wood energy consumption rose from 75 million tonnes to 130 million tonnes between 1960 and 1980. See Energy Information Administration, *Estimates of U.S. Wood Energy Consumption from 1949 to 1981*, 1982.

34 See Howard Raiffa, *Memoir. Analytical Roots of a Decision Scientist* (2011), p. 110.

35 Cesare Marchetti, 'Geoengineering and the energy island', in W. Häfele et al., 'Second Status Report on the IIASA Project on Energy Systems, 1975', IIASA Research Report 76–1, 1976, pp. 220–44.

36 Eglė Rindzevičiūtė, *The Power of Systems. How Policy Sciences Opened Up the Cold War World* (Ithaca, NY, 2016).

37 Wolf Häfele, 'The Fast Breeder as a Corner Stone for Future Large Supply of Energy', IIASA Research Report 73–5, 1973; Wolf Häfele and Alan S. Manne, 'Strategies for a Transition from Fossil to Nuclear Fuels', IIASA Research Report 74–7, 1974; 'Proceedings of IIASA Planning Conference on Energy Systems', 17–20 July 1973, p. 9.

38 Paul S. Basile, 'An integrated system approach: experience at IIASA', in B. Bayraktar, E. Laughton and L. Ruff (eds), *Energy Policy Planning, NATO Conference Series* (New York and London, 1981), pp. 287–305; Wolf Häfele (ed.), *Energy in a Finite World. Paths to A Sustainable Future* (Cambridge, MA, 1981).

39 Dennis Meadows, 'A critique of the IIASA energy models', *The Energy Journal*, 2, 3, 1981, pp. 17–28.

40 Bill Keepin, 'A technical appraisal of the IIASA energy scenarios', *Policy Sciences*, 17, 3, 1984, pp. 199–276.

41 Brian Wynne, 'The institutional context of science, models, and policy: the IIASA energy study', *Policy Sciences*, 17, 3, 1984, pp. 277–320.

42 C. Marchetti, 'On strategies and fate', *Physics in Technology*, 8, 4, 1977, pp. 157–62; C. Marchetti, 'A personal memoir: from terawatts to witches. My life with logistics at IIASA', *Technological Forecasting and Social Change*, 37, 1990, pp. 409–14.

43 Arthur Gerstenfeld, 'Technological forecasting', *Journal of Business*, 1971, pp. 10–18; Erich Jantsch, *Technological Forecasting in Perspective*, OECD, 1967, p. 271.

44 John C. Fisher and Henry Pry, 'A simple substitution model of technological change', *Technological Forecasting and Social Changes*, 3, 1971, pp. 75–88.

45 John C. Fisher, *Energy Crises in Perspective* (New York, 1974).

46 Vaclav Smil, *Energy Transitions. Global and National Perspectives* (Santa Barbara, CA, 2016), pp. 84–90; *idem, Growth from Microorganisms to Megacities* (Cambridge, MA, 2019).

47 Marchetti is close to Robert Hefner III, an oil geologist who became a billionaire thanks to ultra-deep gas drilling. Heffner is also a member of the IIASA board. His book *The Grand Energy Transition. The Rise of Energy Gases, Sustainable Life and Growth* (Hoboken, NJ, 2009) is based on Marchetti's theory.

48 C. Marchetti and N. Nakicenovic, 'The dynamics of energy systems and the logistic substitution model', IIASA Research Report 79–13, 1979; Marchetti, 'On strategies and fate'.

49 C. Marchetti, 'Energy systems – the broader context', *Technological Forecasting and Social Change*, 14, 3, 1979, pp. 191–204.

50 Vaclav Smil, *Energy Transitions. History, Requirements, Prospects* (Santa Barbara, CA, 2010), pp. 67–9.

51 Smil, *Energy Transitions. Global and National Perspectives*, pp. 84–90; *idem, Growth From Microorganisms to Megacities.*

52 Svante Lindqvist, 'Changes in the technological landscape: the temporal dimension in the growth and decline of large technological systems', in O. Granstrand (ed.), *Economics of Innovation* (Amsterdam, 1994), pp. 271–88.

12. *'Play the technology card'*

1 It would appear that $80 billion was originally planned. In the end, less than $1 billion will be spent because of the oil counter-shock. See: https://www.documentcloud.org/documents/4807362-National-Commission-on-Air-Quality-Carbon#document/p255/a463673.

2 *Hearings before the Committee on Energy and Natural Resources, US Senate, Effects of Carbon Dioxide Buildup in the Atmosphere, 3 April 1980* (Washington DC, 1980), p. 4. The Geophysicist Gordon MacDonald, who has been following these issues since the mid-1960s, confirms this point: it was because of the second oil crisis and the return of coal to favour that the climate issue received renewed attention. He began by

working on voluntary climate change. In a 1966 report that he co-signed, the issue of *inadvertent* climate modification by CO2 was already studied: see *Weather and Climate Modification*, vol. 2 (Washington DC, 1966), p. 83.

3 Climate Research Board, National Research Council, *Carbon Dioxide and Climate: A Scientific Assessment*, 1979, p. 2; Thomas Peterson et al., 'The myth of the 1970s global cooling scientific consensus', *Bulletin of the American Meteorological Society*, 89, 9, 2008, pp. 1325–38.

4 https://www.climatefiles.com/exxonmobil/1982-exxon-memo-sum marizing-climate-modeling-and-co2-greenhouse-effect-research/. In October 1982, the oil major financed a conference organized by the climatologist James Hansen. His experts presented an article criticizing an earlier article (from 1979) minimizing the greenhouse effect on the oceans. Cf. Brian P. Flannery, Andrew J. Callegari and Martin I. Hoffert, 'Energy balance models incorporating evaporative buffering of Equatorial thermal response', in James Hansen and Taro Takahashi (eds), *Climate Processes and Climate Sensitivity* (Washington DC, 1984), pp. 108–17.

5 Committee on Nuclear and Alternative Energy Systems, *Energy in Transition 1985–2010* (Washington DC, 1980), p. 57.

6 Climate Research Board, *Carbon Dioxide and Climate: A Scientific Assessment*, p. viii.

7 *Hearings before the Committee on Energy and Natural Resources*, pp. 169–171.

8 US Senate, *Carbon Dioxide Accumulation in the Atmosphere, Synthetic Fuels and Energy Policy* (Washington DC, 1979), p. 22.

9 Roger R. Revelle and Donald C. Shapero, 'Energy and climate', *Environmental Conservation*, 5, 2, 1978, pp. 81–91. In 1982, Revelle explained that global warming also had a positive effect and in 1992 that it was 'by no means certain'. Cf. Roger Revelle, 'Carbon dioxide and the world climate', *Scientific American*, 247, 2, 1982, pp. 35–43; *idem*, 'What can we do about climate change?', *Oceanography*, 5, 2, 1992, pp. 126–7.

10 US Senate, *Carbon Dioxide Accumulation in the Atmosphere, Synthetic Fuels and Energy Policy*, p. 27.

11 Ibid., pp. 116–21. William Kellogg worked with Carroll Williams to organize the major *Study of Man's Impact on Climate* (SMIC) conference in 1971.

12 J. A. Laurmann, 'Fossil fuel utilization policy assessment and CO_2 induced climate change', in J. Williams (ed.), *Carbon Dioxide, Climate and Society* (Oxford, 1978), p. 253.

13 World Meteorological Organization, *World Climate Conference. Declaration and Supporting Documents* (Geneva, 1979), p. 4.

14 World Climate Programme, *Report of the International Conference on the role of Carbon Dioxide and of other Greenhouse Gases in Climate Variations and Associated Impacts, Villach, 9–15 October 1985*, World Meteorological Organization, 1986, p. 44.

15 Department of Energy, *Carbon Dioxide Effects Research and Assessment Program, Progress Report*, 1979.

16 National Academy of Sciences, *Changing Climate: Report of the Carbon Dioxide Assessment Committee* (Washington DC, 1983). The Climate Research Board of the National Academy of Sciences was created in 1977.

17 Jill Williams, Wolfgang Häfele and W. Sassin, 'Energy and climate. A review with emphasis on global interactions', WMO, *World Climate Conference*, pp. 154–64.

18 World Climate Programme, *Report of the International Conference on the Role of Carbon Dioxide*, p. 33: 'With respect to POLICY, IIASA provides us both with the intellectual strength and the outreach into both the world of intellect and the world of decision makers. By illuminating the policy issues and options, IIASA could lay the groundwork for addressing in a deliberate manner the third domain I identify as being of importance to our deliberations.'

19 Williams (ed.), *Carbon Dioxide, Climate and Society*, pp. 303–18.

20 Elodie Vieille-Blanchard, 'Les limites à la croissance dans un monde global. Modélisations, prospectives, réfutations', EHESS dissertation, 2011, pp. 568–71; *idem*, 'Croissance ou stabilité? L'entreprise du Club de Rome et le débat autour des modèles', in Amy Dahan (ed.), *Les modèles du futur. Changement climatique et scénarios économiques: enjeux scientifiques et politiques* (Paris, 2007); Béatrice Cointe, Christophe Cassen and

Alain Nadai, 'Organising policy-relevant knowledge for climate action: integrated assessment modelling, the IPCC, and the emergence of a collective expertise on socioeconomic emission scenarios', *Science & Technology Studies*, 32, 4, 2019, pp. 36–57, and Christophe Cassen and Béatrice Cointe, 'From the limits to growth to greenhouse gas emissions pathways: technological change in global computer models (1972–2007)', *Contemporary European History*, 31, 2022, pp. 610–26.

21 William D. Nordhaus, 'The allocation of energy resources', *Brookings Papers on Economic Activity*, 3, 1973, pp. 529–76. Nordhaus thanks Alan S. Manne, Harvard Professor of Operations Research and a specialist in nuclear economics. See also William D. Nordhaus, 'Resources as a constraint on growth', *American Economic Review*, 64, 2, 1974, pp. 22–6.

22 William D. Nordhaus, 'Can we control carbon dioxide?', IIASA Working Paper, WP-75-63, 1975, p. 34.

23 William D. Nordhaus 'Strategies for the control of carbon dioxide', Cowles Foundation Discussion Paper, no. 443, p. 55.

24 Alan S. Manne, 'Waiting for the breeder', IIASA Research Report, RR-74-5, 1974.

25 Robert White, 'Climate at the Millennium', WMO, *World Climate Conference*, p. 5.

26 Antonin Pottier, *Comment les économistes réchauffent la planète* (Paris, 2016). See also Pierre Matarasso, 'La construction historique des paradigmes de modélisation intégrée: William Nordhaus, Alan Manne et l'apport de la Cowles Commission', in Dahan (ed.), *Les modèles du futur*.

27 Edward David Jr, 'Inventing the future: energy and the CO_2 greenhouse effect', in James Hansen and Taro Takahashi (eds), *Climate Processes and Climate Sensitivity* (Washington DC, 1984), pp. 1–5.

28 In Hansen and Takahashi (eds), *Climate Processes and Climate Sensitivity*, p. vii.

29 Proceedings of the National Commission on Air Quality. Carbon Dioxide Workshop, St Petersburg, Florida, 29–31 October 1980, p. 98 (http://www.climatefiles.com/exxonmobil/1980-national-commission-air-quality-carbon-dioxide/). This document was mentioned by Nathaniel Rich, *Perdre la terre* (Paris, 2019).

30 *Hearings before the Committee on Energy and Natural Resources*; David Rose and Marvin Miller, 'Global Energy Futures and CO2 induced Climate Change', MIT Department of Nuclear Engineering, 1983.

31 http://www.climatefiles.com/exxonmobil/co2-research-program/1981-internal-exxon-co2-position-statement/.

32 Melvin Calvin, 'Renewable fuels for the future', in S. W. Yuan (ed.), *Energy, Resources and Environment* (New York, 1982), pp. 11–21.

33 Edward David, 'Strategies for fossil fuel technology. Multiple options for unpredicted futures', in S. W. Yuan (ed.), *Energy, Resources and Environment* (New York, 1982).

34 https://www.bp.com/en/global/corporate/energy-economics/statistical-review-of-world-energy.html.

35 The absence of a convincing solution for the waste and the accident at Three Mile Island demonstrated the fatal flaws of the Westinghouse reactor, the only one to have achieved any degree of commercial success. Carroll Wilson, 'What went wrong?', *Bulletin of Atomic Scientists*, 35, 6, 1979, pp. 13–17.

36 Quoted in World Coal Study, *Coal. Bridge to the Future: A Report of the World Coal Study* (Cambridge, MA, 1980), p. 5.

37 World Coal Study, *Future Coal Prospects: Country and Regional Assessments* (Cambridge, MA, 1980), p. 98.

38 It should be noted that the 'bridge' figure has also been used to justify gas expansion. Cesare Marchetti was not wrong on this point, and his curves showed just how important gas would become by the year 2000. Marchetti was close to Robert Hefner III, a geologist turned billionaire and pioneer of ultra-deep gas drilling. Heffner went on to become a member of the IIASA board. His book, *The Grand Energy Transition*, was full of praise for Marchetti's systems theory, which also had the merit of presenting the rise of gas in historical terms: Robert Hefner, *The Grand Energy Transition. The Rise of Energy Gases, Sustainable Life and Growth* (Hoboken, NJ, 2009).

39 Wolf Häfele (ed.), *Energy in a Finite World. Paths to A Sustainable Future* (Cambridge, MA, 1981), p. 28. At IIASA, for example, interest in the issue of global warming began very early on. See Williams (ed.), *Carbon Dioxide, Climate and Society*.

40 Naomi Oreskes and Erik Conway, *Merchants of Doubt: How a Handful of Scientists Obscured the Truth on Issues from Tobacco Smoke to Global Warming* (New York, 2010); Neela Banerjee et al., 'Exxon: The Road Not Taken', Inside Climate News, 2015; Benjamin Franta, 'Early oil industry knowledge of CO2 and global warming', *Nature Climate Change*, 8, 2018, pp. 1024–5; Rich, *Perdre la terre*; Christophe Bonneuil, Pierre Louis Choquet and Benjamin Franta, 'Early warnings and emerging environmental accountability: Total's responses to global warming, 1971–2021', *Global Environmental Change*, 2021.

41 In 2022, 88% of the company's investments were in gas and oil.

42 Ralph Rotty and Alvin Weinberg, 'How long is coal's future?', *Climate Change*, 1, 1977, pp. 45–57.

43 Gordon MacDonald, 'The long term impact of atmospheric carbon dioxide on climate', JASON Technical Report, April 1979, p. 19; This is why MacDonald, a member of JASON, explained to the Senate committee that mankind could slow warming but probably not stop it. *Hearings before the Committee on Energy and Natural Resources*, p. 104.

44 Stephen Siedel and Dale Kayes, 'Can we delay a greenhouse warming?', *Environmental Protection Agency Report*, 1983, pp. 5–13. On this report see Joshua Howe, *Behind the Curve. Science and the Politics of Global Warming* (Seattle, WA, 2014), p. 134.

45 National Academy of Sciences, *Changing Climate*, p. 481. On this report see Naomi Oreskes, Erik M. Conway and Matthew Shindell, 'From Chicken Little to Dr. Pangloss: William Nierenberg, global warming, and the social deconstruction of scientific knowledge', *Historical Studies in the Natural Sciences*, 38, 1, 2008, p. 113.

46 Romain Felli, *the Great Adaptation. Climate, Capitalism and Catastrophe* (London, 2021).

47 Edwin Keitz and Dorothy Berks, 'Living with climate change. Phase II', Mitre Corporation, 1976.

48 'Report of Panel III. Environmental effects on the managed biosphere', in US Department of Energy, *Carbon Dioxide Effects Research and Assessment Program. Workshop on Environmental and Societal Consequences of a Possible CO2-Induced Climate Change*, Annapolis, Maryland, 2–6 April 1979 (Washington DC, 1980), p. 46.

Notes to pp. 198–200

49 Klaus Michael Meyer-Abich, 'Socioeconomic impacts of climatic changes and the comparative chances of alternative political responses. Prevention, compensation and adaptation', in US Department of Energy, *Carbon Dioxide Effects Research and Assessment Program. Workshop on Environmental and Societal Consequences*, pp. 348–62.

50 National Academy of Sciences, *Changing Climate*, p. 475.

51 https://www.climatefiles.com/exxonmobil/1984-exxon-presentation-on-co2-greenhouse-and-climate-issues/.

52 William Kellogg, 'Mankind's impact on climate: the evolution of an awareness', *Climatic Change*, 10, 1987, pp. 113–36.

53 Ibid.

54 Probably the most detailed work on the origin of the IPCC is David George Hirst's 'Negotiating Climates: The Politics of Climate Change and the Formation of the Intergovernmental Panel on Climate Change (IPCC), 1979–1992', PhD dissertation, University of Manchester, 2014. See also Shardul Agrawala, 'Context and origins of the Intergovernmental Panel on Climate Change', *Climatic Change*, 39, 1998, pp. 605–20; Tana Johnson, *Organizational Progeny: Why Governments are Losing Control over the Proliferating Structures of Global Governance* (Oxford, 2014), pp. 103–33; Howe, *Behind the Curve*, pp. 154–62.

55 World Climate Programme, *Report of the International Conference on the role of Carbon Dioxide*, pp. 11, 44. In his autobiography, Bert Bolin contrasts Tolba's speech with his own perception of things. Cf. Bolin, *The History of the Science and Politics of Climate Change. The Role of the Intergovernmental Panel on Climate Change* (Cambridge, 2007), p. 38.

56 Jill Jaeger, (ed.), *Developing Policies for Responding to Climatic Change*, 1988, p. v.

57 World Meteorological Organization, *The Changing Atmosphere/ L'atmosphère en évolution*, Toronto Conference, 27–30 June 1988, pp. 28, 43, 311.

58 Letter from Richard J. Smith (Department of State) to Richard Hallgren, 27 January 1988. See Ronald Reagan Presidential Library, Tyrus Cobb Collection, Global Climate Change (1), box, RAC Box 2.

59 'US strategy for implementation of Intergovernmental Panel on Climate Change (IPCC)', 15 October 1988, Ronald Reagan Presidential

Library, Tyrus Cobb Collection, Global Climate Change (1), box, RAC Box 2.

60 Quirin Schiermeier and Bryon MacWilliams, 'Crunch time for Kyoto', *Nature*, 431, 2005, pp. 12–13; Marie-Hélène Mandrillon, 'La Russie et le protocole de Kyoto: une ratification en trompe-l'œil', *Critique internationale*, 29, 2005, pp. 37–47. Izrael was highly critical of the work of Group I and its computer-modelling tools, while defending the study of palaeoclimates, a subject on which Soviet science was more advanced. See Katia Doose, 'Modelling the future: climate change research in Russia during the late Cold War and beyond, 1970s–2000', *Climatic Change*, 171, 2022; Benjamin Beuerle, 'From continuity to change: Soviet and Russian government attitudes on climate change (1989–2009)', *Climatic Change*, 176, 2023.

61 Memorandum from Frederick Bernthal to Richard McCormack, 9 February 1989. https://nsarchive2.gwu.edu/NSAEBB/NSAEBB536–Reagan-Bush-Recognized-Need-for-US-Leadership-on-Climate-Change-in-1980s/documents/Document%208.pdf.

62 https://nsarchive.gwu.edu/sites/default/files/documents/4911013/Document-07–Memorandum-William-A-Nitze-to-Topic.pdf.

63 https://nsarchive.gwu.edu/sites/default/files/documents/4911012/Document-06–Briefing-Memorandum-re-environmental.pdf.

64 https://www.ipcc.ch/site/assets/uploads/2018/05/fourth-session-report.pdf.

65 Jeremy Leggett, *The Carbon War. Global Warming and the End of the Oil Era* (New York, 1999), p. 14; https://www.ipcc.ch/site/assets/uploads/2018/05/fourth-session-report.pdf.

66 'In the 19th century, the world was going through a serious energy crisis, the whale shortage, fortunately Rockefeller saw this crisis as an opportunity.' See Frederick M. Bernthal, 'U.S. Climate Change Policy', *Current Policy*, 1216, 1989.

67 https://adst.org/OH%20TOCs/Reinstein-Robert-and-Kinney.pdf. This is a two-part interview with Stephanie Kinney, who is also a member of the negotiating team and Group III of the IPCC.

68 'The debate [on global warming] persists in many areas', 'temperature measurements are clouded by the urban heat effect', 'the sun plays a

more important role than CO_2'. See Robert A. Reinstein, 'A possible way forward on climate change', *Mitigation and Adaptation Strategies for Global Change*, 9, 2004, pp. 295–309.

69 https://adst.org/OH%20TOCs/Reinstein-Robert-and-Kinney.pdf.

70 Ibid.

71 Dominique Pestre, 'Les entreprises globales face à l'environnement, 1988–1992. Engagements volontaires, management vert et labels', *Le Mouvement Social*, 271, 2020, pp. 83–104.

72 https://adst.org/OH%20TOCs/Reinstein-Robert-and-Kinney.pdf.

73 Pottier, *Comment les économistes réchauffent la planète*.

74 William Nordhaus, 'The ghosts of climates past and the specter of climates future', in Nebjosa Nakicenovic, William Nordhaus, Richard Richels and Ferenc L. Toth, (eds), *Integrative Assessment of Mitigation, Impacts, and Adaptation to Climate Change*, IIASA, Proceedings of a Workshop held on 13–15 October 1993, p. 42. In October 1992, Nakicenovic and Nordhaus invited 80 experts, mainly economists, to IIASA to discuss the 'possible costs and benefits of reducing CO_2 emissions'. The invitation was made on behalf of IIASA, the National Science Foundation and the IPCC's Energy and Industry Subgroup, the future Group III.

75 IPCC, Report of the Third Session of the WMO/UNEP Intergovernmental Panel on Climate Change, Washington, 5–7 February 1990, p. 16: https://www.ipcc.ch/site/assets/uploads/2018/05/third-session-report.pdf.

76 James P. Bruce, Hoesung Lee and Erik F. Haithes, *Economic and Social Dimensions of Climate Change* (Cambridge, 1995), p. 387. In support of this recommendation: the Nordhaus models and the then recent models by Richard Richels. This former student of Alan S. Manne, an employee of the Electric Power Research Institute, had previously made a name for himself for his economic work in favour of fast-breeder reactors.

77 Frequency of the expression 'energy transition' in the Google corpus.

78 Kari de Pryck, *IPCC. La voix du climat* (Paris, 2022).

79 Samuel Randalls, 'History of the $2°C$ climate target', *Wiley Interdisciplinary Review on Climate Change*, 2010, pp. 598–605; Stefan C. Aykut and Amy Dahan, Le régime climatique avant et après Copenhague: sciences,

politiques et l'objectif des deux degrés', *Natures, Sciences & Sociétés*, 19, 2011, pp. 144–57; *idem*, *Gouverner le climat?* (Paris, 2014); Hélène Guillemot, '2 degrés, 1.5 degrés, neutralité carbone . . . Petite histoire des objectifs climatiques à long terme', in Marta Torre-Schaub (ed.), *Droit et changement climatique. Regards croisés à l'interdisciplinaire* (Paris, 2023).

80 IPCC, *Climate Change 1995. Economic and Social Dimensions of Climate Change* (Cambridge, 1995), pp. 387–9. See also Jean-Charles Hourcade and Thierry Chapuis, 'No-regret potentials and technical innovation', *Energy Policy*, 23, 4, 1995, pp. 433–46; Minh Ha-Duong, Michael Grubb and Jean-Charles Hourcade, 'Influence of socioeconomic inertia and uncertainty on optimal CO2-emission abatement', *Nature*, 390, 1997, pp. 270–73.

81 I would like to thank Jean-Charles Hourcade, former director of the CIRED and former lead author of Group III of the IPCC, for the long and fruitful discussions I had with him on this point.

82 https://www.iamconsortium.org/.

83 Lisette van Beek et al., 'Anticipating futures through models: the rise of Integrated Assessment Modelling in the climate science–policy interface since 1970', *Global Environmental Change*, 65, 2020.

84 IPCC, *Climate Change 2022. Mitigation of Climate Change*, p. 25, Summary for Policy Makers, C.3.5.

85 Mathilde Fajardy et al., 'BECCS deployment: a reality check', Grantham Institute Briefing Paper, no. 28, 2019.

86 President's Science Advisory Committee, 'Restoring the Quality of our Environment. Report of the Environmental Pollution Panel', The White House, 1965, p. 127.

87 Freeman Dyson, 'Can we control the carbon dioxide in the atmosphere?', *Energy*, 2, 3, 1977, pp. 287–91.

88 https://www.climatefiles.com/denial-groups/global-climate-coalition-collection/climate-position-statement/.

89 This expression with a bright future can be found in the titles of two of his articles, in 1975 and 1977. The first is about hydrogen atomic power stations built in the middle of the oceans, the second about underwater lakes of CO2. See Cesare Marchetti, 'Geoengineering and the energy island', in W. Häfele et al., 'Second Status Report on

the IIASA Project on Energy Systems, 1975', IIASA Research Report 76–1, 1976, pp. 220–44 and *idem*, 'On geoengineering and the CO2 problem', *Climatic Change*, 1, 1977, pp. 59–68 See also William Nordhaus, 'Can we control carbon dioxide?', IIASA Working Paper, WP-75–63, 1975.

90 It is in 2024 that for the first time an integrated assessment model explored the hypothesis of degrowth for a wealthy country, in this case Australia. Cf. Jarmo S. Kikstra et al., 'Downscaling down under: towards degrowth in integrated assessment models', *Economic Systems Research*, 2024, pp. 1–31. The authors generated 51 scenarios with growth rates ranging from +3% per year to −5% per year. Simply halting the growth of Australia's GNP reduces renewable energy requirements by 40% (though production still needs to be quadrupled by 2030 . . .) as well as reducing mineral extraction and the use of biomass energy.

91 'Confidential: Options for reducing greenhouse gases from vehicles', Note by the Secretary of State for Transport, 12 April 1989, PREM 19/2655. Digitized document available on the Thatcher Foundation website.

92 'Confidential: Climatic change: paper by ministry of agriculture and food', 13 April 1989, PREM 19/2655.

93 'Confidential: Carbon dioxide and climatic change', 13 April 1989, PREM 19/2655.

94 See 'Responses within the international framework', 13 April 1989, p. 4, PREM 19/2652. See also Dr D. J. Fisk, 'Climate Warming', Speech to the Royal Institute of International Affairs, 11 October 1988.

95 Christophe Bonneuil, 'Genèse et abandon d'une politique climatique, 1988–1992', *20&21, Revue d'histoire*, 3, 159, 2023, pp. 79–95.

96 Letter from Dominic Morris to Roger Bright, Department of Environment, 13 January 1989, PREM 19/2652.

Conclusion

1 IEA figures. See https://www.iea.org/fuels-and-technologies/electricity. Since 2000, three times as many coal-fired power stations have

been opened worldwide as have been closed. New capacity: 1.5 TW, closed: 0.45 TW. Calculation based on data from https://globalenergymonitor.org/projects/global-coal-plant-tracker/.

2 Zhang Shuwei, 'Why China's renewables push fuels coal power investment', *China Dialogue*, March 2023.

3 https://www.reuters.com/sustainability/climate-energy/china-climate-envoy-says-phasing-out-fossil-fuels-unrealistic-2023-09-22/.

4 https://www.eia.gov/outlooks/ieo/pdf/IEO2021_Narrative.pdf.

5 From Ethiopia to Switzerland, France, Brazil and Uruguay.

6 According to the IEA and the World Steel Association, hydrogen steel should account for only 8% of the world's steel by 2050 See https://worldsteel.org/wp-content/uploads/Fact-sheet-Hydrogen-H2-based-ironmaking.pdf. To arrive at a 'net zero' scenario, the IEA recently revised upwards (44%) the production of steel using hydrogen in 2050. The use of coke would be systematically coupled with carbon capture and storage. See https://www.iea.org/reports/steel-and-aluminium.

7 Wang et al., 'Efficiency stagnation in global steel production urges joint supply- and demand-side mitigation efforts', *Nature Communications*, 12, 2021, p. 2066.

8 IEA, *Iron and Steel Technology Roadmap Towards More Sustainable Steelmaking*, 2020.

9 Calculation based on EU data for 2020. It takes 55 kWH to produce one kilo of hydrogen and 50 kilos of hydrogen to produce one tonne of steel: https://www.europarl.europa.eu/RegData/etudes/BRIE/2020/641552/EPRS_BRI(2020)641552_EN.pdf. Hydrogen is an indirect greenhouse gas: by combining with hydroxide (OH-) radicals in the atmosphere to form water, it disrupts the chemical reactions that break down methane. Matteo B. Bertagni, Stephen W. Pacala, Fabien Paulot and Amilcare Porporato, 'Risk of the hydrogen economy for atmospheric methane', *Nature Communications*, 13, 2022.

10 Stefan Pauliuk, Tao Wang and Daniel B. Müller, 'Steel all over the world: estimating in-use stocks of iron for 200 countries', *Resources, Conservation and Recycling*, 71, 2013, pp. 22–30.

11 In the 1960s, the construction of roads in northern France led to massive recycling of this bulky residue. See Nelo Magalhães, 'Matières à

produire l'espace. Une histoire environnementale des grandes infrastructures depuis 1945', dissertation, Université Paris-Cité, 2022.

12 Cuihong Chen et al., 'A striking growth of CO2 emissions from the global cement industry driven by new facilities in emerging countries', Environmental Research Letters, 17, 2022; https://www.iea.org/reports/cement. In the early 2000s, most Chinese cement was still produced in vertical kilns, a legacy of the Great Leap Forward. In 2020, 99% of Chinese cement was produced in modern rotary kilns. See Andrew Rabeneck, 'The transformation of construction by concrete', in Robert Carvais et al. (eds), *Nuts and Bolts of Construction History*, vol. 2 (Paris, 2012), 2, pp. 627–36; Xiaozhen Xu et al., 'Modernizing cement manufacturing in China leads to substantial environmental gains', *Communications Earth & Environment*, 3, 2022.

13 Livia Cabernard, Stephan Pfister, Christopher Oberschelp and Stefanie Hellweg, 'Growing environmental footprint of plastics driven by coal combustion', *Nature Sustainability*, 5, 2022, pp. 139–48; https://www.oecd.org/environment/plastics/increased-plastic-leakage-and-greenhouse-gas-emissions.htm.

14 https://www.mckinsey.com/industries/chemicals/our-insights/climate-impact-of-plastics.

15 Mickaël Correia, *Criminels climatiques. Enquête sur les multinationales qui brûlent notre planète* (Paris, 2022), pp. 78–90. Even if the European Union succeeds in driving combustion-powered cars off the Continent after 2035, they will still find vast markets in countries with inadequate electricity grids. This is the reassuring message that European Commissioner Thierry Breton recently sent to car makers.

16 Yunhu Gao and André Cabrera Serrenho, 'Greenhouse gas emissions from nitrogen fertilizers could be reduced by up to one-fifth of current levels by 2050 with combined interventions', *Nature Food*, 4, 2023, pp. 170–78.

17 Vaclav Smil, *How the World Really Works* (London, 2022).

18 The 'residual' emissions reported by countries vary widely between Belgium (9%), France (18%) and Australia (30%). The reality is likely to be at the higher end of this range. See Holly Jean Buck, Wim Carton,

Jens Friis Lund and Nils Markusson, 'Why residual emissions matter right now', *Nature Climate Change*, 9 March 2023.

19 Aljoša Slameršak, Giorgos Kallis and Daniel W. O'Neill, 'Energy requirements and carbon emissions for a low-carbon energy transition'. *Nature Communications*, 13, 2022. This means that 3% of fossil fuels would have to be channelled into the production of renewable infrastructures.

20 Geoffrey Jones and Loubna Bouamane, 'Power from Sunshine: A Business History of Solar Energy', Working Paper, Harvard Business School, 2012.

21 Walter Polakov, *The Power Age: Its Quest and Challenge* (New York, 1933), p. 70.

22 See IEA, *Global Energy Review. CO2 Emissions in 2021* (Paris, 2022).

23 T. Norgate and N. Haque, 'Energy and greenhouse gas impacts of mining and mineral processing operations', *Journal of Cleaner Production*, 18, 3, 2010, pp. 266–74.

24 Concrete consumes three times less energy than bricks. Ignacio Zabalza Bribián, Antonio Valero Capilla and Alfonso Aranda Usón, 'Life cycle assessment of building materials: comparative analysis of energy and environmental impacts and evaluation of the eco-efficiency improvement potential', *Building and Environment*, 46, 5, 2011, pp. 1133–40; G. P. Hammond and C. I. Jones, 'Embodied energy and carbon in construction materials', *Proceedings of the Institution of Civil Engineers – Energy*, 161, 2, 2008, pp. 87–98.

25 At the beginning of the 21st century, a third of the world's housing was made of rammed earth and a sixth of bamboo, materials that are particularly economical in terms of CO2. By the early 2000s, bamboo structures were home to 1 billion people, a rather extraordinary feat given that this plant accounts for just 1% of the world's forest cover. INBAR/FAO, 'World Bamboo Resources. A Thematic Study Prepared in the Framework of the Global Forest Resources Assessment 2005', 2007, p. 31.

26 'The Materials Which Make Up Your Telephone and Where They Come From', *From the Far Corners of the Earth*, Western Electric Corporation, 1927.

27 It should be noted that metaphors derived from the earth system sciences can just as easily feed the convenient vision of rapid technological change. This is what Tim Lenton, a specialist in the 'tipping points' of the earth system, recently did when he applied this notion to the energy transition. This could happen much faster than we think, thanks to a 'cascade of tipping points'. See 'The Breakthrough Effect. How to Trigger a Cascade of Tipping Points to Accelerate the Net Zero Transition', January 2023. This report, the result of a partnership between the University of Exeter and the Bezos Earth Fund, caused great enthusiasm at the recent Davos Forum. https://www.systemiq. earth/wp-content/uploads/2023/01/The-Breakthrough-Effect.pdf.

28 Calculations based on the database of the Carbon Dioxide Information Analysis Center of the US Department of Energy (https://cdiac. ess-dive.lbl.gov).

29 In 2021, gas accounted for 30% of European emissions, which represent 9% of global emissions. Of the gas consumed in the European Union, 45% was Russian.